MW01156807

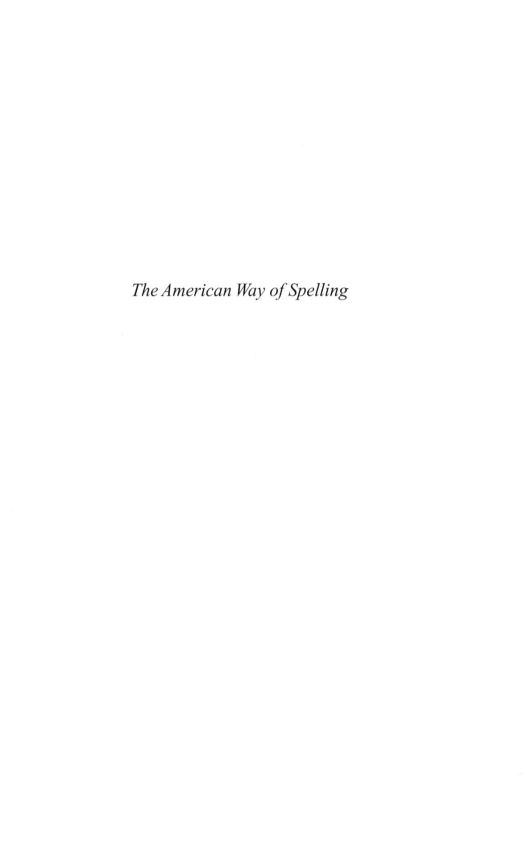

The American Way of Spelling

THE AMERICAN WAY OF SPELLING

The Structure and Origins of American English Orthography

RICHARD L. VENEZKY

THE GUILFORD PRESS
New York   London

© 1999 The Guilford Press
A Division of Guilford Publications, Inc.
72 Spring Street, New York, NY 10012
http://www. guilford.com

Printed in the United States of America

This book is printed on acid-free paper.

Last digit is print number: 9   8   7   6   5   4   3   2   1

Library of Congress Cataloging-in-Publication Data

Venezky, Richard L.
   The American way of spelling : the structure and origins of
American English orthography / Richard L. Venezky.
     p. cm.
   Includes bibliographical references and index.
   ISBN 1-57230-469-3
   1. English language—United States—Orthography and spelling.
2. Americanisms.   I. Title.
PE2817.V46   1999
421'.54—dc21   99-18154
                                            CIP

The lines from "y is a WELL KNOWN ATHLETE'S BRIDE," copyright 1931, © 1959,
1991 by the Trustees for the E. E. Cummings Trust. Copyright © 1979 by George James
Firmage, from *Complete Poems: 1904–1962* by E. E. Cummings, Edited by George J.
Firmage. Reprinted by permission of Liveright Publishing Corporation.

The lines from Mayakovsky's "My University" are reprinted by permission of
HarperCollins Publications, Inc.

For my parents, with love

About the Author

Richard L. Venezky is the Unidel Professor of Educational Studies at the University of Delaware, where he holds joint appointments in linguistics and computer and information sciences. In addition to his academic position, he works with the U.S. Department of Education in Washington, D.C., and directs an educational technology project for the Organisation for Economic Co-operation and Development in Paris. He lives in Newark, Delaware, and in Sag Harbor, New York, with his wife, Councilwoman Karen G. Venezky.

Preface

> . . . everyone . . . has to admit that of all
> languages of culture English has the most
> antiquated, inconsistent, and illogical spelling.
> —ROBERT E. ZACHRISSON (1930), 10

Can *ghoti* be pronounced as *fish*? Why is <o> short in *glove, love,* and *dove* (noun) but long in *rove, cove,* and *dove* (verb)? Why do names like *Phabulous Phoods, Starzz, Science Fare* (a cafeteria), and *Hi-Ener-G* stand out? And why do English words carry such extra baggage as the silent <b>'s in *debt, doubt,* and *subtle,* the silent <k>'s in *knee* and *know,* and the silent <n>'s in *damn* and *autumn*?

Answers to these and many other questions about the ways in which English words are pronounced and spelled are the concerns of this book. My primary audience consists of linguists, lexicographers, educators, and psychologists who study reading and reading acquisition. But I also write for those who are just curious about our spelling system—who are not specialists in phonology or perception, but want to know how the current system works and perhaps a little about its history.

Educators, philologists, and spelling reformers have from the darkest periods of the Middle Ages joined in the assault on the "antiquated," "inconsistent," and "illogical" spelling with which the English-speaking world is burdened.[1] By the middle of the 11th century, the Anglo-Saxons, working with an Irish-flavored Latin alphabet, had established orthographic practices that were consistent enough not only to serve their own needs, but also to serve as a basis for the Norwegian and Icelandic orthographies.[2] But then Norman invaders, trained on the orthography of the Continent, took immediately to reforming English spelling. New letters were introduced, a few old letters were discarded, and many new words were imported, each endowed with an Anglo-Norman flavor. In time the Anglo-Norman language disappeared, but Anglo-Norman graphic practices had settled in as a permanent part of English spelling.

When the Anglo-Norman scribal conversions ended, a neoclassical assault on English orthography began. New words were imported with clean, Latin or Greek spellings; old words were refitted to parade their classical origins. But even though <t> was substituted for quite a few <c>'s and <s>'s, and some <b>'s and <h>'s were inserted where they didn't belong, the old system was still visible through the neoclassical sheen. Grammarians of the 16th and 17th centuries, aroused by "the gros and disgrac'ful barbarismes" of the existing orthography, labored religiously to convert their compatriots to new spelling systems,[3] but they were no more successful than were Benjamin Franklin, George Bernard Shaw, or the editors of the *Chicago Tribune,* all of whom tinkered with spelling reform centuries later.

For several centuries grammarians approached the study of English orthography with the purblind attitude that writing serves only to mirror speech, and that deviations from a perfect one-letter–one-sound relationship were contrary to nature's way. With the rise of comparative philology in the early 19th century, however, a new era arose. Instead of contempt, dispassionate analysis was in vogue for the orthography. But this approach was short-lived. The 19th-century philologists soon decided that the letters weren't really the sounds and relegated the orthography to the back porch of the new linguistic science. With structural linguistics came even harsher treatment. "Writing is not language," claimed one of the dicta of the new science, "but merely a way of recording language by means of visible marks."[4] With these words orthography lost whatever appeal it may have had as an object of legitimate analysis of linguists, and was thus left to the disdain of the spelling reformers, who tried only to replace the system with something more "regular."

Even so astute a scholar as Leonard Bloomfield added his authority to the drive for spelling reform:

> Although our writing is alphabetic, it contains so many deviations from the alphabetic principle as to present a real problem, whose solution has been indefi-

nitely postponed by our educators' ignorance of the relation of writing and speech. . . . The difficulty of our spelling greatly delays elementary education, and wastes even much time of adults. When one sees the admirably consistent orthographies of Spanish, Bohemian, or Finnish, one naturally wishes that a similar system might be adopted for English.[5]

Whatever may have been the relationship between writing and sound when Irish scribes first rendered Old English into Latin script, and whatever may have been the reasons for the subsequent development of this system, the fact is that the present orthography is not merely a letter-to-sound system riddled with imperfections. Instead, it is a more complex and more regular relationship, wherein phonemes and morphemes share leading roles.

More than 35 years ago, Project Literacy at Cornell University initiated a series of linguistic and psychological studies of English orthography. Through the work of Charles Hockett and Eleanor Gibson, analyses were done of the spelling–sound correspondences found in English monosyllables and of the influence of spelling–sound regularity on the recognition of printed words.[6] From my involvement as a student in Project Literacy, and in particular from my work with both Hockett and Gibson, I developed an interest in English orthography that led in time to the publication of *The Structure of English Orthography*.[7] Since that time I have been involved in the study of how children learn to read and how different orthographies function. The current text is a return to the basics of English spelling, the subject that occupied so much of my time in the 1960s. It both expands and reworks my earlier text, incorporating a variety of new topics and rewritten in a language that I hope can be understood by educators as well as by the linguists and psychologists to whom the earlier text was addressed. Language arts teachers and curriculum designers should find most of this text informative; however, a few chapters contain technical treatment not oriented to educational practice.

Some will want to read this book from beginning to end, digesting each chapter in turn, preparing notes on the data and arguments, and perhaps formulating counterarguments along the way. Others will browse as if on the World Wide Web, selecting a passage here or there, following a link through the index or table of contents to a related passage, and occasionally returning to the early chapters for a definition, a pronunciation, or a new initiating link. I invite all such navigational modes. This book is meant both as a reference text and an educational form of recreation, but it falls far short of what consumer software people are calling *edutainment.*

As a sampler of what is to come, consider the *ghoti* issue. This was supposedly offered by George Bernard Shaw[8] as proof of the chaotic nature of English spelling. Shaw was an unflinching advocate of spelling reform and left a portion of his estate to promote that end. Shaw should have stayed with theater, however, and avoided forays into orthography. *Ghoti* can be pronounced *fish* no more than bulls can fly or crocodiles sing. Yes, <gh> is pronounced /f/ in *rough* and *tough,* but at the beginnings of words <gh> can only be pronounced /g/ as in *ghost, gherkin,* and *ghoul.* The letter <o> in *women* is pronounced as <i> in *tip,* but *women* is the only word in the English language in which this correspondence between spelling and sound occurs—a singularity from which no other words take their clues for pronunciation. And <ti> can sound like <sh> in *ship* only in endings such as <tion> and <tient>. At the end of a word, <ti> cannot be pronounced like <sh>.

I present this answer now mainly to alert readers to this book's position on spelling reform. Yes, the flaws in the spelling system will be revealed; but this text is not a tirade against the current system, nor does it advocate reform. We suffer daily such forms as *deceit* and *receipt, deign* and *disdain,* and *moveable* and *immovable,* but there is far more to the total system than what is revealed by the spelling reformers' litany of orthographic irregularities. Although adjustments to the current spellings can be justified, the demand that English spelling, by necessity, must be a one-letter–one-sound system cannot be. English spelling has many irregularities, but it is a more regular system than the spelling reformers admit, and it presents to the reader far more than just a guide to pronunciation. Such spellings as *knife, autumn,* and *conic* reflect language history and provide clues to word identity. We might eliminate these trappings and thus simplify the early stages of learning to read, but this would be at the expense of competent silent reading, where the eye and not the ear is carrying the main burden of word identification. More is said on this topic in Chapter 12.

If you are still wondering whether orthography is an issue for academics alone—a system through which linguists and educators are allowed to fiddle harmlessly with letters and sounds in return for a survival income—come with me to a restaurant to read the menu. I've taken one from a favorite spot in Union Station in Washington, D.C., where hundreds of people every day come and order snacks, drinks, and meals. Look at this menu, this farrago of imported nomenclature: *enchiladas, pizza, hummous, filet, cappuccino, mocha.* Observe the different pronunciations of <ll> in *quesadilla* and *mozzarella;* notice the silent letters in *almond, salmon, filet, pernod, raspberry, Beaujolais, crumb, herb, Bordeaux, cabernet, pinot,* and *liqueur.*

Attend to the different pronunciations of <ch> in *orchid* (part of the name of a drink), *mocha, cheese, brochette, chateau,* and *spinach.* Work out the letter–correspondences in *noir* (of *pinot noir*), *parmesan,* and *Cointreau.* Wow! What a cross-section of patterns! Final <e> pronounced in *cafe, sesame,* and *guacamole;*

silent in *cheese, romaine, compote,* and *Lite.* Nonstandard final <c> patterns in *blanc, franc,* and *Potomac.*

Admittedly, foreign words tend to appear in restaurants and bars in America, but orthographic challenges can also be found in mass transit passenger safety instructions (*knee, debris*), prayer books (*psalm, hymn, Esther*), and calculator operation manuals (*rightmost, pseudorandom, answer*). Our lexicon, the treasure of words that we encounter daily in print, is rife with spelling challenges. Any time you are engaged with print, you are confronted with an orthography that demands some special knowledge to be rendered into sound. This book will either make you feel more at home with its peculiarities or drive you to join a spelling reform society.

The synchronic material presented here was initially gathered from a lexicon of approximately 20,000 words, selected from the *Thorndike–Century Senior Dictionary.*[9] The letter–sound patterns found in these words were later augmented with patterns derived from more recent data bases, as well as from the 1933 reissue of the *Oxford English Dictionary* (*OED*; Murray, Bradley, Craigie, & Onions, 1933), and the 1972–1986 *Supplement* (Burchfield, 1972–1986); the *OED,* of course, is unmatched as a source of information on the English language.[10] The extent to which I am indebted to its editors for information on spellings, etymologies, and historical phonology far exceeds the number of references to the *OED* in this book.

My plan is to provide a general introduction to the characteristics of American English orthography in Chapter 1, followed by two chapters on variations in spelling practices: use of homophones, British–American spelling differences, misspellings used commercially, and a few other such examples. These chapters are followed by an introduction to the English sound system (Chapter 4) and to the writing system (Chapter 5). Chapter 6, which covers the history of the orthography—its origins and evolutions—serves as a launching point for four chapters on the patterns and rules that relate spelling to sound. Concluding the text are chapters on spelling reform and the teaching of reading.

A NOTE ON SYMBOLS AND TERMINOLOGY

Throughout this text, letters and combinations of letters, as they are spelled, are enclosed within arrow brackets (< >), full words that contain examples of spellings are in italics, and pronunciations are enclosed in slant lines as is customary for linguistic works (e.g., /s/). In technical terms, these slant lines signal phonemes—that is, classes of sounds that contrast with other classes of sounds to separate meanings. The alternative is the square bracket treatment (e.g., [s]), which signals sound without making a strong statement about what contrasts with what within the entire phonological system. Occasionally square brackets are used so that we can converse about sounds that do not necessarily separate meaning in English, such as the different pronunciations of <p> in *pin, spin,* and *stop.* Pronunciations are based loosely on Kenyon and Knott's *A Pronouncing Dictionary of American English.*[11] Chapter 4 explains in some detail the pronunciation scheme adopted here. Letter–sound correspondences, which are the primary interest of this book, are represented as <a> → /e/, which says that the letter <a> is pronounced /e/ (as in *late*). Sound-to-spelling correspondences, which occur less frequently here, are represented as /e/ → <a>.

For reasons explained later, the term *graphemes* is occasionally used to refer to letters and *phonemes* to sounds (actually *sound classes*). Nevertheless, the more common terms—*letters* and *sounds*—are preferred. Other terms that will occur on occasion are *morphemes* and *morphophonemes.* Morphemes, like phonemes, are linguistic creations. They identify minimal units of meaning, such as the common sense of *water* or the plurality marker at the end of *toys.* The word *toys* is assumed to be composed of two morphemes: one that carries the meaning of *toy* and one that marks plurality, which in this case is the sound /z/. (Other pronunciations of the regular plurality morpheme are /s/ as in *bats* and /ɪz/ as in *matches*.) Since morphemes are not the focus of this book, and little linguistic knowledge is required to understand the limited use of this term, we won't worry about such issues as how many morphemes are represented by words like *confluence* and *shepherd.*

A morphophoneme is another linguistic creation, invented to bring order to chaotic situations. In English pronunciations, the regular noun plural is sounded as at the ends of *vats, dogs,* or *judges.* For convenience of conversation, linguists posit a unit {S} to stand for all three of these realizations of the regular noun plural. This unit (set off in this book by curly brackets, as just seen) is called a morphophoneme because on the one hand it varies across different forms of the same morpheme, and on the other hand it relates to phonemes. In this case, the morphophoneme is mapped into three different phonemes (or phoneme sequences) according to the sound immediately preceding it. Once again, this is not a term that appears very often, but it plays an important role in Chapter 10.

The urge to introduce more symbolic notation in the name of brevity or economy has been checked by the force of a statement made by the linguist Einar Haugen, when mathematics was still relatively foreign to linguistic descriptions: "Present-day descriptions bristle like a page of symbolic logic and lack entirely the leisurely, even charming quality of the traditional grammars. I would not go back to those grammars, but only suggest that economy may not always be a virtue."[12]

ACKNOWLEDGMENTS

Many people have read and commented on earlier drafts of this book, or offered suggestions for revising and updating the earlier text on which this is loosely based. I am grateful to all of them for the time that they spent and the advice that they offered: Virginia Berninger, Robert Calfee, Frederic Cassidy, Richard Jain, Sidney Landau, Dominic Massaro, Banu Oney, John Sabatini, and Toni Healey. To Toni Healey, in particular, I am grateful for a careful reading of Chapter 6. What remains as misleading, erroneous, or incomplete in that chapter, however, is strictly my own doing. I am especially appreciative, as well, of the critical comments received from two anonymous reviewers, one for The Guilford Press and one for another publisher, and of the assistance received from The Guilford Press's editorial staff, including Chris Jennison, Marie Sprayberry, and William Meyer, who with care and intelligence significantly increased the accuracy, consistency, and coherence of this book.

Parts of this book were drafted while I was a Benton Visiting Scholar at the University of Chicago, and parts were also written while I was a visiting scholar in the U.S. Department of Education in Washington, D.C. I am grateful to the Benton Foundation and to various offices within the Department of Education, as well as to the Unidel Foundation and the College of Education at the University of Delaware, for generous support and encouragement. Support was also received over the past decades for orthographic research from the U.S. Office of Education, the National Institute of Education, and Ginn & Company.

RICHARD L. VENEZKY
University of Delaware

NOTES

1. These descriptions of English spelling can be found in, among other sources, Bloomfield (1933), Hart (1569/1955), Lounsbury (1909), Zachrisson (1930).
2. See Flom (1915).
3. Butler (1634/1910), 16.
4. Bloomfield (1933), 21.

5. Bloomfield (1933), 500f.
6. See, for example, Gibson et al. (1963) and Hockett (1963).
7. Venezky (1970).
8. The claim that Shaw originated this spelling is made in, among other sources, Dickson (1992), 205; Shipley (1997), 74; and Tauber's introduction to Shaw (1963), xvii. However, no published work by Shaw has yet been found with this spelling, and one of Shaw's biographers attributes it not to Shaw but to an "enthusuastic convert" (Holyroyd, 1991, 501).
9. In the *Thorndike–Century Senior Dictionary* (Thorndike, 1941b), the most common 20,000 words according to the Thorndike frequency count are identified. I have omitted many low-frequency words from that list, especially proper nouns, and have included a number of words not included in the original Thorndike list.
10. It is the 1933 reissue of the *OED* that is hereafter referred to in both text and Notes as the *OED*. (The 1933 reissue and the *Supplement* were combined for the 1989 2nd edition [Simpson & Weiner, 1989].)
11. Kenyon and Knott (1951).
12. Haugen (1951), 222.

Contents

Demere rebus tumultum.
(You have to separate things from the
noises they are making)

—ANONYMOUS

CHAPTER 1

Overview

Let us discard orthography, the terror of all
human beings from birth. . . .
—GABRIEL GARCÍA MÁRQUEZ
(1997), E13

This chapter lays down some basic principles of English orthography and attempts to characterize this marvelously variegated system of communication.
A metaphor based on costuming is offered well into the chapter for those
who yearn for familiar footing in this tramp through the winding paths of letters and sounds. But its usefulness (like that of all metaphors) diminishes
rapidly with information about the real thing, and by Chapter 2 it is all but
forgotten. The principles and arguments offered here define an attitude toward English orthography and establish a roadbed for traveling through the
remaining chapters.

A FRAMEWORK FOR ANALYSIS

Orthography concerns letters and spellings, the representation of speech in writing. That's not exactly what this book is about, however. Here only one direction
in the speech–writing relationship—that from writing to speech—is stressed.
Some might call this *pronunciation* as opposed to *spelling,* but I have no shame

in calling it *orthography,* even though a complete, bidirectional treatment is not offered. There are plenty of notes throughout on spelling per se, however.

The framework that most closely approximates the approach adopted here is the functionalist approach presented by Joseph Vachek, among others.[1] This view insists that the written norm is a system unto itself and not simply an adjunct to speech. The role of orthography, according to one linguist, is "to speak quickly and distinctly to the eyes."[2] English orthography is not a failed phonetic transcription system, invented out of madness or perversity. Instead, it is a more complex system that preserves bits of history (i.e., etymology), facilitates understanding, and also translates into sound.

The Alphabetic Base

English orthography is fundamentally *alphabetic,* as opposed to *syllabic* or *logographic.* These three classes represent the traditional classification of writing systems. Alphabetic systems contain symbols that mostly relate directly to speech sounds (i.e., phonemes). Syllabic systems, such as the Japanese Katakana and the Cherokee syllabary, are characterized by symbols that relate to syllables or syllable-like units, usually consisting of a consonant and a vowel. In logographic systems such as Chinese, symbols relate to meaningful entities in the language: words, morphemes, or the equivalent. This three-part classification system appears to have wide acceptance, yet it does not provide for incomplete alphabetic systems like Hebrew. Gelb, among others, finesses this issue by declaring ancient Hebrew to be a syllabary—a position that is not totally defendable.[3] But we do not need to resolve this issue here. Regardless of the full set of classes selected for the world's writing systems, English will remain alphabetic.

The Symbol–Sound Mismatch

I have just said that English orthography is fundamentally alphabetic. *Fundamentally* is one of those hedge words, often inserted when purity remains unrealized. A complete analysis of the current writing system would reveal several deviations from a pure alphabetic principle. Capital letters, for example, signal word type or sentence position, as opposed to sound. The apostrophe, that little supplementary stroke, signals several nonphonetic features: possession (e.g., *gorilla's beat*), contraction *(don't),* and most commonly elision *('til we meet again),* but it also occurs like a silent letter at the end of an occasional personal name *(Dontae').* Moreover, one letter, <x>, usually translates into two sounds (e.g., *exit, luxury*), and some letters occasionally translate into no sound (e.g., <p> in *psychology,* <n> in *hymn*).

These are minor aberrations compared to the quantitative mismatch between the 26 letters commonly deployed for English sounds and the 40-plus basic sounds or phonemes of General American speech. Part of the solution to this mismatch has been to combine letters such as <c> and <h> to represent sounds that neither bear any relationship to nor can be derived from the separate sounds of the letters from which they are composed. In Spanish, many double-letter combinations (e.g., <ch, ll, rr>) are considered single units and until recently were assigned independent positions in the alphabetical scheme.[4] Combinations such as <ch, sh, th, oo> labor as diligently as the single letters for the cause of English spelling, but are not afforded independent status in dictionaries or other alphabetical orderings. A second mechanism for bridging the letter–sound mismatch is to allow letters to take on multiple sounds, sometimes using context to indicate which sound is currently appropriate. Thus, an initial <th> corresponds to /ð/ in function words (e.g., *the* and *then;* except *through*); elsewhere in an initial position, it corresponds to the voiceless form /θ/.

Beyond the 26 Letters

English orthography did not emerge from the head of Zeus with the present display of 26 letters. In the earliest writings only 22 appeared, including a joined character (i.e., a *ligature*), <æ>. In time new letters were borrowed or invented— thorn (þ), eth (ð), yogh (ȝ), zed (z), jay (j)—and two-letter combinations (digraphs) were introduced (e.g., <th>). Later, especially with moveable-type printing, non-Roman characters were cast aside. In the evolution of the present 26-letter system, extra symbols were also introduced: The hyphen, apostrophe, dieresis, and other punctuation marks, along with features such as italics and boldface, were adopted.[5]

Beyond the specific marks placed on the page are formatting conventions such as paragraph indentation, which are also part of the writing system but not of the orthography. This book covers the 26 letters and those few marks such as the apostrophe ('), dieresis (¨), and tilde (~) that directly signal pronunciation or word identity. A few words are said in a later chapter about the ligatures <æ> and <œ>, which pop up now and then, particularly in British writing, for words of Latin and Greek extraction. Otherwise, stage center is occupied by the 26 letters and their more popular combinations.

General Principles

Given the alphabetic base—the 26 letters plus the punctuation marks and other extra equipment of the writer's arsenal—and the mismatch in size between the spelling and sound inventories, how does English orthography go about its business? And how does it differ in intentions and style from other alphabetic systems? To answer these questions, seven principles of English orthography are set forth, followed by the promised metaphor. These frame the discussions that follow in Chapters 2 through 12.

1. Variation Is Tolerated

Not only are foreign spelling patterns admitted into English, but alternate spellings of words are tolerated. *Moneychanger* is acceptable as one word, as *money-changer,* or as two separate words without hyphen. *Tinker's dam* is as acceptable as *tinker's damn,* and *propellant* must share the altar of correctness with *propellent.* There are perhaps over 2,000 such compounds for which the major American collegiate dictionaries give different spellings.[6] Many of these differences are over compound words: whether to merge the components into a single word, to write them as hyphenated words, or to give them as separate words. Other differences reflect British–American variations (e.g., *labour–labor*), and others, like *propellent–propellant,* are of a miscellaneous class.

Neither Great Britain nor the United States has tolerated a language academy or any other body authorized to legislate on spellings. The U.S. Board on Geographic Names, appointed by executive order of Benjamin Harrison in 1890, has been allowed to establish spelling preferences for U.S. place names, but no other institutions have been empowered to dictate the orthography of the general lexicon.

2. Letter Distribution Is Capriciously Limited

For reasons that are deeply rooted in the history of English orthography, many letter combinations that are common in other alphabetic writing systems are shunned in English. The doubled letters <aa> and <ii>, for example, are discouraged, occurring only in a small number of recent borrowings. Similarly, the consonants <h, j, k, q, v, w, x, y, z> are discouraged from doubling. Exceptions exist, particularly for <v> <z>, but these are a small, static group.

Among the other restrictions are limits on word positions for doubled consonants (they cannot occur initially in words, as they do in Spanish) and for certain single letters. For example, <u, v, j, q> rarely occur in final position. As Chapter 3 demonstrates, these restrictions allow the generation of pronounceable pseudo-words with varying degrees of approximation to correct spelling.

3. *Letters Represent Sounds and Mark Graphemic, Phonological, and Morphemic Features*

Unlike a phonetic alphabet, present-day English orthography contains both *relational units* and *markers*. Relational units map directly into sound. The <b> in *bird,* the <ch> in *much,* and the <ou> in *mouse* are the workhorses of the spelling–sound system. A marker is an instance of a letter that has no pronunciation of its own; instead, it marks the pronunciation of another letter, indicates the morphemic status of a word, or preserves a graphemic pattern.

In *guide* <u> marks hard <g>, as opposed to its soft pronunciation as in *germ, gibe,* and *gyp;* in *running* the added <n> marks the checked pronunciation of <u>, as opposed to its free pronunciation as in *super;* and in *nurse* the final <e> indicates that <s> is not a plural or verbal ending. Markers, however, are not unique to English. In Italian, for example, an <h> is added after a <c> to preserve the /k/ pronunciation before <i> (e.g., *chiamare,* "call, name"), and after a <g> to preserve the /g/ pronunciation before the same letters (e.g., *larghezza,* "width"). Markers are common to other orthographies, as are diacritics for similar functions. For example, the cedilla is added to a <c> in French to mark its /s/ pronunciation in environments where it would otherwise be pronounced /k/ (e.g., *ça*).

4. *Etymology Is Honored*

English has always had rather loose immigration regulations for vocabulary. Words, unlike people, have been forever welcomed, regardless of their origins. Neither quotas nor IQ tests have ever been required for admission to the lexicon. And unlike the melting-pot emphasis on assimilation in most of American history, orthography has been unencumbered by pressures to shed its alien appearance. Consequently *bijou, chalet,* and *chauffeur* retain their French garb, *trekked* smacks of Dutch (via Afrikaans), *ohm* and *Fahrenheit* are still German, and *vodka* remains recognizably Russian.

All these words could have been rendered into English orthography, but over the last several centuries foreign spellings have been allowed to coexist with native ones. This might lead to the assumption that with etymology considered, letter–sound translation (including stress placement) would be simplified. Some linguists, for example, propose a Romance stress rule and a Germanic stress rule, depending on lexical origin.[7] There are numerous cases, however, where words of Latin origin follow the Germanic stress pattern.[8] In addition, when sound changes occur in a language, words borrowed from that language into

English before a particular change may follow one pattern, and words borrowed after the change may follow a different pattern.

Extensive borrowing over a long period of time—with different retention patterns for spellings and changing spelling–sound relations in the original languages—frustrates not only the use of etymology for predicting spelling–sound patterns, but the entire enterprise of orthographic rule making. Consonant sequences proscribed in the core vocabulary finagle their way into common usage (e.g., *schlemiel, tsunami, atlatl*), and rare vowel patterns may find new favor (e.g., *cru, Chianti*). In proper nouns in particular, almost any Romanized spelling is admitted into English print.

Rather than yielding to these interlopers and parvenus, and forsaking any attempt to define an English orthographic style, we assume here that the average reader can distinguish between a native spelling such as *chair* and a clearly foreign spelling such as *atlatl*. This does not eliminate the *chief–chef* problem, but it does allow patterns to be defined in spite of such anomalies as *tchotchkes* and *llama*. At best, however, only the more extreme zones are distinguished along a continuum from native (or naturalized) to foreign; the gray, muddled middle zone is acknowledged but not finely divided.

5. *Regularity Is Based on More Than Phonology*

As explained in connection with several of the other principles, the patterns within English orthography require attention to morphology and phonotactics, as well as to phonology. Some final consonant clusters such as <mn> contain silent letters that would be irregular from a strict spelling-to-sound perspective. When morphologically related words are considered, however, such as *damn–damnation,* a regular pattern appears. Similarly, all of the single-letter vowel spellings have two pronunciations, as discussed in Chapter 9. If only the letters and their pronunciations are considered, the correspondences appear to be irregular. However, these too become generally regular when certain graphemic and morphological features are observed. The full range of features that must be considered to determine what is regular is the subject of Chapter 10.

Left undiscussed in the remainder of this book are several characteristics of regularity that no rational person would expect to see broken in an operational writing system. One is the preservation of order between a word's spelling and its pronunciation. A letter–sound system that was egregiously non-order-preserving would not work. Yet as obviously desirable as order preserving is for a practical orthography, it is occasionally violated in English. The first infraction is in words for which <wh> is still pronounced as two separate sounds, /hw/. The sequence <hw>, which was common in the earliest English writings, was later reversed to

<wh>, supposedly to separate <w> from perceptually confusable vowel letters that often followed.[9]

A second infraction is in the terminal spelling <le>, which is pronounced /əl/ (or as a syllabic consonant). As with <hw> and <wh> spellings, an earlier <el> spelling was reversed to <le>. The *Cursor Mundi,* written about 1300, has *batel* (battle); Wyclif's Sermons, from c. 1375, use *botelis* (bottles). A small number of spellings with final <re> are also reversals, but these occur only after a <c> or <g>, such as in *ogre* and *acre,* which might be mispronounced if followed by <e>. With these not too spectacular exceptions, English orthography is order-preserving; that is, the sounds are sequenced in pronunciation in the same order as in their spellings.

A second assumption is that letters are seldom wasted. Once functional units are defined for letters within a word, almost all serve some function. Similarly, sounds rarely appear from nowhere. Some silent letters are exceptions to this principle, as are occasional British place names such as *Cholmondeley* (/čʌm lɪ/) and *Marjoribanks* (/mǎč bæ̀ŋks/), but most silent letters either preserve a word's derivation or morpheme identity and are pronounced in an affixed form (e.g., *gnostic–agnostic, autumn–autumnal*). (The letter <x> is an oddity for English orthography because it regularly maps to two separate consonants, but this is not considered an exception to the present principle.) Among the single-word exceptions is *eighth,* where the <t> maps to /t/ by itself and to /θ/ as part of the digraph <th>.

6. *Visual Identity of Meaningful Word Parts Takes Precedence over Letter–Sound Simplicity*

We might respell *boys* as *boyz* and *matches* as *matchiz* to improve translation to speech, but this would remove the visual identity of the noun plural morpheme. Similarly, *sane* might be respelled as *sain* to make it parallel with *rain,* but this would obscure its relationship to *sanity.* The present system, short of misleading the voice, favors the eye over the tongue and glottis. One result of favoring visual identity is the retention of silent letters, particularly when related forms assign sounds to the letters. Thus we have *damn–damnation, hymn–hymnal, gnostic–agnostic,* and *sign–signal.* But not all silent letters can be so justified. The <l> in *could, would,* and *should,* for example, is not pronounced in any related form; nor is the <b> in *subtle,* unless variant pronunciations of the distantly related *subtile* are considered. Another result is alphabetic morphemes, such as <d> and <ed> for the past tense of verbs and the multifunctional <s> and <es>, as in *runs, houses,* and *John's.*

Not only is morpheme identity usually preserved in prefixing and suffixing, but visual discrimination of *homophones* (i.e., two or more words with different meanings but the same pronunciations) is encouraged through different spellings. *Bell* and *belle* are distinguished by an otherwise unneeded <e>; *in* and *inn* by an extra <n> at the end of the latter; and *quartz* and *quarts* by a seldom-used <z>. Homophones, more than any orthographic mechanism, reveal the enormous variability of English letter–sound patterns. Consider, for starters, the different mechanisms available for distinguishing homophones:[10] doubling a final consonant (*ad–add, in–inn, pit–Pitt, web–Webb*), doubling a final consonant and adding a final <e> (*bar–barre, mat–matte, step–steppe*), added a final <e> (*aid–aide, by–bye, main–Maine*), changing final <c> to <ck> (*bloc–block, sac–sack, tic–tick*), changing <c> to <k> (*disc–disk, scull–skull*), and various other schemes (*bah–baa, beau–bow, bizarre–bazaar*). These mechanisms evolved over the past 500 years as the influence and importance of English expanded and print became dominant in everyday affairs.

7. English Orthography Facilitates Word Recognition for the Initiated Speaker of the Language, Rather Than Being a Phonetic Alphabet for the Nonspeaker

Stress and syllable boundaries in English are not marked and are often unpredictable, so that *object* may be either a noun, with stress on the first syllable, or a verb, with stress on the second syllable. *Hothouse,* without knowledge of the boundary between the <t> and the <h>, might induce a pronunciation of the digraph <th>. The <s> at the end of *boys, choices,* and *cats* has three different pronunciations that every native speaker of English manages to keep straight without conscious knowledge of the rules involved. For the nonspeaker, correct pronunciation requires, first, an understanding of when a terminal <s> signals certain morphemic functions such as noun plural; and, second, the pronunciation of the sound before the <s>.

These are a few but not all of the problems that English orthography poses when one assumes that it behaves like the International Phonetic Alphabet (IPA; see Chapter 4) or some other phonetic transcription scheme. An ostrich, viewed as an imperfect horse, also leaves much to be desired. Among two-toed flightless ratite birds, however, it ranks at the top of its class. Similarly, English orthography suffers abuse and scorn from those who see it for what it is not and probably was never intended to be.

THE COSTUME ANALOGY

Given this set of principles, a simple analogy based upon a parade of marching bands might capture some of the flavor of English orthography. Imagine a parade where several such groups could be identified by similarities in dress. One might be a native Anglo-Saxon group with distinctive hats, shoes, pants, dresses, and accessories. Another might be a classical (Latin–Greek) group and another a Romance group, each with distinctive uniforms. These would represent the main vocabulary sources for present-day English.

But now picture another group dressed primarily in classical garb, but with hats and accessories in the Anglo-Saxon pattens. This group would represent words such as *beauty, virtue,* and *necessary,* which are Latin in origin but have adopted an Anglo-Saxon stress pattern. Similarly, a marcher in Romance raiment might have Anglo-Saxon shoes, representing French words such as *manner* in which a native spelling pattern (the double <n>) has been introduced. There would even be a few people tramping along in Anglo-Saxon dress, but with a classical scarf or belt, representing naturalized words such as *debt* and *doubt* that were respelled during the neoclassical revival to emphasize their Latin heritage. This melange of dressing styles represents the major sources for present-day English orthography, but enlivened by naturalization, adaptation, and other forms of cross-fertilization.

ASYMMETRY OF READING AND SPELLING

In the IPA and in a small number of orthographies, including Finnish and Turkish, each symbol or symbol sequence has a single pronunciation, and each phoneme has one and only one symbolic representation. But as every schoolchild knows, English spelling is not simply the mirror image of English reading. Some letters have two or more pronunciations, and each of these pronunciations often has two or more other spellings, leading to a spaghetti-like tangle that defies two-dimensional representation. Consider the network shown in Figure 1.1, which is a small piece of the total spelling-to-sound and sound-to-spelling system for English.

Figure 1.1 begins with the spelling <c>, which has three common nonzero pronunciations: /k/, /s/, and / š/, and one rarer one, / č/. Each of these sounds, in turn, has a bevy of different spellings. The sound /k/, for example, is commonly spelled not only <c> as in *coal,* but also <ck> as in *pick,* <k> as in *kid,* and <q> as in *liquor,* not to mention spellings such as <kh> as in *khaki,* <kk> as in *trekking,* <cc> as in *accord,* and <ch>as in *chord.* And so on for the other <c> pronunciations.

What makes the reading–spelling systems so asymmetrical (and so complex from either a spelling or a reading perspective) is a small number of special properties of English writing:

1. Markers such as consonant doubling and final (silent) <e>. Consonant dou-

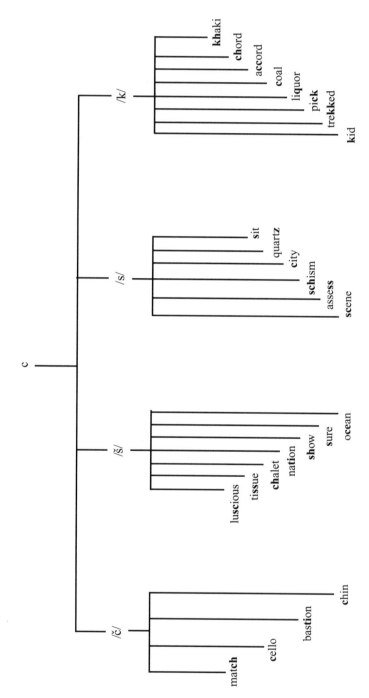

Figure 1.1. Pronunciations of the letter <c>, and the possible spellings for these pronunciations (excluding the silent <c>, as in vi**c**tuals).

bling, which indicates a *short* (i.e., checked) pronunciation of the preceding vow-el spelling, ensures that for a large number of consonant sounds in medial and for a few in final position, at least two common spellings will exist. Silent <e> ensures at least two common pronunciations for <e>, as represented by its pronunciations in *fret* and *time*. Because of the digraph vowel spellings, at least two different spellings exist for most *long* (i.e., free) vowel sounds (e.g., *boat, note*).

2. Survival of different spellings for sounds that are no longer distinct. Seven hundred years ago, for example, <ee> and <ea> were pronounced differently. By the end of the 17th century the sounds represented by these two symbols had merged, but since English and American spelling conventions were highly stable by then, no respelling occurred.[11]

3. Borrowed spellings. Over the past 900 years, a great many words have been borrowed with spelling–sound correspondences that differ from native ones. For example, <ie> was a common spelling in French loan words for the vowel sound /i/ as in *achieve, grief,* and *relief.* This duplicated the native <e . . . e> spellings that were common until the end of the 16th century, and the <ee> spellings that replaced them in all but a small number of native words (e.g., *deep, seek, here, mete*). Similarly, Greek and Latin words with <ch> spellings for /k/ have been borrowed (e.g., *chemical, chord*), as well as French words with <ch> spellings for /š/ (e.g., *champagne, chalet*), thus contrasting with native patterns such as *king* and *ship.* Had the English maintained tighter immigration laws for their vocabulary, we might have a simpler and more symmetrical system today.

4. Scribal pedantry. Among the more peculiar spelling–sound patterns in English is the <t> → /š/ pattern, which occurs before unstressed high front vow-els or glides: *nation, constitution.* Most of these words were spelled with a <c> (e.g., *nacioun*) until the end of the 14th century, when the <t> spelling began to appear. (It did not become established, however, until the time of Shakespeare.) Its origins are in the period of neoclassical enthusiasm, when large numbers of Greek and Latin words were imported into English and when many words were respelled to show their true or imagined classical origins.

5. Graphical constraints. For various reasons that are discussed more fully elsewhere in this book, English scribes developed restrictions on vowel and con-sonant doubling and on which letters could occur in final position in English words. Thus no digraph doubles, and among the single-letter functional units, <a, h, i, j, k, q, u, v, w, x, y> rarely if ever double. In addition, <b, c, d, g, m, n, p, r, t> rarely double at the end of a word. Among the consonants, this leaves only <f, l, s> to double at the ends of words. The exceptions are mostly the result of intentional lengthening of two-letter content words (*ebb, add, odd, egg, inn*), shortened forms (*mitt* from *mitten*), proper names (*Finn, Watt, Crockett, Pitt*), imitative words (*burr, purr*), or homophone discriminations (*butt–but*).

As a result of doubling restrictions, three pseudogeminates, <ck, dg, tch>, were adopted in the 15th century. The digraph <ck> replaced <kk>; <dg> replaced <gg> when it represented /j/; and <tch> replaced <cch> when it represented /č/. Over time two less frequently occurring spellings, <pph> and <rrh>, were added to this list. These occur only after single-letter vowels with checked pronunciations and therefore function as compound units, as do geminate consonant clusters.

LOOKING AHEAD

With this overview behind us, we move to some of the more interesting aspects of variability in English spelling: homophones, British–American differences, place names, and foreign patterns in words for food and drink. Then we explore invented or nonstandard spellings as used for trade and advertising names, and pseudowords invented by psychologists and educators for experimental purposes. These next two chapters explore the richness of both variability and irregularity—features denied to many other writing systems.

NOTES

1. The most comprehensive statement of Vachek's views can be found in his 1989 monograph, *Written Language Revisited.* Several of his earlier works may also be of interest, including *Selected Writings in English and General Linguistics* (1976), "Two Chapters on Written English" (1959), and "On the Interplay of External and Internal Factors in the Development of Language" (1962).
2. Frinta (1909), cited in Vachek (1973), 19.
3. Gelb (1963). The contrasting view, that ancient Hebrew was an alphabetic writing system, is found in Jackson, (1981).
4. In April 1994, the Association of Spanish Language Academies voted to drop <ch> and <ll> from the Spanish alphabet. The practical effect of this move was to shift <ch> and <ll> from separate entry status in dictionaries (and children's alphabet books) to inclusion under <c> and <l>, respectively. According to a brief note in *The New York Times* ("In Spanish," 1994), the decision "was taken mainly to simplify dictionaries and make Spanish more computer compatible with English." This is, I suppose, another example of imperialism via the Internet.
5. On the development of the alphabet and spelling within English, see Scragg (1974), and the *OED* under the entries for the separate letters. For the development of punctuation symbols and practices, consult Parkes (1993).
6. Deighton (1972).

7. Chomsky and Halle (1968).
8. Friederich (1958).
9. See Venezky (1993).
10. A more comprehensive list of homophones and homographs is presented in Whitford (1966).
11. See Dobson (1957) and Scragg (1974), 48–49.

CHAPTER 2

A Celebration of Variation

y is a WELL KNOWN ATHLETE'S BRIDE
(lullaby)
& z
= an infrafairy of floating
ultrawrists who
lullabylullaby
—E. E. CUMMINGS (1991), 319

Principle 1, as presented in Chapter 1, is that "Variation is tolerated." This is an egregious understatement, in that variation is actually invited in English orthography. In languages that have single spellings for each sound (Finnish and Turkish are prime examples), double entendres and other plays on words such as *Bagel Buoy* (a deli in Sag Harbor, New York), *READ*WRITE*NOW!* (a literacy program of the U.S. Department of Education), and *The Write Stuff* (a stationery store in Newark, Delaware) cannot occur. Nor can styles or nationalities be distinguished through spelling differences, as they are in the English-speaking world. A theater in the United States that uses the spelling *theatre* is aligning itself with the British stage, and an American in England who insists on *meter* rather than *metre* is declaring something about his or her American heritage. These and other variations in spelling constitute the first stop on our tour of American English spelling. First is a revisiting of homophones, those alike-sounded words that have first appeared in Chapter 1. Our goal here, though, is not simply to goggle at their multiplicity, but to explore the orthographic redundancy that allows differently spelled homophones to exist.

Then comes a different type of variation—that of spellings for which the Atlantic Ocean holds apart competing renditions. This is a short tour, a brief excursion through a self-contained landscape. From there we enter the domain of place names and the U.S. government agency established by executive order at the end of the 19th century to regulate their spellings. Finally, we glide into the orthography of American cuisine, in an expansion on the spellings from a restaurant menu that are discussed at the end of the Preface. This is done for fun as much as for revelation, but it pulls together a wide range of patterns and exemplifies, as suggested in Chapter 1, how international American spelling has become.

A HARMONY OF HOMOPHONES

Modern dictionaries do not fully agree on how to define *homophone*. Some require only that two words be pronounced alike but have different meanings to qualify, regardless of their spellings; others designate as homophones two or more words that sound alike but differ in meaning, derivation, or spelling.[1] For now we are primarily interested in the subset of homophones that are sounded alike but spelled differently, as opposed to *homographs,* which are words that are spelled and sometimes pronounced alike but have different meanings. The conversation here centers on the orthographic mechanisms and redundancies that allow differently spelled homophones to exist. We'll start with a few examples to challenge our ability to think outside of the box:

Rod–rod
all ready–already
I'll–aisle
E's–ease
C–sea–see

The first pair (*Rod–rod*) reveals a simple orthographic device (capitalization) that allows for a bevy of homophones: *Peg–peg, Ball–ball, Watt–watt, Mike–mike,* and so on. Sometimes another spelling difference is also present, as in *Finn–fin* and *Eve's–eaves,* but we'll come to these by and by. In a few cases (e.g., *Watt–watt*), a pair has resulted from a unit of measurement and its eponym. A few more of these exist (e.g., *ohm,* named after Georg Simon Ohm), as well as a few near-misses, such as *volt,* named after Alessandro Volta. But all in all, this is not a large class if it is restricted to personal names and to acronyms (e.g., *WAC–wack*). However, when place names are counted, the class mushrooms considerably. Among the cities and towns in the state of Illinois, for example, are *Anchor, Apple River, Atlas, Banner, Bath, Beach, Berry, Big Foot, Big Rock, Birds, Bishop Hill, Blue Mound, Bluffs, Bluff Springs*—and that's not even through the B's.

A second type of homophone is found in *I scream–ice cream* and *all ready–already,* although one might argue that under some sentence conditions, these homophones have slightly different stress patterns. Given that we can utter these in at least one context where they are truly identical, we will ignore this slight inexactitude. This class is not large, and in fact one must strain a little to generate exemplars: *all ways–always* and *a rye–awry* are a start. The reader is challenged to find longer examples to compete with this one:

> *The sons raise meat.*
> *The sun's rays meet.*[2]

Contracted forms represent a third mechanism from which homophones can derive. Some examples, besides *I'll–aisle,* include *you'll–Yule, we've–weave, we'll–weal, can't–cant,* and *he'll–heal.* Closely related to contractions, which bring together two or more words, are elided forms such as *o'er,* in which a sound and its spelling have been left out. *O'er* is homophonic with both *ore* and *oar.* Similar are *'twill* (it will) and *twill.* Given the limited number of contractions commonly used in English, this class is also relatively small.

Two of the examples above (E's-ease, C-sea-see) both use the names of letters of the alphabet—one with just the name itself (C-sea-see), and one with the plural of the name (E's-ease). Of the letter names alone, at least 15 have homophonic matches among words that rank at least one level above esoteric. For the plurals, *B's, C's, E's, I's, J's, K's, M's, N's, O's, P's, Q's, T's, U's, X's,* and *Y's* have common homophonic matches, and a few others could be included with a little stretching (e.g., *G's, L's*). Admittedly, the use of letter names is stretching the definition of *homophone,* although all of the letters of the alphabet are entries in major commercial dictionaries.

All of the remaining homophones—that is, the great majority of them—differ by consonant or vowel units, or both. In the listings that follow, consonant alternations are given first, followed by vowel alternations. In general, pure examples of each class are presented first; that is, the first exemplars are word pairs that differ only by the single feature that the class represents. Then, typically, a few exemplars that differ by the class feature and one or more other features are presented.[3]

Consonants

Geminates

In the class of geminates are pairs like *ad–add, in–inn, canvas–canvass, but–butt,* and *bus–buss.* Only a few have contrastive medial consonants (e.g., *canon–cannon, Mary–marry*), although the latter also has an upper-case–lower-case difference. When less pure examples are admitted, a larger group results: *medal–meddle, pend–penned, rigor–rigger, bowl–boll, manor–manner, carat–carrot,* and more. The gemination of a final consonant in what would otherwise be two-letter words is discussed in a later chapter. Medial geminates contrast with single consonants because of borrowings, mainly, but in a few cases they are results of the peculiar vowel lengthenings and shortenings that occurred (or didn't occur) from the late Old English period through the early Middle English period.

Silent Letters

Homophonic pairs can result from initial, medial, or final silent letters: *wreck–reck, Psalter–salter, knave–nave, wrap–rap; straight–strait, taught–taut; dam–damn, plumb–plum, hi–high.* With multiple differences, pairs such as *knell–Nell, pshaw–Shaw, reign–rain, coo–coup, core–corps, him–hymn, wry–rye, know–no, knows–nose, gnu–new, wrapped–rapt,* and *sign–sine* occur. Many of these result from the loss of pronunciation in English of the first consonant in certain initial consonant clusters (/gn/, /kn/, /wr/), or of a medial palatal (/x/). Some result from borrowings (e.g., *damn, hymn*), and some are the results of scribal tampering (e.g., *plumb*).

Added Morpheme

When the past-tense <ed> pronounced /t/, or the plural or third-person singular, present indicative <s> pronounced /s/, is added to a word, a potential homophone results. Examples of the former include *guessed–guest, leased–least, missed–mist,* and *paced–paste;* examples of the latter include *cokes–coax, lacks–lax, locks–lox, minks–minx,* and *tacks–tax.* For a variety of reasons—doubling patterns for final consonants, <x> spelling of /ks/ within a morpheme—no pure contrasts exist in this group. Homophones can also occur for morphemic <s> pronounced /z/ (e.g., *ads–adze, pries–prize, rows–rose*), but all of these are also impure. Morphemic <er> can also create homophones, as in *cougher–coffer.*

Variant Consonant Spellings

By far the largest group of homophones that differ by consonant spellings occur because of alternate spellings for consonant sounds, aside from silent letters, geminates, and added morphemes. One large subgroup of these contains different spellings for /k/: <c, ch, ck, k, q> in particular.[4] The letters <k> and <c> alternate in *ark–arc, Frank–franc, ranker–rancor,* and *skull–scull;* <ck> and <c> alternate in *dock–doc, flock–floc, lack–lac, Mack–Mac, sack–sac, tack–tac,* and *tick–tic;* <ck> and <q> alternate in *clack–claque;* <ck> and <ch> alternate in *check–Czech;* <k> and <q> alternate in *mask–masque,* and *peak/peek–pique;* <ch> and <q> alternate in *choir–quire;* and <c>, <ck>, and <q> alternate in *sac–sack–saque* (all terms that derive ultimately from Latin *saccus*).

The other common contrasts are <c> and <s>, which alternate as spellings for /s/ (e.g., *cell–sell, cider–sider, cede–seed, cellar–seller, Ceres–series,* and *Greece–grease*); <s> and <z>, which alternate as spellings for /z/ (e.g., *phase–faze, raise–raze,* and *raiser–razor,* as well as the cases cited above for morphemic <s>); and <f> and <ph>, which alternate as spellings for /f/ (e.g., *file–phile, faze–phase, fill–Phil, filter–philtre, profit–prophet, flocks–phlox,* and *frays–phrase*).

Less frequent consonant alternations include the following:

> <f> or <ff>–<gh>: *draft–draught,* plus *coffer–cougher* (cited above for morphemic <er>)
> <g>–<dg>: *pigeon–pidgin*
> <g>–<j>: *gym–Jim*
> <r>–<rh>: *rime–rhyme*
> <sh>–<ch>: *shanty–chanty, cash–cache*
> <sh>–<t>: *Marshall–martial*
> <w>–<o>: *won–one*
> <wh>–<h>: *whole–hole, wholly–holy, whore–hoar*

Vowels

Final <e> as a Morpheme Marker

The first class of homophones involving vowel alternations consists of a small number of words where <e> at the end of a word distinguishes it from another word of the same spelling. This class is distinguished from the fourth class described here, in which final <e> is part of a free vowel pattern. Included here are pairs such as *aid–aide, bad–bade, for–fore, grill–grille, be–bee, ho–hoe,* and *we–wee.*

Alternations of <i> and <y>

The number of homophones involving alternations of <i> and <y> is surprisingly small, even when digraphs are included. The most frequently occurring members are *gym–Jim, lie–lye, stile–style, maize–May's, raise–rays,* and *staid–stayed.* Although one of these (*staid–stayed*) results from morphemic <ed> added to a word that ends in <y>, no separate class for these is established because too few occur.

Alternations of <u> and <w>

Like the <i>–<y> class, the <u>–<w> class is quite small; exemplars include *faun–fawn* and *clause–claws* (<au>–<aw>), and *foul–fowl* (<ou>–<ow>).

Digraph versus Final <e>

The fourth class is a relatively large one, composed of mixtures of native words and borrowings. Included are the following:

> <ai> or <ay>–<a . . . e>: *fain–fane, gait–gate, hail–hale, lain–lane, mail–male, fair–fare, hair–hare; frays–phrase, grays–graze, grayed–grade*
> <ea>–<a . . . e>: *great–grate*
> <ea>–<e . . . e>: *Jean–gene*
> <ee>–<e . . . e>: *seed–cede, seen–scene*
> <oa>–<o . . . e>: *load–lode, loan–lone*
> <oo>–<o . . . e>: *moor–more*
> <oo>–<u . . . e>: *loot–lute, shoot–chute*
> <ew>–<u . . . e>: *mews–muse*

Alternate Spellings for /u/

The fifth class, and the following classes up to the miscellaneous class, are composed of the variant spellings for a vowel sound. Not included are the ones already mentioned under other classes. For /u/, a number of spellings alternate, including <oo>–<o> (*too–to*), <you>–<ew>/<yew> (*you–ewe–yew*), <oo>–<ou> (*coop–coupe, root–route*), and <oo>–<oe> (*shoo–shoe*).

Alternate Spellings for /i/

Included in the sixth class are <ea>–<ee> (*beat–beet, feat–feet, heal–heel,* and more), <ea>–<ei> (*sealing–ceiling*), <ea>–<ie> (*lean–lien*), and <ee>–<ie> (*freeze–frees–frieze*).

Alternate Spellings for /o/

The seventh class includes <oa>–<ow> (*groan–grown*), <oa>–<o> (*hoarse–horse*), <ou/ow>–<o> (*four–for, fourth–forth, know–no, low–lo,* and *mourning–morning*), <ow>–<oe> (*row–roe, tow–toe*), and <o>–<o . . . e> (*poll–pole*).

Alternate Spellings for /e/

Only two alternations have been found for the eighth class: <ai>–<ei> (*rain–reign–rein*) and <a . . . e>–<e . . . e> (*crape–crepe*).

Miscellaneous Alternations

/ɪ/: <ea>–<e . . . e>: *hear–here*
/ɔ/: <au>–<a>: *haul–hall, maul–mall*
/aɪ/: <ey>–<ai>: *eyelet–aisle;* <i>–<i . . . e>: *light–lite, might–mite, sight–site*
/ʌ/: <o> or <o . . . e>–<u>: *some–sum, son–sun*
/ʌr/: <er>–<ur>: *Percy–pursy, serf–surf;* <ea>–<u>: *earn–urn*

Homophones in Everyday Life

As a last comment on homophones, here are a few collected from newspapers, TV, magazines, phone books, restaurants, and store signs.

The Good Cents Breakfast (a breakfast special in a motel restaurant)
Second Sonshine (title of a newspaper story about the younger of two sons of a former U.S. president)
Dollars and Sense (title for the financial news section of a TV news program)
I knead it daily (a T-shirt slogan seen in a cafe bakery)
Mane Attraction (title of a magazine story about a salon for long hair)

Paws for Thought (animal grooming business in Chicago)
When in Roam (title of a newspaper article on mobile phones)

SPELLING DIFFERENCES ACROSS THE ATLANTIC[5]

American and British spelling practices derive from the same common stock, but have diverged since the American Revolution in a number of ways, none of which has affected the major patterns of the orthography. These differences, furthermore, vary to some degree according to whose opinion is consulted. *The Oxford Guide to English Usage,*[6] for example, presents a more conservative view of current British spelling than that of the *Collins COBUILD English Language Dictionary,*[7] the *Chambers 20th Century Dictionary,*[8] or the *Cambridge International Dictionary of English.*[9] For American spelling, Lee Deighton lists more than 2,000 words for which the four major collegiate dictionaries in the late 1960s gave alternative spellings, and for almost 1,800 of these words, the dictionaries did not agree on which spelling was predominant.[10]

A somewhat lengthy list of words that are spelled differently in the United States and Britain can be generated from published discussions on this topic.[11] Included are such variations as American *cozy, mustache, pajamas, skeptic,* and *sulfur,* as compared with British *cosy, moustache, pyjamas, sceptic,* and *sulphur.* What is most noticeable about this list is not its length, but its shortness relative to the full vocabulary of the English language. Given the World Wide Web, electronic mail, and fax communications, plus multinational corporations and especially multinational publishing houses, the direction of change is clearly toward consensus rather than wider differentiation.

Compounds and Word Division

Although the differences between American and British spelling practices are not large, some noticeable differences nevertheless do exist. For example, American dictionaries tend to write compounds as single words to a greater extent than British dictionaries do. Nevertheless, the spelling of many compounds, particularly newer ones, is unsettled in America. *American Heritage,* for example, shows all three possible spellings for *secondhand* (i.e., *secondhand, second-hand, second hand*), while all three major U.S. dictionaries disagree on the spelling for *fellow-man,* each preferring a different one of the three options. Hundreds of other compounds show disagreements. In word division, the American scheme is to divide according to pronunciation (e.g., *knowl edge*), while the British appeal first to derivation (e.g., *know ledge*).

Use of Ligatures

With the exception of a few isolated spellings such as *curb* and *jail* (British *kerb, gaol*), all of the British–American spelling differences are in medial or final word positions, and most of the differences are in word endings.[12] One that is not concerns the derivatives of the ligatures <æ> and <œ>. At the end of the 19th century, both American and British spelling retained <æ> and <œ> in classical borrowings, especially for mythological and technical terms (e.g., *Œdipus, amœba*). According to the *OED,* however, there was a tendency, more so in the United States than in Britain, to simplify the two ligatures in familiar or popular words. American practice by the late 1950s, however, had shifted: "Words formerly written with a ligature *æ, œ* are now usually written with the two letters separately. . . . There is a tendency in the US to drop the *e* or the *o,* esp. in common nouns *ecology, gynecology,* but since it is by no means universal and varies in different words, no rule can be given."[13]

The U.S. Government Printing Office's *Style Manual* proscribes ligatures in anglicized or Latin words, but suggests following the appropriate national practice for other foreign words. In contrast, the 1993 edition of *The Chicago Manual of Style* states that the two ligatures should not be used at all for classical borrowings, recommending <e> where either ligature previously appeared. Only for spelling Old English words in an Old English context is <æ> to be used, and only for spelling French words in a French context is <œ> to be used.[14]

British style has also changed: "In the last twenty years or so, British printers have come to accept the American simplification of the <ae> and <oe> digraphs (or ligatures) in classical borrowings such as *encyclopedia, medieval, fetid,* though many survive, e.g. *archaeology, Caesar.*"[15] More recently, *COBUILD* does not use the ligatures at all. With the ligatures eliminated, British spellings now have two separate letters in their place, while American spellings have replaced both with <e>: American *ameba, diarrhea, gynecology;* British *amoeba, diarrhoea, gynaecology.*

Changes before Suffixes

American and British spelling differ in seemingly contradictory ways in the handling of final consonants and vowels before both derivational and inflectional suffixes. Before <ment> and <ful>, the American style is to double or to retain a doubled <l> (*enrollment, fulfillment; skillful, willful*), while the British style is for a single <l> in each case (*enrolment, fulfilment; skilful, wilful*). On the other hand, the British style is to double a final <l> after a single-vowel spelling, even if the final syllable is not stressed, while American style generally is to double a final consonant only after a stressed single-vowel spelling (American *traveling, marvelous* vs. British *travelling, marvellous*). The British reverence for doubling final <l> extends even to <l> after digraph vowel spellings, giving forms like *woollen* where American spelling admits only *woolen*. (But the British preference is for *paralleled* and *devilish*.)

With words that end in <p>, the British style favors gemination: *kidnapped, kidnapping* and *worshipped, worshipping*. American spelling is more unsettled. The *Collegiate* and *Random House* both prefer *kidnapped, kidnapping*, but *worshiped, worshiping*, while *American Heritage* prefers a single <p> in all four.

The treatment of final <e> after <dg> when adding suffixes also separates American and British spelling. British usage favors retention of <e> in adding <ment> to such words as *abridge, judge*, and *lodge*, while American spelling prefers dropping the <e>: *abridgment, judgment, lodgment*. Sir James Murray, chief editor of the original *OED*, was critical of the American style: "I protest against the unscholarly habit of omitting it from 'abridgement,' 'acknowledgement,' 'judgement,' 'lodgement,' which is against all analogy, etymology, and orthoepy, since elsewhere *g* is hard in English when not followed by *e* or *i* . . . ".[16] In defence of the American style, an equally strong if not stronger argument can be made that <dg> as a spelling unit has only a single pronunciation, which is the soft <g> (/ĵ/), and therefore the <e> is unnecessary. For other words that end in silent <e>, American spelling generally omits the <e> before <able> except after <c> or <g>, while British spelling tends to make exceptions for certain words (American *blamable, namable, ratable* vs. British *blameable, nameable, rateable*).

Word Endings

First, before <r> and <l>, American spelling prefers <o> to the British <ou> (e.g., American *honor, favor,* and *molt* vs. British *honour, favour,* and *moult*). The <ol> spellings are found in only a small group of words—*mold, molder, molt,* and *smolder* being the only common ones. The contrast between <ou> and <o> dates to the period just after the American Revolution, and in particular to the spelling reform efforts of Noah Webster (see Chapter 11). Although neither American nor British usage is totally consistent, American spelling is more so, deviating only on *glamour* and *saviour.* In formal usage, the British prefer <or> for agent nouns (e.g., *actor*) but <our> for abstract nouns (e.g., *ardour, favour, valour*). Before certain suffixes, <our> changes to <or> (e.g., <ation>, <iferous>, <ize>), but before others it remains (e.g., <able>, <er>, <ful>, <ite>).

Nevertheless, exceptions abound: *anterior, saviour, error, horror,* and more. Samuel Johnson omitted <u> in *anterior* and *interior,* but it was excluded from *emperor, orator,* and *horror* by later lexicographers.[17]

A second difference concerns final <er> and <re>. American spelling consistently uses final <er> in preference to <re> (e.g., *center, liter, meter*), while the British are equally consistent in using <re>. One of the few British exceptions occurs for *meter* in the sense of a device (and its verb counterpart). The American usage dates mainly to Noah Webster, while the British usage has developed over the last 350 years. In the 1623 edition of Shakespeare's plays, more <er> than <re> spellings occurred. Nevertheless, by the middle of the 17th century, <re> was the majority preference in England.[18] The American preference for <er> is slightly problematic, because compounds such as *central, metric,* and *fibrous* require reversal to the British style.

A third difference is the contrast between final <ce> and <se>, which varies unsystematically between American and British practices. *License* and *practice* are both noun and verb spellings in America; in Britain the noun spellings are with <ce>, but the related verb spellings are with <se>: *license, practise.*[19] In contrast, the American *defense, offense,* and *pretense* are spelled with final <ce> in Britain. Two other differences are found in the contrasts between <yze> and <yse>, and between <xion> and <ction>. The verbal ending <yze>, which is part of the Greek stem <lyse>, retains the <z> in American practice (*analyze, catalyze, paralyze*), but is usually spelled with an <s> in Britain (*analyse, catalyse, paralyse*). *The Oxford Guide to English Usage* is rather emphatic about this preference: "The spelling *-yze* is therefore etymologically incorrect and must not be used, unless American printing style is being followed."[20] For <xion> and <ction>, American spelling prefers <ction> in many places where British spelling prefers <xion> (*deflection, genuflection, inflection* vs. *deflexion, genuflexion, inflexion*). The trend in British spelling, however, appears to be away from the <xion> spelling. Both *COBUILD* and *Cambridge,* prefer *inflection* over *inflexion.*

This is the view of British–American differences at the end of the 20th century. They are not major in relation to the underlying patterning of the orthography, nor do they affect a large segment of the vocabulary. Nevertheless, they do still yield distinctive spelling and lexicographic practices. As publishing moves online and the World Wide Web becomes the mode of communication around the world not only for academics and professionals, but for homemakers and others the future of these differences is in question. Those that are the least consistent (such as the <our>–<or> differences) may be the first to be leveled, followed by some that affect only a small number of words (such as <re> versus <er>). Stay tuned for the next instal(l)ment in this story.

PLACE NAMES

As a fraternity pledge at Cornell University in the middle 1950s, I was required to learn by heart the name of a lake in Massachusetts, Lake Chargoggaggog-gmanchaugagoggchaubunagungamaug, which we were told meant "You fish on your side, I'll fish on my side, and nobody fishes in the middle." We had a pennant on the wall with this name (quite a long pennant), and pledges were required to recite the name on demand. Years later I learned that this name was a fiction—a monstrosity created, apparently for humor, by a newspaper editor in Webster, Massachusetts, near where the lake is located. The true name of the lake, as shown on modern maps of Massachusetts, is Lake Chabunagungamaug, which apparently means "boundary fishing-place" or "lake divided by islands."

The Lake Chabunagungamaug case is just one of a number of problems in place name spelling that have arisen over the past several centuries, especially with names taken from Native American languages for which few if any speakers remain. In addition, different names have often been given to the same mountain range, river, or even town, as different settlers, railroad agents, or postal clerks have attempted to establish their notions of correct labels. For example, in *The American Language,* H. L. Mencken pointed out that what is spelled *Allegheny* for the river in Pennsylvania is spelled *Allegany* for a county in Maryland, and *Alleghany* for a city in Colorado.[21] But we need not cover such an expanse of territory to witness orthographic confusion. Pennsylvania's Allegheny National Forest is bounded on its north by New York State's Allegany State Park. And just west of Allegheny National Forest is the town of Port Allegany, which sits nearly on the Allegheny River.

Many place names in the United States are taken from native Indian words (e.g., *Chicago, Roanoke*), family names (e.g., *Scottsdale, Harper's Ferry*), or Biblical and mythological names (e.g., *Jaffa, Phoenix*). Many of these were transliterated from languages that either had no writing systems or were written with non-roman letters; in addition, spellings often changed over time. For example, the state of Delaware was named for Thomas West, Lord de la Warre (a governor of Virginia), and was spelled in various ways before the current spelling was settled. Because of these problems in place name spellings, President Benjamin Harrison created the U.S. Board on Geographic Names by executive order in 1890 to ensure "that uniform usage in regard to geographic nomenclature and orthography obtain throughout the Executive Departments of the Government, and particularly upon the maps and charts issued by the Departments and bureaus."[22]

The idea for the board came from Professor Thomas C. Mendenhall, Superintendent of the U.S. Coast and Geodetic Survey Office, who in January 1890 circulated a letter to various government departments and the National Geographic Society, suggesting a board for resolving disputed questions of geographical orthography. Most of the departments that Mendenhall addressed answered favorably, leading him to convene an unofficial board, which met through the spring of 1890 and which became the U.S. Board on Geographic Names upon President Harrison's order later that fall.

During the first 10 years of its existence, the U.S. Board on Geographic Names decided 4,157 cases, in addition to approving spellings for all 2,803 counties then in existence in the United States. Typical of the problems dealt with by the board was the spelling of the name *Wisconsin,* which over the 211 years from the time that French explorers first visited the area until the Territorial Council and House of Representatives passed a resolution on the issue, was rendered as *Ouisconsin, Wiskonsin, Wisconsan,* and probably a variety of other ways. In the preface to the 1831 edition of his spelling book, Noah Webster referred directly to this problem:

> Many of these names still retain the French orthography, found in the writings of the first discoverers or early travellers; but the practice of writing such words in the French manner ought to be discountenanced. How does an unlettered American know the pronunciation of the names, *Ouisconsin* or *Ouabasche,* in this French dress? Would he suspect the pronunciation to be Wisconsin and Waubash? Our citizens ought not to be thus perplexed with an orthography to which they are strangers.[23]

Webster was anxious to establish an American style of spelling, but with or without this motivation, his concern was valid.

An 1822 map of the "Arkansa Territory" uses the spelling *Wisconsan* for the Wisconsin region but shows on another plate the spelling *Wisconsin,* which may have been a spelling error.[24] In contrast, a map published in Detroit in 1830 refers to the "Territory of Michigan and Ouisconsin." When the Wisconsin Territory was created in 1836, the current spelling was applied. However, sufficient disagreement remained that the Territorial Government approved a resolution in 1845 "to declare the name of the Territory 'Wisconsin.'" Even with this resolution, the U.S. Board on Geographic Names found it necessary to include an entry in its *Second Report* on the Wisconsin River: "Wisconsin; river in Wisconsin. (Not Ouisconsin, nor Wiskonsin.)"[25]

The origins of spelling differences for place names were discussed extensively in the board's *Second Report.* One cause was the fact that different exploring expeditions had given different names or different spellings to places, in ignorance of what earlier parties had decided. Several hundred cases from Alaska that the board considered in its first years, representing an admixture of Native, Russian, Spanish, and English nomenclature, derived from this problem. The transliteration of Native American names was a second major source of variation. A third was that railroads and post offices adopted names for their offices or stations that differed from local usage in spelling (or from the local names themselves). Carelessness and ignorance round out the list. On the positive side, the report also noted a tendency "toward the discarding of objectionable names and the adoption of pleasing ones, and toward the simplification and abbreviation of names, particularly as shown in the dropping of silent letters."[26]

Early in its existence, the board adopted nomenclature reforms that included the following:

> (a) avoidance, as far as seems practicable, of the possessive form of names; (b) dropping of the final "h" in the termination "burgh"; (c) abbreviation of "borough" to "boro"; (d) spelling of the word "center" as here given; (e) discontinuance of the use of hyphens in connecting parts of names; (f) simplification of names consisting of more than one word by their combination into one word; and (g) avoidance of the use of diacritic characters.[27]

Apparently one of the decisions of the board was to accept the name Lake Webster as a replacement for Lake Chabunagungamaug—a decision that has since been reversed.

In 1911, under pressure from various sources, the board was forced to restore <h> to *Pittsburgh*. By executive order of April 17, 1934, the board was abolished and its functions transferred to a newly formed Division of Geographic Names in the Department of the Interior. In 1947 a public law recreated the U.S. Board on Geographic Names, the title under which it functions today. Its present structure includes a Domestic Names Committee, which operates on the principle of formal recognition for present-day local usage, and a Foreign Names Committee, which deals with such issues as Romanization standards. In 1990 the Library of Congress marked the 100th anniversary of the board with a special exhibit, during which time the controversy over the correct name for Lake Chabunagungamaug triggered an exchange in *The New York Times*.[28]

THE ABC'S OF FOOD AND DRINK

We end this leisurely excursion to the islands of orthographic miscellany by coming ashore to an American dinner table. But before enjoying the repast, we must attend to the spellings of the food and drink. Unlike Tantalus,[29] however, who can never quite reach the water he stands in or the fruit that dangles in front of his eyes, you will be free to nosh, chop, gnaw, munch, guzzle, scoff, nibble, taste, and devour as you choose once this chapter is completed. We'll start with the offerings from two menus encountered on a recent journey: one (which has been introduced in the Preface) from a restaurant in Union Station, the rail hub of our nation's capital; and the other from a pub in a working-class neighborhood in Wilmington, Delaware, where the journey began. From these we will expand our purview to include other menus, a seed catalog, and some cookbooks.[30] Our goal is to demonstrate how global the orthography of food and drink has become in America. As a starter, gaze at the full range of origins of the terms on these two menus:

> Arabic: *hummous, mocha*
> British English: *draught*
> Chinese: *tea* (by way of Dutch), *ketchup*
> French: *Cabernet, Cajun, chef, croutons, mayonnaise, romaine, sautéed, Sauvignon* (and more)
> German: *deli, kraut, hamburger, schnapps*
> Greek: *pita*
> Hebrew: *Reuben*
> Hindi: *punch*
> Italian: *antipasto, marinara, mozzarella, parmesan, pepperoni, pizza, salami* (and more)
> Japanese: *teriyaki*
> Latin: *orchid, soda*
> Portuguese: *buffalo*
> Spanish: *chili, jalapeño, quesadilla, salsa, tuna*
> Turkish: *coffee*

Amazing! Thirteen different languages, not counting American and British English. With cookbook recipes included, this number climbs further: for example, African (Ibo) *okra,* Native American (Narragansett) *squash,* and Brazilian (Tupi) *cayenne.* Two spelling reform creations also occur on the two menus, *Lo-Cal* and *Lite* (as in *Miller Lite*), as does one foreign marker, the tilde (*jalapeño*). The cookbooks offer two more such markers, the cedilla (e.g., *niçoise*) and the acute accent (e.g., *purée, frisée*). Markers for two different pronunciations of <g> occur in *George* and *Guinness.* In the former, an <e> marks the soft pronunciation while in the latter a <u> marks the hard pronunciation. Similarly, <e> serves various marking functions in *cheese, lettuce, romaine, Lite,* and *sausage.*

Silent letters abound: <l> in *almond* and *salmon;* <p> in *raspberry;* <t> in *Cabernet* and *filet;* <d> in *Pernod* and *sandwich;* <h> in *herb;* <b> in *crumb;*

and <ll> in some pronunciations of *quesadilla.* In *cheese, chef,* and *mocha,* <ch> takes on all three of its pronunciations; in *mozzarella* and *quesadilla* <ll> takes on two different pronunciations; and <c> takes on three in *lettuce, cafe,* and *cappuccino.* The pronunciation of <zz> in *buzzing* and *fizzle* is different from that of *mozzarella* and *pizza,* and the <u> in *guacamole* shows one of its rare occurrences as /w/ when not preceded by <q>. Finally, <th> is /t/ in *thyme.*

In *cheese, lettuce,* and *sausage,* final <e> is silent; in *cafe, guacamole,* and *sesame,* it is pronounced, but with two different mappings. At a more advanced level, what appear to be stressed vowels in the last syllables of both *lettuce* and *sausage* are in fact unstressed and pronounced /ɪ/. At the level of individual mappings for vowels, variety is everywhere to be found: <e> is /e/ in *filet* and *quesadilla,* /ɪ/ in *jalapeño,* /ɛ/ in *enchiladas,* and /ə/ in *parmesan;* <a> is /ɪ/ in *sausage,* /ə/ in *tuna,* /e/ in *Cajun,* /æ/ in *raspberry,* and /a/ in *guacamole.*

Within the seed catalog and cookbooks, even more variety in American orthography appears. *Rabe,* as in *broccoli rabe,* is one of the few exceptions to the free vowel pattern in monosyllables.[31] *Bibb,* as in *Bibb lettuce,* is a recent addition to the culinary lexicon and represents yet another case of final geminate consonants to distinguish a personal name from a common word with otherwise identical spelling. (Bibb lettuce is named after Major John Bibb, a 19th-century American grower.) *Gnocchi* is a case of silent initial <g> before <n>, but not one that was pronounced at an earlier time in English. (It appears in English writing only at the end of the 19th century, borrowed from Italian.) *Vermouth* adds another <ou> spelling to the /u/ pronunciation list, joining *soup, group,* and a handful of French borrowings, and *cantaloupe* adds another <ou> spelling to the /o/ pronunciation list.

Shiitake, a Japanese borrowing formed from the Japanese *shii,* "chinquapin nut," is a rare case of <ii> as a functional unit. (In *skiing,* the only common word in which <ii> occurs in English, each <i> is mapped into a separate phoneme.) *Niçoise* has <oi> → /wa/, a mapping found only in recent French borrowings; *cassoulet* has <ou> → /ə/, a rare mapping for <ou>. The Italian <cch> (= /k/) spelling abounds, especially in the seed catalog: *finocchio* (also spelled *finochio*), *radicchio, zucchetta, zucchini,* and *gnocchi* (from one of the cookbooks).

LOOKING AHEAD

There is much more that could be pointed out about the spellings of food and drink terms, but the table beckons, the wine is poured, and the repast is fresh from the oven and cutting board. Enjoy! Then move on to Chapter 3, where the world of creative spellings awaits.

NOTES

1. An example of a dictionary with the former requirement is *The Random House Dictionary of the English Language,* second edition, unabridged (Flexner, 1987), hereafter referred to as *Random House;* an example of one with the latter requirement is *Merriam–Webster's Collegiate Dictionary,* 10th edition (Mish, 1993), hereafter referred to as *Collegiate.*
2. I am endebted to Charles Hockett (1958) for this example.
3. A listing of over 1,800 homophones can be found in Whitford (1966).
4. For those speakers who pronounce the <a> in *khaki* as they do in *father,* the <kh> spelling of /k/ can be included, because *khaki* is identical to *cocky.*
5. The discussion that follows is based primarily upon the spellings offered by the three British dictionaries mentioned in the first text paragraph below and cited in notes 7–9, plus three major American dictionaries: the *Collegiate* (Mish, 1993); the *Random House* (Flexner, 1987); and *The American Heritage Dictionary of the English Language,* third edition (Soukhanov, 1992), hereafter referred to as *American Heritage.* British and American style guides consulted for this work include *The Oxford Guide to English Usage,* second edition (Weiner & Delahunty, 1994); the *U.S. Government Printing Office Style Manual* (1973); and a comparative study of spellings in four popular collegiate dictionaries that were copyrighted in the period 1968–1970 (Deighton, 1972). *The Oxford Guide to English Usage* reflects "correct and acceptable standard British English" and "is based largely on the archives, experience, and resources of the Oxford English Dictionary Department of the Oxford University Press, and has the authority of the Oxford family of dictionaries behind its recommendations" (Weiner & Delahunty, 1994, v). British spellings at the end of the 19th century and after the first quarter of the 20th century were also reviewed for contrast and for trends (Craigie, 1927; Matthews, 1892).
6. Weiner & Delahunty (1994).
7. Sinclair (1987). This is hereafter referred to as *COBUILD.*
8. Kirkpatrick (1983).
9. Proctor (1995). This is hereafter referred to as *Cambridge.*
10. Deighton (1972).
11. See especially Mencken (1936), Deighton (1972), and Weiner & Delahunty (1994).
12. Not included here are pronunciation differences for shared spellings (e.g., *schedule*) and morphological differences (e.g., *dreamed–dreamt*).
13. Nicholson (1957), 537f.
14. *The Chicago Manual of Style* (1993), 168.
15. Scragg (1974), 85.
16. Cited in Oxford University Press (1983), 86, fn. 1.
17. See Johnson (1755) and Matthews (1892).
18. See Matthews (1892).
19. But the *Collegiate,* while preferring *license,* also gives *licence* without marking the latter as British.
20. Oxford University Press (1983), 86.
21. Mencken (1936). Besides Mencken's section on place names in this work, there

are a number of mostly older treatments of the subject, as well as an endless collection of archival works listing the place names of specific areas (some of which are available on the World Wide Web). An earlier work of general interest is Stewart (1945). For a more recent account, consult Matthews (1972). For scholarly information on the place names of specific regions, see the *Publications of the English Place-Names Society,* which began to appear in 1924.

22. U.S. Board on Geographic Names (1901), 2.
23. Webster (1831/1962), 17.
24. This is discussed in Smith (1942).
25. U.S. Board on Geographic Names (1901), 133.
26. U.S. Board on Geographic Names (1901), 15.
27. U.S. Board on Geographic Names (1901), 16, with lettering changes.
28. The longer name was included in a September 9, 1990 news article on the Library of Congress exhibit (Sullivan, 1990). This led to a letter to the editor by the curator of anthropology at the Smithsonian Institution, Ives Goddard, (Goddard, 1990) which was published on September 29, giving the full story of the lake's name.
29. On Tantalus, Edmund Spenser wrote in *The Faerie Queen* (1590/1981, II.vii.59): "Most cursed of all creatures vnder skye, / Lo *Tantalus,* I here tormented lye: / Of whom high *Ioue* [Jove] wont whylome feasted bee, / Lo here I now for want of food doe dye." For a brief synopsis of the story, see Norton and Rushton (1952), 86f.
30. The two cookbooks consulted for this chapter were Meyer and Romano (1994) and Williams (1994). Both are highly recommended for either orthographic or culinary purposes. The seed catalog was that of Shepherd's *Garden Seeds* (1998).
31. Also spelled *raab* or *rab,* from the Italian *broccoli di rapa,* "flowering tops of turnips."

CHAPTER 3

Creative Spellings

A boy at Sault Ste. Marie
Said spelling is all Greek to me,
Till they learn to spell "Soo"
Without any u,
Or an a, or an l, or a t.
—ANONYMOUS
(Peter Pauper Press, 1951)

According to Principle 2 in Chapter 1, "Letter distribution is capriciously limited." Some might object to the modifier "capriciously" because some distributional limitations have rational explanations. Yet the distributions of some spelling units in English are unpredictable, bordering on the impulsive. Why, for example, do we allow <e> to double, but fight against <a> doing the same? Why can't <tch> start a word? We have reasons for some distributional limits, but not for all of them. But these limits, rational or not, allow trade and advertising spellings and pseudowords to be created with varying approximations to real English spellings. These creations and the mechanisms used to generate them are the topics of the present chapter.

THE JOY OF CREATION

To invent a new spelling and have it enshrined within a treasury of spellings such as the *OED* may not rank quite as high on the creativity scale as Mozart's 41st

Symphony or the discovery of penicillin, but it is a major feat nevertheless and one to be celebrated. Lewis Carroll did it with *galumphing,* which appeared first in *Through the Looking Glass* ("Jabberwocky") in 1871.[1] Carroll's "Jabberwocky" is built on made-up words: *brillig, slithy, toves, gyre, gimble, wabe, mimsy, borogoves, mome,* and more. Some are patterned after real words (e.g., *brillig, slithy, gimble*); some contain familiar suffixes (e.g., *frumious, uffish, frabjous*); and one is an extension of a noun to a verb (*gyre*). Except for *manxome,* which contains a sequence that occurs in only two English words (<nx>—*anxious, anxiety*), all are orthographically familiar.

A century later, Dr. Seuss followed in the tradition of Lewis Carroll with *There's a Wocket in My Pocket!,*[2] in which are enshrined such classics as *wasket* (in your basket), *nureau* (in your bureau), and *zlock* (behind your clock). Creations that begin with the letter <z> are especially prominent: *zall, zellar, zower, zable, zamp, zelf,* and *zillow* (along with *zlock*). Except for *zlock,* which contains (or implies) an initial consonant cluster that does not occur in English (/zl/), these are all acceptable made-up words or pseudowords.

But poets and children's authors are not the only ones who traffic in new spellings. Drug companies invent new spellings every day for their products; *Xanax, Advil, Tagamet,* and *Prozac* are creatures of the companies' spelling machines. These and other commercial spellings are the subjects of the next section. Following that is a discussion of what psychologists and linguists call *pseudowords*—that is, made-up words or nonsense words.

TRADE, ADVERTISING, AND PERSONAL NAME SPELLINGS

Of interest in this section is the entire class of trade, advertising, and personal name spellings. Special attention is given to that segment characterized by deviations and violations of standard orthography—that is, names and phrases like *Uneeda* biscuit, *U-All-No* after-dinner mint, *Exxperience the Freedom* (a slogan for Dos Equis XX imported beer), and *Publick House.* Brander Matthews, writing at the end of World War I, claimed that "apparently the invention of trade names is not a customary procedure on the part of foreign advertisers. The British, although less affluent in this respect than we are, seem to be a little more inclined to employ the device than their competitors on the Continent."[3] Perhaps the best evidence for the existence of a special class of commercial spellings is their appearance in satires, parodies, and cartoons. A satirical essay in *The New Yorker,* for example, spoofed such creations with the labels *Phabulous Phoods, Joxx Cologne,* and *Chateau X-ellente.*[4] Personal names are included here, not because in general they represent deliberate attempts to attract attention, but because they often violate basic spelling patterns in what appears to be an attempt to distinguish themselves from common words that would otherwise be spelled the same: for example, *Ladd* versus *lad* or *Bil* versus *bill*. In some cases, however, it is difficult to determine if a foreign name has been adopted or if an unusual spelling has been created (e.g., *Djuna*).

One writer has portrayed advertising spelling as an alternate spelling system that exists in complementary distribution in a speech community with the formal system—a form of what linguists call *diglossia*.[5] Exactly what to call this type of spelling is problematic. Trade and advertising spellings as well as spellings of personal names are mixtures of standard and nonstandard spellings, with the latter reserved almost exclusively for products with mass appeal. Elegant and expensive items are rarely, if ever, given names with nonstandard spellings and orthographically deviant forms. *Cheez-It, Bake-N-Serv,* and *Dan-Dee Lunch* do not suggest formal dining or expensive cuisine as well as *Chef Milani's Salad Dressing* or *The Four Seasons* (a New York City restaurant). In addition, more than trade names are involved as rap stars (*Snoop Doggy Dogg, Ice-T*), private individuals *Jhane, Dontae',* and business establishments (*Sit-N-Bull Saloon*) have often adopted the same mechanisms to create their identities. For now I refer to these as *commercial spellings,* covering trade names of products, services, business establishments, and performing groups and individuals, with the understanding that the nonstandard spellings are of primary interest here.

Louise Pound, a dialectologist and linguist, analyzed commercial spellings in separate studies spanning the period 1913–1925 and found a significant increase in intentional misspellings between 1913 and 1923. Writing when the phonograph had just come of age as a home entertainment medium and when the first recordings of Louis Armstrong, Bix Beiderbecke, and The Original Dixieland Jass [*sic*] Band were released, Pound suggested that "it may be that our audacities of spelling are merely a phase of the general jazzing' (as critics call it) of language, as well as of music, manners, and morals, consequent upon the war.[6] Her 10 classes of misspellings included a variety of vowel and consonant changes and omissions (e.g., *Trufit* shoes, *Az-Nu* enameling, *Dyanshine* shoe polish), misspellings for alliteration (e.g., *Kooper Kettle Klub* cigars), simplifications (e.g., *E. Z. Walker* shoes, *Ride Rite* springs), and some miscellaneous alterations (e.g., *Shu-Wite, Rev-O-Noc*). In a later article, Pound elaborated on <k> misspellings in advertising: *Klaudia the Kute Kid of the Circuit, Kwality Kut Klothes, Klip-Klap Snaps,* and so on. She speculated that "Simplified orthography for advertising is perhaps the most important legacy of the defunct spelling reform movement."[7]

A more recent study of 1,512 modified advertising spellings also focused on the devices used for orthographic modification.[8] The classes created included shortening (e.g., *akuret, blok, flo*), schwa deletion (e.g., *chik-n, flav-r*), reduction of past participles (e.g., *dipt, hop'd, tipt*), use of homonyms (e.g., *hart, lox*), <gh> deletion (*Brite, Delite, do* [for *dough*]), and use of older spellings (e.g., *Olde Thyme Shoppe, Towne House*). The largest categories of products with intentional misspellings were household maintenance items (22.4 percent), foods and beverages (17.9 percent), and hobby and recreational items (12.0 percent).

Rock and rap groups have for several decades adopted modified spellings (e.g., the *Beatles*), but more recently the tendency has escalated. Among the names touted in the late 1980s and early 1990s were *Phat Mac Kerouac, Phish, Guns N' Roses, Motley Crüe, Black Crowes, Kix,* and *Hi-Five,* matching older ensembles like the *Byrds* and the *Monkees*. Among the rock and rap song titles incorporating similar orthographic license were "*U Can't Touch This,*" "*I Would Die 4 U,*" and "*Cum on Feel the Noize.*"[9] Although rock and rap performers might use modified orthography as a defiance of standards, commercial spellings have already reached a level of common acceptance that removes most of this appeal.

Drug names, as a class, show a heightened propensity for orthographic innovation, adopting just about every opportunity offered by standard spelling for personal tailoring. *Garlique, Tears Naturale* (eyedrops), *Arrid,* and *Sportscreme,* are examples of what can be found on the shelves of any well-stocked drug store. Names with <y> are especially prevalent: *Tylenol, Kyolic, Benadryl, Phyto-Nutrients, Hytone,* and *Caladryl* constitute a representative listing from a pharmacy in my home town. Most drug names bear a scientific demeanor, but some (such as *Tears Naturale*) are faux French, and a few are draped in a modern, hip mantle: *Perigard, N'Ice, ReNu* (contact-lens-wetting solution), and *Sportscreme.*

Whether commercial spellings will have an impact on standard orthography remains to be determined. One of the few modified spellings to become an accepted variant spelling is *donut,* which is included in current American dictionaries as well as the *OED.* The irony of this transition is that with formal acceptance, most of the impact of the advertising form is lost. Commercial spellings succeed to the degree that they are distinctive to the eye through their use of nonstandard or unexpected spellings, but still readily pronounceable through understandable letter–sound conversions.

Current uses of nonstandard spelling for commercial recognition can be classified into a small number of groups. These are summarized next, with examples of the more common representatives of each.

Early English

The first group consists of respellings that smack of an earlier period—the *Ye Olde Shoppe* variety of orthography. Two mechanisms account for almost all the members of this class: the addition of <k> to final <ic>, as in *Publick;* and the addition of a final silent <e>, as in *Olde* and *Towne,* with doubling of a final consonant when required for proper pronunciation of a single-letter vowel spelling (e.g., *Shoppe*). This is a relatively small group of observed spellings, primarily found on restaurants, shops, and housing developments. Exuded is a whiff of pre-Victorian rural life, of an earlier, gentler period when craft was still authentic and trustworthy.

Letter Names and Numbers

Letter names substituting for words or word parts are common among product brand names, companies, and performers or performing groups: *Bar-B-Q, U-All-No, Bake-N-Serv, E. Z. Walker, La-Z-Boy, Uneeda, Chik-N, X-Press Delivery, Sit 'n' Stroll, Ice-T, Al E. Gator Show.* Many of these include other deviations from standard spelling to differentiate themselves, and some border on rebus writing. The letter <N> as a substitute for *and* is common, as is <U> for *you;* otherwise, no pattern of usage emerges from the examples found. But just as variation occurs with the spellings of many compound words, similar indecision can be observed in the use of letter names to represent words and word parts. For example, the substitution of <EZ> for *easy* occurs as a two-letter word, in caps (*EZ Auto Repair*), as two hyphenated letters (*E-Z Kleen Maintenance*), as two letters with periods after each (*E. Z. Walker*), and as two letters separated by a space (*E Z Button Co.*).

The letter <N> appears to be the most versatile letter for word or syllable representation, commonly appearing as a substitute for *and* (*Spin 'N' Dance, Shop-N-Save, Grin 'n' Bare It*), but also making cameo appearances for *in* (*Keep-N-Touch Communications, N-Charge Construction*), *on* (*N'Site Productions*), and even for <ing> (*Sit-N-Bull Saloon*). Unlike the <EZ> style substitutions, <N> represents shortened phonological forms in all of these cases. It also suffers from the lack of a standard spelling: Compare *Spin 'N' Dance, Shop-N-Save, Shop-N-Bag Super Market, Grin 'n' Bare It,* and *Sit 'n' Stroll* (the last two being the only cases found with a lower-case <n>). In *Brite-N Clean,* the Latin style of adding the coordinating conjunction as a suffix appears to be adopted, although here it is suffixed to the first of two cojoined words rather than to the second (cf. *Senatus populusque Romanus,* "The senate and the people of Rome").

The <T> group is nearly as large as the <N> group, but it derives from various directions, and not all of its members fit the patterns assumed for business spellings. In *T-ball, T-bill* (also *T-bond, T-man*), *T cell, T-group, t quark,* and *T-unit* the <T> or <t> is an abbreviation of a word (for *tee, Treasury, thymus-derived, training, top,* and *terminable,* respectively). In *T-bar, T-bone steak, T-shirt,* and *T square,* the <T> stands for a particular shape, and in *T stop* and *t-test,* <T> or <t> stands for different variables used in photography and statistics.

An alphabet might be composed of trade and advertising names that start with letters used for their names. *A-Korn Roller, B-Line Systems Inc., C-Food Express, D-Lux Motel,* and *EZ Auto Repair* initiate the string. Other letters collected include <G> (*G-Pop's Beauty Supplies Depot*), <K> (*K-9*), <M> (*M-backe House of Hope*), <U> (*U-Haul, U Ride*), <X> (*Xcel Laboratories*), and <Y> (*Y Care*). The letter <X> is probably the most frequently appearing, occurring in such names as *Xcel Laboratories, Xchanger Corporation, Xclusive Limousine Service, Xpedite Systems Inc., Xpert Carpet Service, Xtend Communications,* and *Xxtra Painting Service.* Running a close second is <U>: *U-Haul, U Ride, U-Save Sewerage and Drainage, U Send Me Travel Etc., U-Comtu-EZ.*

Numbers are rare in trade spellings or in any other deliberate attempts to deviate from standard orthography. Universally familiar is a World War II spelling, *K-9,* which curiously is missing from almost all modern dictionaries. Among the few other names containing numerical substitutions are the title of a pop song, "*I Would Die 4 U*"; a cafe in a trendy department store on Fifth Avenue in New York City, *Cafe on 5ive;* and a sports TV program, *NBA 2night.* All these spellings could be classed according to the size of the unit that the letter name or number represents. *Ice-T, Uneeda,* and *U-All-No* represent the word class, while *EZ, K-9, 2night,* and *Xpedite* represent the syllable class. *Cafe on 5ive* is more sophisticated because a visual, not a pronunciation, effect is intended.

Doublings (Geminates)

A small splash can always be made by doubling letters that do not normally double in English spelling. Some are clear violations, such as <x> and <y>, which have been observed in a few forms: *Exxon, Exxperience, Exxit* (a store name), *Xxtra Painting Service, Flyy Girl* (title of a novel), and *Skyy* (a brand of vodka). Foreign names bring doubled <a> and <u> (*Maaco, Saab,* and *Ruud Waterheaters*), and personal names bring a number of letters that do not normally double in final position (*Ladd, Webb, Gregg, Capp, Watt*). Doubled <h>, <j>, <q>, and <w> remain to be observed but probably have occurred somewhere in the English-speaking world. (Doubled <v> will probably also attract attention, in spite of a small number of legitimate <vv> spellings.)

Related to the <x> and <y> cases are spellings such as *barooom* and *sloooow,* which occur in advertisements but not as product names. These draw on more common forms, such as *brrr* and *oooh!,* and are relatively frequent. Slightly different are the cases of letters that can double in English, but generally are not doubled in the positions where the trade names double them (e.g., *Snoop Doggy Dogg*).

Simplified Spellings

Simplified spellings constitute the largest class of commercial spellings, containing everything from the deletion of silent <gh> in <igh> and <ight> spellings (*Hi-Tech, Brite, Prestolite, Delite*) to deleting <e> in forms like *Trufit, Tru-View, Dubl-duti, Conectiv,* and *Serv* (as in *Bake-N-Serv*). Also included often are <k> or <c> for <ck> (*Sunpak, Gyplak, Phone Jak, Tanlac, Rev-O-Noc*), <o> for <ow> (*Evenflo*), <t> for the past tense (*dipt, tipt*), and various miscellaneous replacements such as *Az-Nu, U-All-No, Microglas, Cheez-It, Do* or *Doh* (for *dough,* as in *Play-Doh*), *Trublepruf,* and *Shu-Wite.* The last two of these represent somewhat deviant spellings, because the pronunciations do not match those of the intended words. Less frequently occurring are <f> for <gh> (*I Mak M Laf*), <e> for <ea> (*Def Leppard*), and <u> for <ew> (*ReNu*).

Within this class are a number of simplifications that violate structural regularity principles. For example, *Conectiv, Bake-N-Serv, ReNu, Shu-Wite,* and *Tru-View* have words that end in <u> or <v> but should have a final <e>; *Def, Laf,* and *Microglas* have single-consonant endings where geminates are required; and *Sunpak* ends in <k> where <ck> is required.

Run-Ons and Contractions

In another group of terms, either two words are spelled as one or sounds are deleted. In the first group are *Fixit, Lettuce Entertain You, Mixit Entertainment, Securcar Inc., Payless Submarine, Outta Space Antiques,* and *U-Comtu EZ,* along with *Gufohedake Brane Fude,* which was the center of an early 20th-century fraud suit. In the latter are the <N> forms cited earlier, such as *Spin 'N' Dance,* and such forms as *Read 'Em and Reap* and *K'Nex* (a construction toy).

Diacritics

A few uses of diacritics for name differentiation have been observed, including the macron (*Thōz Nuts, DēLonghi, Westvāco*), apostrophe (*Dontae'*), and dieresis (*Motley Crüe*). This is relatively rare, however.

Infrequent Letters

A few letters such as <k, q, x, y, z> tend to stand out because of their low frequency of use in standard spelling. Consequently, many commercial names incorporate these in obvious ways: for example, *Kan-Do Group, Kwik Klean, Flex-lex, Lux, Ax Nu, Sudz Coin Laundry, Wordz* (as in *Play on Wordz*). The <k> forms tend to introduce <k> for <c>, while the <y> forms introduce <y> where <i> would be expected, and the <z> forms have <z> for more common <s>. The letter <q>, which appears to have limited favor, is a substitute for <k> or for <c> or <ck> pronounced /k/. The letter <x> gives a Grecian gloss to a product name, perhaps suggesting some chemical or physical process in its origins.

Exotic Homonyms

Exotic homonyms include attempts to incorporate French and other foreign spellings (*Over the Ranbeaux, Jazz'E Junque, Tru-Colour*) or to syllabify with a hyphen (*Un-Scene Records, Rock-it Cargo*). Of a rarer type is *pohmp*, in "We're going to pohmp you up," found on a sign in a bookstore. Altogether, this is a small class.

High-Tech Compounds

Spellings such as *ThinkPad, UltraFinder, VoiceNet,* and *InFocus* represent a recent trend that is patterned after naming conventions in certain computer programming languages. In the earliest programming languages (e.g., FORTRAN, ALGOL), names of variables, functions, and programs tended to be short and case-invariant. FORTRAN, in particular, had severe restrictions on the length of such names. As programming became more sophisticated, names of variables (and functions and programs) became more descriptive of the qualities or processes they represented, and therefore longer. Many of these were multi-words, but since space marked the end of a name, the words had to be connected. This led to names such as *WORDSIZE, typeofaccount,* and *numberrequired.*

The C programming language introduced the convention of connecting parts of a name with an underline: *send_wait, ADD_FORCE_TO_HOST, window_id_format.* But as early as 1980 a few programming languages, led by the Mesa language developed at Xerox PARC, began to use internal capitals to mark the first letter of a word: *ReadFile, FileData, ProcessState.* By the mid-1980s this convention became common, and within a few years a large number of technical products were named using the same convention: *DerbyTech Com-*

puters, TouchStone, ProTech, and *CompuAdd.* From computer-related products the convention spread to other technical products and corporation names, and then to nontechnical use, such as *SkyMall Calling Card, MellonBank, SelfCare,* and *PowerBar.* These are related to the run-on terms described above, except that no sounds or spellings are deleted and each component word begins with a capital letter. A newer convention is to borrow World Wide Web and e-mail addresses for names (e.g., *biztravel.com, amazon.com, @Home*).

A RECLASSIFICATION

As a group, these spellings can be gathered into four categories according to their orthographic legality. First are the completely legal—that is, regular spellings such as *Beatles, Kox,* and *Tylenol.* These violate neither structural regularity patterns nor spelling-to-sound patterns. Next are the marginal spellings—the ones that are in the gray zone between legal and illegal. Included here are the run-ons such as *Mixit* and contractions such as *Read 'Em and Reap.* In the third category are clear violations of either structural or letter–sound patterns. *Sudz, Exxon, Microglas, Phone Jak, Serv,* and *Wordz* are examples of structural violations; *Mak* (for *Make*), *Copytex, Shu-Wite,* and *Trublepruf* are examples of letter–sound violations. In the fourth class are the spellings that introduce symbols not ordinarily used in spelling (e.g., *Thōz Nuts, 2night*) or that require a different letter–sound system, such as letter name forms like *C-Food* and *E. Z. Walker.*

The computer-influenced spellings such as *InfoTips, MellonBank,* and *biztravel.com* fit into this fourth category. They represent the most rapidly expanding convention for the present, but like most other types of creative spellings, they are limited in application. Drug names, for example, still tend toward the high-tech look, with <y>'s and <x>'s in abundance. What have not been explored in depth here are the types of violations that do not occur. For example, no creative spellings that start with pseudogeminates have been observed, nor any that begin with true geminate consonants, except for one case of <xx>.

An issue that remains to be explored is the range of images that different types of creative spellings create or attempt to create. Forms like *zlock, brillig,* and *mimsy* appear playful and amusing; *Publick* and *Ye Olde,* in contrast, invoke images of an American colonial setting, with horse-drawn wagons, gabled houses, and blacksmith shops. *Ice-T* is cool, while *Cafe on 5ive,* for those who know Fifth Avenue near Central Park in New York City, is friendly but elegant. Exactly how spellings like *K'Nex, U-All-Know,* and *Sudz Coin Laundry* appeal to different age, sex, and income groups remains to be explored. Perhaps there is a grant to be had for exploring this topic with focus groups, scalings, and other market analysis strategies.

PSEUDOWORDS

The second major category of creative spellings to be discussed here is composed of made-up words or *pseudowords*. For at least 90 years psychologists and linguists have been inventing different types of spellings as stimuli for studies of word perception, letter–sound knowledge, and familiarity with print, as well as for testing decoding ability (see Chapter 12). The term *pseudoword* is applied to any invented spelling that is created to be an approximation to English spelling. A *pseudohomophone* is a spelling, such as *fone* or *shert,* that sounds like a real word when pronounced but is not a spelling found in a common dictionary.

Pseudowords can be orthographically regular (e.g., *swaner, mauton*) or irregular (e.g., *blou, heeck*), and pronounceable (e.g., *selom, sliv*) or unpronounceable (e.g., *rbleyfg, wnraes*). Thus one can invent pseudohomophones that are either orthographically regular (e.g., *trane, gest*) or orthographically irregular (e.g., *tchane, ttrik*). The main concern of this section is the generation of good-looking pseudowords—that is, the rules that allow a psychologist or linguist (or anyone else who strays into this business) to generate pseudowords that are acceptable as English spellings. By extension, knowing what is acceptable leads to knowing what is not acceptable so that illegal pseudowords can be generated by breaking one or more of the rules for generating regular pseudowords. First, though, here is a little history of this topic.

The earliest published study that used pseudowords to study perception of printed words was by Walter F. Dearborn in 1906.[10] Dearborn was a student of James McKeen Cattell at Columbia University, where he received his PhD in psychology in 1905. Assisting him at Columbia with his reading studies were not only Cattell, but also R. S. Woodworth, Edward L. Thorndike, and Raymond Dodge, all leading psychologists of the time and major contributors to the study of reading. Dearborn went from Columbia to the University of Wisconsin; he was serving there as an instructor in educational psychology when his dissertation studies were published. He later became a professor of education at Harvard and coauthor with Irving H. Anderson of an influential textbook on the psychology and pedagogy of reading.[11]

Dearborn created 30 "nonsense" words that he used to study the time required for word perception. Some of these were labeled "normal, common" (e.g., *werq, apli*) and the others "non-normal" (e.g., *ciuo, dpin*). He noted that words that did not contain a normal sequence of letters "disappoint the associative expectancy" and thereby take longer to pronounce.[12] He also noted that some of his creations were more difficult to pronounce than others.

As a pioneer in the use of pseudowords for studying reading, Dearborn is remembered with favor. As a creator of respectable pseudowords, however, Dearborn made no lasting contribution. Of his 30 words, 28 end in vowels, many with two- and three-vowel sequences (e.g., *ruia, tioe, fiea*). Some of his words are unpronounceable (e.g., *fhwe, dpiu, sfag*), and some such as *werq,* which he labeled "normal, common," are orthographically illegal. Nevertheless, the use of pseudowords to study word perception was original with Dearborn, even though nearly a half-century passed before anyone revisited this idea.

The return to using pseudowords came in the 1950s and was due to Claude Shannon's algorithm for generating approximations to English spelling.[13] Psychologists at that time began to use pseudowords in studies of language processing, starting with a study in which second-order (e.g., *nermblim, edingedl*) and fourth-order (e.g., *mossiant, otations*) pseudowords were generated for a free-recall task.[14] A later study generated fourth-order approximations (e.g., *mossia, onetic*), based on the same stimuli and experimental method.[15] Later in the 1960s tables were published of single-letter, bigram, and trigram frequencies for different word positions, using lists of unique English words.[16] These tables as well as the Shannon generation algorithms continued to influence the construction of pseudowords well into the 1980s.

By the 1980s, however, two other techniques were introduced for generating pseudowords. One was based upon altering a single letter in a familiar word (e.g., *plane–plame–dlane*). In this example, the first alteration produces a pronounceable pseudoword, while the second produces an unpronounceable one. The second technique was to use rules for generating pseudowords, based upon patterns of orthographic structure. Although this has been attempted in a number of studies, no full set of rules or patterns for doing this has ever been published. In the section that follows, I sketch an approach to doing this and give at least a subset of the rules.

Preliminaries

Given that English orthography is far from regular, and that through borrowings especially, almost every pattern has at least one exception that occurs in a major dictionary, one can set either loose or strict rules for acceptable pseudowords. For example, one- and two-letter words are restricted to a small set of mostly function words in the English lexicon.[17] In cases where more two-letter words might have occurred, either a final <e> was added (e.g., *rye, foe, roe*) or a final consonant was doubled (e.g., *ebb, odd, egg*). A strict approach to generating pseudowords therefore labels all one- and two-letter creations as irregular. A loose criterion, in contrast, admits as regular *ab, eb, ib, ob, ub, ap, eg,* and so on.

Similarly, a strict rule set does not allow digraph vowels before true geminates or pseudogeminates, thus ruling out words such as *neack, troadge,* and *louffer.* Such a criterion also allows only <ff, ll, ss> to double at the ends of monosyllables, and then only after single-letter spellings. This rule classes seemingly well-formed words such as *burr, err, fizz, razz, butt,* and *watt* as irregular. The justification offered is that although word-final <rr, tt, zz> occur in English, they are (1) rare, and (2) limited mostly to relatively recent borrowings or imitative words. Final <rr> occurs in only three common words (*burr, err,* and *shirr*); final <tt> occurs in four (*boycott, butt, putt,* and *watt*); and final <zz> occurs in five (*buzz, fizz, fuzz, jazz,* and *razz*). Of these latter five, three (*buzz, fizz, razz*) have imitative origins, one is a back-formation (*fuzz*), and one has an unknown but recent origin (*jazz*).

Making rule setting more complex is the question of monosyllabics and multisyllabics that end in a single <f, l>, or <s>. Aside from a small group of exceptions (*if, of, chef, clef, motif*), final <f> occurs only after digraph vowels (e.g., *loaf, woof*) or consonants (e.g., *elf, serf*). Thus, by strict rules, *trif* and *enslaf* would not be well-formed pseudowords. For <l>, monosyllabics, with four exceptions (*gel, nil, pal, til*), end in <ll>; multisyllabics can end in either <l> or <ll>, except for the ending <full>, which becomes <ful>. For <s>, monosyllabics, with the exception of function words (e.g., *as, is, has*) and *bus* and *pus,* end in <ss>, while multisyllabics can end in either <s> or <ss>. Nevertheless, most noninflectional <s> endings are suffixes (<eous, ius, ous, us>), and most <ss> endings are <less>, <ness>, or the female marker <ess> (e.g., *actress, heiress, sorceress*).

A strict criterion also outlaws <u> at the ends of words, and <y> at the beginnings of words as a vowel. For the digraph vowels, the <u> and <i> variants are restricted to preconsonantal positions, and the <y> and <w> variants to all other positions. However, given the high number of exceptions for <ow> before consonants, this exception is allowed.

Further restrictions are applied to consonants. For example, the rarer digraphs and trigraphs are classed as irregular (e.g., <pph>, <kh>), and all the restrictions noted above for <h, j, k, q, v, w, wh> apply. Thus <q> can occur only before <u>, <h> only before vowels, <j> only in initial and medial positions by itself (i.e., <j> is not allowed in consonant clusters), <k> only before <e, i, y> or after digraph vowels at the end of a word, <v> not in final position, and <wh> only in word-initial position. Moreover, neither true geminate consonants nor the pseudogeminates can occur in word-initial position. Beyond these restrictions, consonant clusters are restricted to those generating phonological clusters that are legal in English. This last restriction rules out Dr. Seuss's *zlock,* as well as such abominations as *tlong, dlimpt,* and *frongb.*

Under the assumption that the initial consonant clusters <kn, gn, mn, ps, pt, wr> are fossils of an earlier period when they were pronounceable (or thought to be), no new words with these clusters are allowed. Similarly, <sf> is ruled out because the few common /sf/ initial clusters in English are all spelled <sph>. (A few rarer Italian borrowings have initial <sf>, as does the recent coining *sferics,* but these are not sufficient to class this sequence as a common English initial cluster.) The same reasoning rules out the final clusters <mn> and <gn> and certain initial clusters such as <skw>, since initial /skw/ in English is spelled <squ> (e.g., *squirrel, square*).

Strict rules for final consonants and consonant clusters are equally problematic. For example, final <z> is rare in English words, occurring by itself among common words only in *whiz,* which is possibly of imitative origin; and *quiz,* whose origin is unknown. The letter <z> also occurs in word-final position in four rare clusters: <dz> (*adz*), <ltz> (*waltz*), <ntz> (*chintz*), and <rtz> (*quartz*). Consequently, final <z>, either alone or as the last element in a final cluster, is not allowed under the strict rules. For final consonant clusters, inflectional <s> and <d> are allowed, but only according to the rules given in Chapter 5.

Among the final consonant clusters, frequency and conformity to graphotactical patterning are the main criteria used for selection, which means that some arbitrariness is unavoidable. For example, <lb> is included, even though it occurs in only one common word (*bulb*). This decision is based on both phonological and orthographic patterning: Most of the other <l> + stop clusters occur (<lp, ld, lt, lk>), and <lb> is the only available spelling for final /lb/. Similarly, <g> is allowed to occur after single-letter vowels in monosyllables and multisyllabics, even though few multisyllabics other than compounds contain this ending.

More problematic is final <gh>, which occurs in under 40 common words in final position. Most of these occurrences are after <ou>; a few follow <ei> or <i>. None follows <a, e, o, u>, or <y> or any other digraph spelling except <au> or <ou>. Except in place names, only one example of a final <gh> cluster occurs: <rgh> (*burgh*). Since most of these <gh> spellings are silent (and almost all that are not represent a fossilized correspondence, <gh> → /f/), the decision here is to eliminate final <gh> totally under the strict rules, but to allow it after any vowel in the loose rule set.

With these restrictions, strict rules are listed below for vowels and for initial and final consonants and consonant clusters.

Vowels

All the primary vowel units and all the major secondary units described in Chapters 9 and 10 can be used in pseudowords, but with certain restrictions. For the primary vowel spellings (<a, e, i/y, o, u>), <y> is not allowed at the beginning of a word, and <i> and <u> are not allowed in word-final position. For digraphs, <i/y> and <u/w> alternate as second elements as described in the "Preliminaries" section above. In addition, digraph vowels do not appear before consonant clusters in the same syllable, but the manner in which this is realized in spelling is complicated. For example, <ee> appears before no consonant clusters except (1) those formed through suffixes or compounds (e.g., *seemly, needless, greenhouse*), (2) those formed by the addition of <th> at the end of numerals (e.g., *eighteenth*), and (3) before consonant + <le>, and related inflectional and derivational forms (e.g., *needle, needling*).

Initial Consonants

<b, c, ch, d, f, g, h, j, k, l, m, n, p, ph, r, s, sh, t, th, v, w, wh, x, y, z>

Initial Consonant Clusters

1. <bl, br, chl, chr, cl, cr, dr, fl, fr, gl, gr, pl, pr, phl, phr, sl, sr, shr, tr, thr>
2. <sc, sch, sk, sm, sn, sp, sph, st, sw>
3. <scr, spl, spr, squ, str>
4. <dw, qu, tw>

Final Consonants

1. Unrestricted: <b, ch, d, m, n, p, ph, r, sh, t, th>
2. Restricted: <c> (only after <i>); <f, l, s> (see above); <k> (only after digraph vowels); <ck, dg, ng, tch, x> (only after single-letter vowels)

Final Consonant Clusters

1. <lb, rb, lch, rch, ld, rd, lf, rf, rg, lk, rk, rl, lm, rm, ln, rn, lp, rp, lph, rph, ls, rs, lsh, rsh, lt, rt, lth, rth>
2. <mp, mph, nch, nd, nk, ns, nt, nth, nx, sk, sm, sp, ct, ft, pt, st, xt, thm>
3. <mpt, nct, rld, rpt, rst>

Medial Consonants and Consonant Clusters

All the consonants that can occur initially except <wh> can occur between vowels, with the restrictions that <q> be followed by <u>, and <k> be followed by <e, i>, or <y>. For medial consonant clusters, the main rule is that the cluster must be (1) a legal final cluster (in relation to its preceding vowel spelling), (2) a legal initial cluster, or (3) divisible into a sequence of (1) followed by (2). In addition, the following geminates, along with the pseudogeminates (<ck, dg, tch>), can occur intervocalically after single-letter vowels: <bb, cc, dd, ff, gg, ll, mm, nn, pp, rr, ss, tt, zz>. Before final <e>, many different functional units can occur, including <dg>, which can only be followed by final <e> at the end of a word. On the other hand, <ch, ck, gh, h, j, k, sh, w, x, z> are rarely or never followed by final <e> and are not allowed to do such under the strict rule set. Before final <le>, however, the following consonants and their geminates can occur: <b, c, d, f, g, p, m, s, t>, along with <ck, nk, rk, mp, rt, st, zz>.

These rules for medial clusters are incomplete because a number of patterns involving digraph vowels and consonant clusters are restricted. For example, the final clusters involving <k> have highly constrained use in medial position. A pseudoword such as *tilkament* is outlawed because *tilcament* is the preferred English spelling. (Although <k> does occur in English words before all vowels, occurrences before <a, o, u> are mostly recent borrowings.) Further restrictions are required for repeated occurrences of digraph vowels and for interrelationships between initial and final clusters, but these are left for another time.

Beyond the rules presented here are issues of word aesthetics. A word like *xyclyzutch* is as legal as *ticlamutch,* but the latter is far more attractive and probably would rate far higher on a subjective scaling of closeness to real English words. Use of infrequently occurring letters such as <k, x, y, z> makes a word look slightly strange, as do rare consonant clusters. Nevertheless, the rules presented here can function as a base from which pseudowords are generated and then tested for utility in any particular application.

Pseudowords That Are Legal by Strict Rules

chaish	*phrag*	*sploon*	*entraff*	*conprumely*
folch	*dwoun*	*thriss*	*skifroon*	*reprangest*
selk	*scheim*	*quint*	*inglarm*	*scrongingly*
jaft	*flowm*	*skirld*	*freedle*	*stidentious*
zeap	*glersh*	*chromp*	*scagful*	*maltrinker*

Pseudowords That Are Legal by Loose Rules but Not Strict Rules

eb	*brou*	*kheam*	*graufull*	*untevving*
ig	*cleyt*	*knoap*	*heeddle*	*sleadgary*
loj	*drough*	*loutch*	*rewonj*	*staubbest*
pogh	*sqwel*	*psorch*	*scheldell*	*thangfruzz*
tref	*yblif*	*steelc*	*ghamper*	*ydrosingly*

LOOKING AHEAD

This may be a convenient place to take a break from distributional limits and their consequences. The next two chapters shift from spelling variations and creative spellings to a description of English phonology and to the basics of the writing system. These topics are needed to digest the history of English spelling that follows these two chapters. This history in turn serves as an introduction to the heavy-duty descriptions of orthographic patterns that follow.

NOTES

1. Dodgson [Carroll] (1871/1979), 1605–1606.
2. Geisel [Seuss] (1974).
3. Matthews (1919), 662. Other treatments of commercial spellings can be found in Mencken (1936), 171ff.; Bellamann (1929); Pound (1923, 1925); and Jaquith (1976).
4. Buckley (1996).
5. Jaquith (1976).
6. Pound (1923), 226.
7. Pound (1925), 43.
8. Jaquith (1976).
9. Wloszczyna (1991).
10. Dearborn (1906).
11. Anderson and Dearborn (1954).
12. Dearborn (1906), 65.
13. Shannon (1951).
14. Miller et al. (1954).
15. Wallach (1962).

16. In psychological terms, these are *type* counts as opposed to *token* counts. That is, each unique word is given the same weight as any other unique word, rather than being weighted according to its frequency of occurrence in print.
17. A *function word* is a word like *to* or *and* that serves primarily syntactic functions, as opposed to a *content word* like *toy* or *jump,* which has a referent in the real or imaginary world.

CHAPTER 4

The Sound System

Nor did Pnin, as a teacher, ever presume to
approach the lofty halls of modern scientific
linguistics, that ascetic fraternity of phonemes,
that temple wherein earnest young people are
taught not the language itself, but the method of
teaching others to teach that method; which
method, like a waterfall splashing from rock to
rock, ceases to be a medium of rational
navigation but perhaps in some fabulous future
may become instrumental in evolving esoteric
dialects—Basic Basque and so forth—spoken
only by certain elaborate machines.
 —VLADIMIR NABOKOV
 (1957/1989),10; emphasis added

Principle 3, as presented in Chapter 1, is as follows: "Letters serve both to represent sounds and to mark phonological and morphological features." To understand the sound end of letter–sound correspondences requires some knowledge
of the sound system of English—that is, English phonology. This chapter is an
introduction to the sounds of American English and some of the mysteries of
their articulation. It will not replace a full course on the topic, but it should allow
later chapters to be digested without serious discomfort. The emphasis here is on
what linguists call *articulatory phonetics* (i.e., phonetics as viewed from the
standpoint of the physiological system that produces speech sounds). Other ap-

proaches to this science, including *theoretical phonology* and *acoustical phonetics,* are ignored. Those who have already mastered this topic may want to skip directly to Chapter 5, where the graphemic system is introduced.

REPRESENTATION OF SPEECH

Speech generated in normal conversations results from a continuous set of adjustments to the vocal cords; to the end of the velum, which opens or closes the nasal passage; and to the various oral articulators, particularly the tongue and the lips. Years of experience with print leads us to assume that speech sounds are uttered in neat linear successions, with silences marking the boundaries between words. What reaches the ear, however, is neither so neatly bundled nor so well defined. Some of the cues for adjacent speech sounds overlap in time; boundaries between words are often missing or filled with other speech sounds; and the actual sounds transmitted show enormous variability, especially by position within a word.

Part of learning to speak a language is learning to attend to certain invariants in the speech stream and to ignore much of the messiness and variability. Just as there is more to seeing than what meets the eye, there is more to hearing than what meets the ear. Some parts of the noncritical variations among sounds are discussed later in this chapter, but most are not. Furthermore, since this book is concerned mostly with the problems of mapping the spellings of single words into sounds, many interesting problems related to words in natural speech contexts are ignored. In the discussion that follows, the fiction of neat sequences of sounds within words is maintained—partly because that is what we think we hear, and partly because it is a necessary simplification for making sense of English orthography. In addition, although speech units are best described by features, this level of analysis is not presented here because its complexity far outweighs the potential use that might be made of it.

Systems for Representing Speech Sounds

Since speech sounds dominate the discussion here, a means of representing such entities is required for convenient communication. Fortunately (or unfortunately), various schemes exist for this purpose. What I use throughout the book is a slightly modified version of the International Phonetic Alphabet (IPA), which was first proposed in 1888 by an international association heavily influenced by foreign-language teachers.[1] This is the most commonly used system among linguists, although the actual symbols used for English vary from one school of phonology to another. The system I have adopted is close to that described by J. C. Wells in *Accents of English,* and is the simplest of all commonly used systems.[2] It is sufficient for now to know that speech sounds are represented by many of the letters of the alphabet, plus a few extra symbols, and are enclosed in slant lines. Thus, for example, the initial sound in the word *flummox* is written /f/. Where fine points of pronunciation are at issue, square brackets are used (e.g., [f]). The exact meanings of these different representations are explained below. For those whose curiosity about the specific sounds of English cannot be contained, Table 4.1 shows all the sounds of American English as represented in the IPA, along with equivalent representations in the two most popular dictionary phonetic systems.

Phonetic versus Phonemic

The sound representation scheme used here represents one attempt to record what are called *broad* phonetic distinctions. This contrasts with a narrow transcription scheme that would record *fine* phonetic distinctions. For example, in a narrow transcription scheme, the sound at the beginning of *pin* would be represented as [pʰ] to show that it is aspirated, while the related sound in *spin* would be shown as [p], which implies no aspiration. Finally, the last sound in *stop* would be shown as [ʔp]; this indicates a glottalized stop, which is characterized by a lack of release of air at the end of the sound. However, since these variations are seldom of interest to the nonphonetician, and they do not contrast as do the initial sounds in *pin* and *bin,* they are seldom recorded by nonspecialists.

This reasoning is carried one step further to create classes of sounds that are phonetically similar and, as classes, contrast with each other to separate meaningful elements in the language. Such classes are called *phonemes* and are represented by the same symbols used for the sounds themselves, but enclosed within slanted lines as described earlier (e.g., /p/). Most of the decisions that are required for a phonemic analysis of a language are also required for deriving a broad phonetic representation. However, a phonemic analysis often requires quite arbitrary decisions such as whether to represent the initial sounds in *chin* and *judge* as members of independent phonemes or as combinations of phonemes. As far as I know, there are neither theoretical nor psychological criteria for justifying one choice over the other in many of these situations. In this text, broad phonetic transcriptions are used, although they are presented as phonemic representations.

**TABLE 4.1. Symbols for the Phonemes of American English
in Three Different Systems**

IPA*	Thorndike–Barnhart†	Merriam–Webster‡
æ	a	a
a	o	ä
ɛ	e	e
e	ā	ā
ɪ	i	i
i	ē	ē
ʌ	u	ə
ə	ə	ə
ʊ	u̇	u̇
u	ü	ü
ɔ	ô	ȯ
ju	yü	yü
aɪ	ī	ī
aʊ	ou	au̇
ɔɪ	oi	oi
b	b	b
d	d	d
f	f	f
g	g	g
h	h	h
ǰ	j	j
k	k	k
l	l	l
m	m	m
n	n	n
ŋ	ng	ŋ
p	p	p
r	r	r
s	s	s
š	sh	sh
t	t	t
θ	th	th
ð	~~TH~~	<u>th</u>
v	v	v
w	w	w
j	y	y
z	z	z
ž	zh	zh
č	ch	ch

*The IPA symbols as given here represent a slight modification of the International Phonetic
Association (1989) system.
†The Thorndike–Barnhart symbols are from Thorndike (1941b).
‡The Merriam–Webster symbols are from Mish (1993).

SPEECH PRODUCTION

Speech in all known languages results from control of an airstream that origi-
nates in the lungs; passes through the trachea to the larynx, in which the vocal
folds are located; and then proceeds through the pharynx to the oral and nasal
cavities. These latter three areas are known as the *vocal tract* and are illustrated
in Figure 4.1. The larynx, also known as the Adam's apple or voice box, contains
fine sheets of tissue that can be pulled apart to allow air to flow through unobstructed, or drawn together in various ways to interfere with the airstream. These
elastic sheets are the vocal cords, or vocal folds, and the space between them is
called the *glottis*. Sounds produced with the vocal cords drawn apart so that air

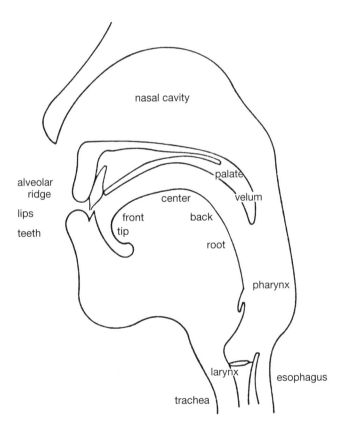

Figure 4.1. The vocal tract. From Kreidler (1989), p. 21. Copyright 1989 by Blackwell Publishers. Reprinted by permission.

passes through unobstructed are called *voiceless* sounds. Those produced with the cords close enough to be set in vibration by the passing airstream are called *voiced* sounds; when the glottis is closed and then released, a *glottal stop* results, as is sometimes heard as the replacement for /t/ in words such as *bottle.* A fourth glottal state, with the front part of the vocal cords closed and the back part open, yields whispered sounds, which are also voiceless.

For most English speech sounds, air flows through the pharynx and then to the oral cavity, with the nasal cavity closed off by the end of the velum. This moveable part of the soft palate can be lowered to allow air to flow into the nasal cavity, or raised to prevent air from entering. Sounds produced with the nasal cavity open are called *nasals,* all of which are consonants. In addition, when, the nasal cavity is opened during the articulation of a vowel in anticipation of a following nasal consonant, a *nasalized vowel* results.

All speech sounds are produced through adjustments to the three main chambers in the vocal tract (the pharynx, the oral cavity, and the nasal cavity) and to the vocal cords. Of the three chambers, the oral cavity carries the highest workload and makes adjustments in the production of all sounds. The nasal cavity can be opened or closed, but no further changes are made to it. The pharynx can be adjusted slightly, affecting mainly its size, but this has little impact on the sounds produced. Within the oral cavity, the primary articulators are the tongue, lips, teeth, and jaw. The tongue—which is the most mobile and most active of these articulators during speech production—can be positioned higher or lower, and toward the front or back of the mouth, to produce different types of resonant chambers. It can also be shaped to force the airstream to move in different directions and with different types of motion or turbulence. The jaw also affects the size and shape of the oral resonant chamber, while the teeth and lips can affect airflow.

TYPES OF SPEECH SOUNDS

English speech is composed of three basic types of speech sounds: *vowels, consonants,* and *glides.* Vowels are produced by a free flow of air from the lungs through the vocal tract, but with the vocal cords vibrating; thus vowels are generally voiced sounds. They also form the centers, or *nuclei,* of syllables. Consonants are produced with constriction or closure of the vocal tract that causes air turbulence. They may be voiced or voiceless, but with the exception of *syllabic consonants* (which are explained later), they cannot form the nuclei of syllables. Glides—of which English has two, /j/ and /w/—share properties of both vowels and consonants. They are articulated like vowels, but require movement of the articulators. Unlike vowels, however, they cannot form the nuclei of syllables. After this chapter, glides are classed as consonants for ease of discussion.

Consonants

Most consonants in English are articulated with the end of the velum blocking the entrance to the nasal cavity. These sounds are called *oral* consonants, in contrast to *nasal* consonants, which are articulated with air passing into both the oral and the nasal passages. Within these classes, consonants are further divided by manner and place of articulation. The manner of articulation distinguishes *stops, fricatives, affricates, liquids,* and *nasals,* as explained further below. Places of articulation are the places in the oral cavity where the main obstructions to air passage occur; terms referring to these places include *labial, bilabial, dental/alveolar, palatal, velar,* and *glottal.* Table 4.2 depicts one scheme for distinguishing consonants by place and manner of articulation; a slightly different scheme is described below.

Stops

When the airflow is completely but momentarily blocked, a *stop* results. English has six contrastive stops: /p, b, t, d, k, g/. The stops /p/ and /b/ are *bilabial;* that is, both lips are used to cut off the airflow completely in their articulation.

TABLE 4.2. Consonants: Place and Manner of Articulation

labials	labio-dentals	dentals	alveolars	palato-alveolars	velars	glottal	
m			n		ŋ		nasal stops
p b			t d		k g		oral stops
	f v	θ ð	s z	š ž		h	fricatives
				č ǰ			affricates
		l	r				liquids

They differ only in that /p/ is voiceless and /b/ is voiced. Similarly, /t/ and /d/ are *alveolar* stops, with the first voiceless and the second voiced. For these, the air-flow is cut off by the tip of the tongue pressing behind the teeth or on the alveolar ridge, which abuts the back of the teeth. Finally, /k/ and /g/ are *velar* stops, with the same voiceless–voiced alternation. Air is cut off in their articulation by the back of the tongue pressing against the soft palate, or velum.

Two variants of these stops merit special notice. One, which is formed by blocking airflow at the glottis, occasionally occurs as an allophone of /t/. This glottal stop is represented by [ʔ] in IPA and can be heard, for example, in some New York City pronunciations of words such as *bottle,* where it replaces the [t]. It is also common in certain interjections, for example, [ʔmʔm]. The other, represented by [ɾ] in IPA, is a form of [t] that occurs particularly in Midwestern speech with such words as *ladder* and *latter.* One phonetician describes it as "a voiced tap of the tongue-tip [against the upper gum]."[3] In following current linguistic practice for English-language studies, this sound is represented as [D].

Fricatives

Fricatives are produced by constricting the oral passage sufficiently to cause turbulence in the airflow. English has nine fricatives, as shown in Table 4.2. The ones articulated closest to the front of the mouth, /v/ and /f/, are *labiodental;* that is, they are pronounced by constricting the airstream with the upper front teeth and the lower lip. The only difference between the two phonemes is that /v/ is voiced and /f/ is voiceless. Similarly, /ð/ is a voiced and /θ/ is a voiceless dental fricative, articulated with the top front portion of the tongue forcing air to pass between it and the upper gums and then out between the teeth. With the tongue as described, its tip may touch the upper incisors or extend between the upper and lower incisors; this is the reason for the occasional label *interdentals.*

To turn to sounds produced further toward the back of the mouth, /z/ is a voiced and /s/ is a voiceless alveolar fricative, articulated with the grooved blade of the tongue against the alveolar ridge of the upper palate. This tongue position forces air against the edges of the teeth, generating a hissing sound. Nearly identical to /z/ and /s/ are the *palatoalveolar* fricatives /ž/ and /š/, which are articulated with the front of the tongue raised toward the rear portion of the alveolar ridge, just in front of the palate. As with /z/ and /s/, /ž/ is voiced and /š/ is voiceless. Last in the fricative sequence that extends from the lips backward into the mouth is the voiceless /h/, which in standard English has no voiced counterpart. Unlike all other consonants, /h/ has no fixed placed of articulation. Although the nasal cavity is always closed off and the glottis is usually half-open, the position of the tongue and lips during articulation of /h/ is determined by the following vowel (or semivowel). Following standard classification schemes, it is classed here by place of articulation as *glottal.*

Affricates

Affricates are compounds of a stop followed by a fricative, and in some phonetic marking schemes they are represented as such. English has only two, both palatoalveolar: the voiced /ǰ/ as in *judge,* and the voiceless /č/ as in *chair.* These can be represented as /dž/ and /tš/, but for English these sequences offer no advantage over the simpler /ǰ/ and /č/.

Fricative and Affricate Subclassifications

Within the combined group of fricatives and affricates, several subdivisions have special significance. Depending on acoustical properties, the sounds /f, v, s, z, š, ž, č, ǰ/ are labeled *stridents,* while the remaining three, /ð, θ, h/, are called *nonstridents.* Of more direct importance to letter–sound mappings are the *sibilants,* /s, z, š, ž, č/, and /ǰ/, so named for the high-pitched hissing that they share. Words that end in these sounds, if they take the regular plural or possessive endings, spelled <s/es> or <'s/s'>, have /ɪz/ rather than /s/ or /z/.

Liquids

Liquids are a special class of consonants in which the obstruction of air is significantly less than for all the other classes. English has two liquids: /l/, which is articulated with air rushing off the sides of the tongue, and /r/, which can be pronounced either as a retroflexed sound or as a flapped sound. When the tongue tip is curled back into the mouth or when the tongue is bunched upward in the back of the mouth, a retroflexed /r/ results. The flapped /r/, which is rare in American English, results from the tongue tip tapping quickly against the alveolar ridge.

Nasals

Nasals are produced like voiced stops, but with air passing through both the oral and the nasal cavities. The three nasals, /m, n/, and /ŋ/, are produced with closure at the bilabial (/m/), alveolar (/n/), or velar (/ŋ/) position. Although these three nasals appear parallel to /b, d/, and /g/, one major difference exists: /ŋ/ cannot appear at the beginning of a word or syllable. In fact, it can occur only after a vowel at the end of a morpheme or before /k/ or /g/ (e.g., *ring, wrangle, monk, lynx, uncle*).

Semivowels

Semivowels, which are also called *glides,* are rapidly articulated vowel-like sounds; however, unlike vowels, they cannot function as syllable nuclei. English has two semivowels, /j/ and /w/, representing the initial sounds in *yeast* and *wagon.* Both occur at the beginnings of syllables before vowels, and after vowels as off-glides or as the second elements of true diphthongs. The semivowel /j/ begins with the front of the tongue raised toward the hard palate and the tip of the tongue resting behind the lower front incisors. During articulation, however, the articulators change to the position of the following vowel. For /w/ the lips are initially rounded, and the back of the tongue is raised part of the way toward the velum. As the sound is articulated, the articulators are repositioned for the vowel that follows. (When semivowels occur after vowels, the initial articulatory states just described represent the terminal states for the vowel articulations.) Given the mode of articulation for semivowels, it is best to consider them in terms of movements rather than as steady-state positions.

The semivowels (and vowels), along with the nasals and liquids, compose a class of sounds called *resonants* or *sonorants* because of their loudness, length, and resonance. The remaining consonants (i.e., the fricatives, stops, and affricates) are called *obstruents.* Another grouping places the semivowels with the vowels and fricatives as *continuants.*

Vowels

Vowels are produced with vocal cord vibration (i.e., they are voiced) and with the vocal tract more open than it is for other classes of sounds. English vowels are characterized by three basic dimensions: degree of *lip rounding, tongue placement,* and degree of *muscle tension.* Lip rounding is treated as an all-or-none factor. A small number of vowels are produced with the lips rounded (/o, u, ʊ, ɔ/, and /oi/); the rest are produced with unrounded lips. This is in some sense an incidental feature, because the vowels that are rounded are also characterized by additional features that separate them from the other vowels. Tongue placement refers to the position within the mouth of the body of the tongue: front, central, or back, and high, mid, or low. Muscle tension refers to the amount of tension of the tongue muscles and of other muscles in and around the vocal tract, and, like lip rounding, is treated as an all-or-none factor (tense vs. lax). A classification of American English vowels by degree of lip rounding and tongue placement is shown in Figure 4.2. This vowel set represents General American speech, a dialect spoken through a wide area of the country outside of eastern New England and the South.[4]

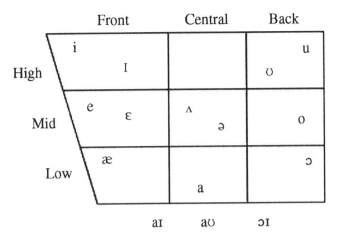

Figure 4.2. The vowels of American English.

Tense–Lax Distinction

The vowels in *beat* and *bit* are identical for tongue position (high, front) and lip rounding (none). They differ, however, because for *beat* the tongue muscles are tense while for *bit* they are lax. Similarly, the vowels in *bait–bet* and *food–foot* differ by the same contrast, with the first of each pair tense and the second lax. With tense vowels, the larynx tends to rise, and the muscles that lead from the chin back to the neck tend to bulge. (Observe yourself in a mirror saying *beat–bit* deliberately.) Variable muscle tension as a basic characteristic of vowels is found in few other languages. German has it, but not to the same degree as English. Consequently, non-native speakers of English tend to have difficulty in distinguishing and producing vowel pairs that differ only by tension: /i/–/ɪ/, /u/–/ʊ/, and /e/–/ɛ/.[5] A second factor associated with the tense–lax distinction is that monosyllables in English do not end with lax vowels. Thus words like *be, bay, boo,* and *bow* (= /bo/) exist, but no equivalent forms with lax vowels do.

Monophthongs and Diphthongs

Most vowels are articulated with a single steady state for the vocal tract; others begin with the articulators in a steady-state position but end with them in a glide position. The former are called *simple vowels* or *monophthongs,* the latter *diphthongs.* The vowels in *sit, set, sat, saw, sot, bush, but,* and *suppose* (first vowel) are almost always simple. Those in *brow, boy,* and *buy* are almost always diphthongs and are distinct from the vowels composed of their first elements.

(The hedging here is due to dialect differences.) Thus, /aʊ/ and /aɪ/ are distinct from /a/, and /ɔɪ/ is distinct from /ɔ/. The vowels in *beat, bay, boo,* and *bow* (as in *bow and arrow*) usually have off-glides, but they are slight, and the distinction between the pure (nonglided) and the glided pronunciations of these sounds is not meaningful. Therefore, they are represented here as simple vowels: /i, e, u, o/. In other representation schemes they are shown with off-glides: for example, /iy, ey, uw, ow/.

Mid-Central Vowels

Finally, there exist three mid-central vowels. The first is /ʌ/ as in *hut,* which is a lax vowel found only in stressed positions. The second is a weak, neutral, un-stressed vowel, called *schwa,* and is represented as /ə/. This is the vowel heard at the beginning of *away* and at the end of *soda.* It is the largest source of problems not only for spelling-to-sound translation (reading), but also for translation in the other direction (spelling). The third is the tense, /r/-colored vowel heard in stressed positions, as in *bird, worm,* and *burn.* It is often represented as /ɝ/, which indicates clearly that it is not two sounds in succession, but a single sound. Its unstressed, lax variant is /ɚ/, which is heard at the end of *actor* and *butter.* In /r/-less speech, a tense, mid-central vowel /ɜ/ replaces /ɝ/.

For a variety of reasons, dictionary editors and others of similar persuasion prefer to represent these sounds as if each were a sequence of vowel + /r/ : /ʌr/ for the stressed form and /ər/ for the unstressed one. The argument made is that /ər/, for example, does not occur in English except across a syllable boundary, and therefore no ambiguity results from its deployment for /ɚ/. (Across syllable boundaries, words such as *arrive* and *arrest* have /ə/ + /r/ in succession, and they do not coalesce into /ɚ/.) To make the representation here as simple and as ac-cessible as possible, the /ʌr/ and /ər/ representations are used. In addition, the distinction between /ʌ/ and /ə/ is retained, even though an argument could be made for treating the two as the members of the same phoneme.

Free–Checked versus Long–Short

Because of the importance of syllable structure in English, the classification of vowels according to whether they can end a syllable (*free*) or not (*checked*) has special significance. The checked vowels are /ɪ, ɛ, æ, ʊ, ʌ/; the remainder are free. The free–checked distinction should not be confused with the traditional classification of certain vowels as *long* or *short.* The terms *long* and *short* as ap-plied to English vowel sounds in educational literature and in dictionaries are neither historically accurate nor mnemonically useful. Although some of the

Modern English long–short pairs have developed from Middle English vowels which apparently differed only by quantity (commonly called length), this is certainly not true of all such pairs.[6] Modern English long <u> (/ju/), for example, has developed primarily from /u/ in French borrowings. Middle English long <u> (/uː/) has become Modern English /aʊ/ as in *house.* Anglo-Norman scribes imported the French spelling <ou> for Middle English /u/ in the 12th century, but left untouched the spelling <u> for short <u> (/u/), thus destroying for posterity a graphemic identity between the long and short <u> sounds and their reflexes in Modern English.[7]

Long and short vowels are defined today in terms of spellings: They are the primary pronunciations of the spellings <a, e, i, o, u>. The other English vowels, however, seem to have no place in this scheme. How, for example, are /ʌ/ and /ɔ/ classed? To answer this question by appeal to phonetic length is not justified by the classifications of the other vowel sounds. For two spellings, <a> and <o>, the long vowels are on the average phonetically shorter than the short ones.[8] Furthermore, since vowel length varies according to the following sound, almost all long vowels are pronounced in some environments with durations that are shorter than the maximum durations of their corresponding short vowels. The preference here, therefore, is for *free–checked* rather than *long–short.*

UNITS, PROCESSES, AND SEQUENCES

The segmental speech sounds just described occur within units called *syllables,* and where words have more than one syllable, prominence or *stress* is applied to one or more of the vowels within the syllables. Syllables have characteristic structures, based in part upon the places where vowels can occur (as explained above), and in part on the allowable consonant sequences. The patterns or rules that describe these sequences comprise *phonotactics.* Sounds tend to influence each other within words and sometimes across words, leading to additions, deletions, and modifications of articulation. Some of these changes occurred over the past 1,300 years and account for many of the peculiarities of English orthography, and some are still active in modern speech. These topics are discussed below.

Syllables

A *syllable* is a sequence of one or more sounds with a single vowel or syllabic consonant as a nucleus and (optionally) consonants or glides as beginnings (onsets) or endings (codas). Syllables are easy to count, since each vowel or syllabic consonant in a word represents a different syllable. Syllable divisions, however, are far more problematic, because English does not have a distinctive syllable articulation pattern. Acoustically, the transition from one syllable to the next is seldom marked by zero speech output. A slight dip in energy may occur, but in general, articulation continues as the articulators move from the position required at the end of one syllable to that required at the onset of the next. Furthermore, many syllable boundaries can switch without causing a difference in word perception. Thus, for instance, *walking* can be divided as /ˈwɔk ɪŋ/ or as /ˈwɔ kɪŋ/. Where unpronounceable consonant sequences occur, syllable boundaries may be forced, as in *picture* (/ˈpɪk čər/), where the division can be only between the two medial consonants, since syllables can neither begin nor end with /kč/. Occasionally a switch in a syllable boundary is accompanied by a sound change, as is represented by the two different divisions of *zero:* /ˈzɪr o/ and /ˈzi ro/. The switch from the lax /ɪ/ to the tense /i/ occurs because stressed syllables in English cannot end with lax vowels.

Stress

Stress is an important characteristic of English words, primarily because it cannot always be predicted reliably from a word's spelling. *Stress* refers to the relative prominence of a syllable, achieved during articulation through control of a vowel's pitch, loudness, or length. Two marked levels of stress, *primary* and *secondary,* are shown by short vertical marks—the former placed above the line, the latter below. Thus the phonemic representation of *independent,* with secondary stress on the first syllable, primary stress on the third, and the remainder unstressed, is /ˌɪn dɪ ˈpɛn dənt/.

In many cases, unstressed vowels can vary freely across /ɪ, i, ə/. The second syllables in *heated, roses,* and *pencil,* for example, can be pronounced with either /ɪ/ or /ə/. Similarly, the first syllables in *begin, resign,* and *defend* can vary among /ə, ɪ, i/. In the development of letter–sound rules here, only a single pronunciation is claimed for these, but the possibility of free variation is noted.

Phonotactics

Every language has preferred arrangements of sounds that are embodied in both articulatory and perceptual encodings. English phonology, for example, admits complex initial consonant clusters, as in *squirrel* and *spring.* Native speakers of English, through practice that starts at an early age, learn both the articulatory movements required to produce these clusters with grace and rapidity, and the feature extractions required to recognize them in fast, connected speech. Many other languages, including Hebrew, do not admit consonant clusters of this complexity. Whether speakers of Hebrew are at a special disadvantage in learning English because of this mismatch is an empirical issue that remains to be resolved.

English has a rich and complex set of initial and final consonant clusters, but not all possible consonant sequences are allowed. The initial cluster /tl/, for example, is not permitted in English words, yet is common in many Native American languages of the coastal Northwest. Initial /vr/, which is allowed in French (e.g., *vrac, vrai, vrillon*) does not occur in English except in *vroom,* which entered the vocabulary in the 1960s and is often pronounced /varum/ rather than /vrum/.

The allowable sequences of sounds in a language comprise its *phonotactics.* These rules or patterns define what commonly occurs in different positions in spoken words, and therefore they are important for understanding orthographic patterns. For English, furthermore, historical phonotactics is important because the orthography preserves patterns like initial <gn> and <kn>, which were once pronounced but are no longer so. How and why phonotactics change over time are no more understood than why women's hemlines lengthen or shorten from season to season. Contact with other languages may cause subtle shifts in articulation that lead eventually to major changes in sound sequencing, or large numbers of immigrants may, because of difficulties in pronouncing specific sound sequences, produce different patterns that come to be imitated by native speakers.

Whatever the causes, sequences that once occurred in English, such as initial /hn/ (*hnutu,* "nut") and /kn/ (*know*), are no longer admissible. As stated earlier, the former has no reflex in current spelling but the latter does, as do /wr/ and /gn/, which have also lost their initial elements. But not all strange and unpronounceable spellings are remnants of earlier pronunciations. The <b> spellings in *debt, doubt,* and *subtle* (and *subject*) are scribal insertions in imitation of real or imagined classical origins. Similarly, <p> was added to earlier *tarmigan* in mistaken enthusiasm for a Greek root.[9] Of especial interest for spelling are the allowable consonant sequences in word-initial and word-final positions, because these positions contain many of the problematic spelling–sound correspondences. An understanding of them is also critical for deciding what is English-like and what is not in psychological studies of orthographic processing, although unfortunately no simple, clear division is possible. Although an exhaustive treatment is not warranted, especially for the reader mainly interested in orthography, the more common properties of these schemes deserve some attention. These are sketched below.

Initial Clusters

The two-element initial clusters are of two types: *stop-first* and *fricative-first.* Stop-first clusters combine all six stops /p, t, k, b, d, g/ with the liquids /r/, /l/ and glides /j/, /w/, but with the rule that sequences articulated at the same place in the mouth are not allowed. This yields the forms shown below, where the illegal clusters are marked with asterisks. Note that /gj/ does not occur in word-initial position, but does occur in syllable-initial position in *ague.* Also, several of the /j/ clusters are dialectal, occurring in some dialects but not in others (e.g., *Tuesday, due*).

Initial stop-first clusters

/pr/	*price*	/kr/	*crayon*	/dr/	*drug*
/pl/	*please*	/kl/	*clean*	*/dl/	
/pj/	*pew*	/kj/	*cute*	/dj/	*due*
/pw/	*pueblo*	/kw/	*quick*	/dw/	*dwarf*
/tr/	*tray*	/br/	*break*	/gr/	*green*
*/tl/		/bl/	*blue*	/gl/	*glass*
/tj/	*Tuesday*	/bj/	*beauty*	(/gj/	*ague*)
/tw/	*twin*	*/bw/		/gw/	*guano*

Fricative-first clusters do not pattern as neatly as the stop-first clusters. The largest group according to unique word counts (i.e., types) consists of clusters in which /s/ combines with the voiceless stops, /p, t, k/ (as in *spin, stick,* and *skin*). The fricative /s/ also combines with two nasals, /n/ and /m/ (as in *snow* and *smoke*). It combines with /f/ in a small number of Greek borrowings (e.g., *sphere, sphinx, sphincter*) and in a few rare Italian forms (e.g., *sfumato, sforzando*), almost all of which are technical terms. Other common fricative-first clusters include /fr, fl, fj/ (*fright, flight, few*); /šr/, /ər/ (shrank, thrash); and /hw/ (*when*), for <wh> words that have retained an /hw/ pronunciation. Rarer clusters, generally evidenced by single examples, include /ɵw/ (*thwart*); /vr/ (*vroom*), which has been mentioned above; and a brace of borrowings, including the Yiddish /šl, šm, šn/ words (such as *schlemiel, schlepp, schmaltz, schmear,* and *schnorer*), many of which have spread beyond the Borsht Belt into everyday English.

English also admits three-element initial clusters, which are formed from a subset of the clusters with voiceless stops, prefixed with /s/. Of these, /skl/ is extremely rare, and /stw/ is a hole in the pattern since no rule outlaws it.

Three-element initial clusters

/spr/	*spring*	/str/	*string*	/skr/	*screw*
/spl/	*splash*	*/stl/		/skl/	*sclerosis*
/spj/	*spew*	/stj/	*stew*	/skj/	*skewer*
*/spw/		/stw/		/skw/	*squirrel*

Final Clusters

If the initial clusters appear to be messy, organizing the final clusters ranks with the Herculean labors. English appears to have weak constraints on clusters that can occur after vowels (i.e., postvocalic clusters); it allows an amazing variety of these, multiplied further by morphemic endings such as /s, z, t, d, θ/. If we ignore the morphemic endings, some flashes of order appear in the mist. Among the most prolific final clusters are the /l/ and /r/ combinations, which include every sound class except the glides.

Final clusters starting with /l/ or /r/

/lp/	*kelp*	/rp/	*harp*
/lt/	*belt*	/rt/	*art*
/lk/	*balk*	/rk/	*ark*
/lb/	*bulb*	/rb/	*orb*
/ld/	*bald*	/rd/	*yard*
/lθ/	*wealth*	/rg/	*Borg*
/lm/	*film*	/rm/	*arm*
/ln/	*kiln*	/rn/	*torn*
/lf/	*elf*	/rf/	*wharf*
/lv/	*solve*	/rv/	*carve*
/ls/	*false*	/rθ/	*Barth*
/lǰ/	*bilge*	/rz/	*Mars*
/lč/	*belch*	/rs/	*horse*
		/rč/	*porch*
		/rǰ/	*large*

A second group of clusters contains sequences composed of nasals followed by their coarticulated stops. The full set, shown below, has been reduced in modern American English by the leveling of final /ŋg/ to /ŋ/ and of final /mb/ to /m/. However, the spellings for these clusters remain, as in *thing* and *bomb*.

Final clusters starting with nasals

/nt/	pint	/nǰ/	binge
/nd/	find	/mp/	amp
/nč/	bench	/ŋk/	think

In addition, three-element clusters are formed by adding /t/ to the end of /mp/ and /ŋk/, yielding /mpt/ (*attempt*) and /ŋkt/ (*distinct*).

A third group is composed of /s/ plus the voiceless stops /p, t, k/, and is symmetrical.

Final clusters including /s/ plus a voiceless stop

/sp/	asp	/ps/	apse
/st/	past	/ts/	Betts
/sk/	task	/ks/	axe

Other final clusters include /ft/ (*raft*), /pt/ (*apt*), and /kt/ (*act*); a host of /ɵ/ forms, such as /pɵ/ (*depth*) and /rmɵ/ (*warmth*); and a scattering of oddities, such as /ðm/ (*rhythm*), /lts/ (*waltz*), /rts/ (*quartz*), and /ŋst/ (*angst*). In medial positions across syllable boundaries, any combination of final and initial clusters can occur, so that an enumeration of them is unnecessary. Finally, to round out the phonotactics for consonants, three sounds are restricted to word-initial or syllable-initial positions (/h, j, w/), and one is restricted to any position except word-initial (/ž/).

Loss of Sounds

Sounds have been deleted from English words as far back as records or reconstructions can reach. No single rule or tendency can account for any significant portion of these changes, although simplification of sound sequences, particularly consonants, has been the result of many changes. However, why certain consonant sequences such as initial /hr/ and /hn/ were leveled (/hr/ to /r/ and /hn/ to /n/), while /hw/ survived intact, has yet to be answered satisfactorily. The leveling of /hr/ occurred at the end of the Old English period, before the orthography became fixed; thus no trace of the earlier pronunciation is preserved in spelling. In contrast, the dropping of initial /k/ and /g/ before /n/, as in *knee* and *gnat,* occurred after the orthography had become relatively stable, and therefore both earlier pronunciations are reflected in the current spellings.

Historical changes account for silent <gh> in words such as *light* and *fight;* for the silent <h> in words such as *shepherd* and *prohibition;* and for a variety of other silent letters, as will be explained in Chapter 6. Sound changes active today account for a different set of sound deletions, most of which have not yet reached the lofty status of "accepted" in standard English. Many involve sequences of three consonants where the middle element tends to be deleted. In *cents, facts,* and *lists,* for example, a medial /t/ tends to be dropped, giving /sɛns/, /fæks/, and /lɪs/. In *months* and *fifths,* the same process leads to the deletion of /ɵ/, giving /mʌns/ and /fɪfs/.

Assimilation

In most languages evidence can be found of the modification in the articulation of one sound due to anticipation of a following sound. In Latin, for example, the final consonant in the prefix *cum-* has been modified to match the place of articulation of the consonant that follows. Thus, before bilabials it has remained /m/, as shown by the modern English forms *combine* and *compare.* Before alveolars it has shifted to /n/ (e.g., *contact, condemn*), and before velars it has become /ŋ/ (e.g., *congress, conquer*). The process by which the articulation of a sound is modified to match better the articulation of an adjacent sound is called *assimilation.* In English, most assimilation is regressive; that is, sounds tend to be modified in anticipation of sounds that follow. For example, the nasal consonant in *length* (/lɛŋɵ/) moves frontward in anticipation of the dental position of /ɵ/ to /n/, giving /lɛnɵ/. We can view this as fallout from overly rapid articulation: We are so anxious to get out the next sound that we start preparing the vocal tract for it before the current sound is completed.

Assimilation can also be either progressive or reciprocal.[10] Progressive assimilation has led to part of the pronunciation pattern for the morpheme ending <ed>, which originally was a separate syllable ending in /əd/. In time, the vowel was lost except after words ending in /d/ or /t/. Then the final /d/ assimilated to the consonant preceding it by becoming voiceless /t/ after voiceless consonants (e.g., *kissed, hoped*), but remaining voiced otherwise. Reciprocal assimilation accounts for one of the sound–letter oddities in English: the mapping of initial <s> in *sure* and *sugar* to /š/. In both instances, an earlier /sj/ changed, through reciprocal assimilation, to /š/. This same process has led to the American pronunciation of *issue,* /'ɪšu/, which contrasts with the British pronunciation, /'ɪsju/.

Palatalization

Palatalization (also called *assibilation*), a form of reciprocal assimilation, is important for both modern English speech and for the history of English phonology. It also accounts for many of the more complex letter–sound correspondences involving the letters <d, t, s, z, x> and the vowels that follow them in particular environments. Jespersen, in discussing 17th century consonant changes in English, described the process thus:

> Under this name [assibilation] it is convenient here to comprise two changes, /sj/ and /zj/ > (š, ž), and /tj/ and /dj/ > (tš, dž). In the first, we have a sort of complete assimilation of the two sounds. In the second change, the off-glide from the more or less palatalized stop /t, d/ has developed into the sibilant, which has in most cases absorbed the following /j/.[11]

Two phonetic tendencies combined in palatalization. The first was the shift of unaccented /ɪ/ before another vowel to /j/, so that the number of syllables in the word was reduced by one. Then, through assimilation, the changes from /sj, zj, tj, dj/ to /š, ž, č, ǰ/, respectively, occurred. Palatalization generally took place before an unstressed vowel; compare, for example, the stress on /u/ in the following lists:

Palatalized	Unpalatalized
credulous	*credulity*
cynosure	*pursuit*
capitulate	*presume*
schedule	*importune*
assiduous	*assiduity*
treasure	*institute*

In modern speech, palatalization can occur across word boundaries in phrases such as these:

raise you [as in poker]	/réžə/
bet you	/béčə/
this year	/ðíšɪr/
lead you	/liǰə/

For this to happen, one of the tongue-tip consonants, /z, s, d, t/, must occur at the end of a word, and the following word must start with /j/. Even under these conditions, however, the change is optional. In words like *issue, treasure,* and *credulous,* palatalization was completed hundreds of years ago. British English, however, has retained /sj/ in *issue, sexual,* and *sumac,* while American English generally has /š/ except for *sumac,* which has /š/ or /s/. In *schedule,* British English has what Kurath calls a "peculiar /š/ for earlier /s/."[12]

Dissimilation, Epenthesis, and Metathesis

The opposite of assimilation, *dissimilation,* has had a less pronounced impact upon letter–sound patterns. It is evidenced today mostly in substandard pronunciations of such words as *police* and *believe,* where /ə/ has been deleted before a stressed vowel, yielding the monosyllabic /plis/ and /bliv/. Two other types of sound changes that have had a minor impact on English orthography are *epenthesis* and *metathesis.* The first results in an inserted sound, usually between consonants, that shares one or more features of each of its neighbors. Thus, for instance, some pronunciations of *prince* have an epenthetic /t/: /prints/. This results from maintaining the stop closure of the /n/ and at the same time anticipating the voicelessness of the following /s/. Metathesis, which involves inverting the order of articulation of two sounds, has both a historical and a current importance. Some Old English forms (e.g., *brid*) changed through metathesis to their current forms (e.g., *bird*). Today metathesis occurs primarily in substandard pronunciations, such as *preform* for *perform* and *percipitation* for *precipitation.*

Morphophonemics

The alternation of sounds in related words—for example, *food–feed, sane–sanity,* and *breath–breathe*—comprises a special area of phonology called *morphophonemics.* In preserving the visual identity of morphemes, English orthography has developed a large number of patterns that are important for letter–sound mappings. Almost all such patterns are traceable to sound changes that separated formerly identical sounds. Of particular interest for the present work are alternations such as *breath–breathe,* where the same spellings map into different sounds in related forms.

Some alternations (e.g., *write–written*) occurred in early stages of English or its parent languages, but the conditions that led to the changes have long since vanished. Other alternations (e.g., *sane–sanity*) appear to be active, so that words created or imported into English now would be expected to follow these alternation patterns. That is, if a word such as *blane* were adopted as an adjective, its <ity> form would most probably have a checked pronunciation of <a> and be spelled *blanity.* In Chapter 10 this topic is explored in more detail.

LOOKING AHEAD

There is much more to English phonology, but what has been presented here should suffice for understanding the phonological side of spelling–sound translation treated in the remainder of this text and for appreciating the importance of

Principle 3. For a better grounding in the fundamentals of phonetics and phonemics, the reader is encouraged to consult the various references cited in the notes for this chapter. From here we move to the graphemic base for letter–sound correspondences, and especially to the issue of which units to select as basic to this translation process.

NOTES

1. A brief history of the International Phonetic Association (Association Phonetique Internationale) and the IPA is given in International Phonetic Association (1949). A more extensive treatment is found in Albright (1958). Current revisions to the IPA chart, including reclassification for sounds, are described in International Phonetic Association (1989); see also Pullum (1990).
2. Wells (1982).
3. Kreidler (1989), 109.
4. For descriptions of other English dialects, see Wells (1982).
5. Technically, /o/ and /ʌ/, as well as /æ/ and /a/, are also distinguished by a tense–lax difference. For a fuller discussion of this topic, see Giegerich (1992).
6. The terms *Old English, Middle English,* and *Modern English* are explained in Chapter 6. For now it is sufficient to know that Old English refers to the earliest period of the English language, extending from the late seventh century until about 1100. Middle English follows, continuing until about 1500, and is followed by Modern English. The period from 1500 to perhaps 1600 is often referred to as early Modern English.
7. The terms *long* and *short* were employed for describing vowel sounds as early as the first century B.C. by the Greek grammarian Dionysius Thrax (see Dionysius Thrax, 1874, 328). This terminology was borrowed by the Latin grammarians Donatus and Priscian (c. 1000). Latin and Greek grammars were the philological staples of the English until the 16th century, when from the Renaissance gushed a stream of English grammars, orthoepical works, and spelling reform tracts. By this period, however, the former distinction of quantity between English vowels, if there ever were a pure quantitative distinction, had been obliterated by the Great Vowel Shift. Nevertheless, long and short vowels were an integral part of the Latin grammars upon which the first English grammars were modeled, and these terms were thought by the 16th-century English philologists to be inspired by heaven to the same extent as language itself.
8. See Peterson and Lehiste (1960).
9. According to the *OED, ptarmigan* was used in Lowland Scotland before 1600 and was spelled with an initial <t>. Its origins are obscure, but a classical source is unlikely. The <p> first appeared in a work published in 1684 and became standard in English by the second half of the 18th century.
10. Reciprocal assimilation is also referred to as *bidirectional* (e.g., Giegerich, 1992) or *mutual* (e.g., Kreidler, 1989).
11. Jespersen (1909/1961), 341.
12. Kurath (1964).

CHAPTER 5

The Writing System

English spelling is unusual because "our
language is a rich verbal tapestry woven together
from the tongues of the Greeks, the Latins, the
Angles, the Klaxtons, the Celtics, the 76'ers and
many other ancient peoples, all of whom had
severe drinking problems."
—DAVE BARRY (quoted in Lyall, 1993), C5

The first part of Principle 3, concerning representation of sound, has motivated
Chapter 4. This chapter is concerned with the remainder of Principle 3—that is,
with how the orthography is organized to represent sound, and also to mark
graphemic, phonological, and morphological features. The goal here is to define
units of analysis for the remaining chapters: letters and letter sequences that signal sound directly or indicate the sound correspondences or morphological status
of other letters or letter sequences, or that preserve graphemic patterns.

DESIGN ISSUES

Defining Basic Graphemic Units

Even from the direct letter-to-sound standpoint, the writing system is more complex than is revealed in the notion that there are 26 letters, or *graphemes,* which

through careful manipulation are mapped into the phonemes of English. Between the enumeration of the 26 letters and the consideration of correspondences to phonemes, a number of complexities must be untangled. One is the designation of the spelling units themselves. Obviously, there are more than 26 functional units; <th, ch, oo>, for example, are as basic to the current orthography as <a, b, t>. But are <tch, ck, dg> primitive units on a level with <a> and <th>, or are they in some sense compound units, whose correspondences to sound can be predicted from their immediate constituents?

To map spelling into sound, graphemic words must be segmented into their basic graphemic units. This requires schemes for handling letters like the final <e> in *rove* and the <b> in *debt*. Is the <e> in *rove* connected to <o>, forming the discontinuous unit <o . . . e>, or is it part of the unit <ve>, or is it a unit by itself? Similarly, how is the <b> in *debt* to be handled—as part of the unit <eb>, or as part of <bt>, or as a separate unit? Are the silent <e> in *rove* and the silent <b> in *debt* equivalent? The solutions to these problems should be not only consistent with the way similar letters are handled, but also general enough to handle new cases that may arise. They cannot be settled satisfactorily by simply labeling all unpronounced letters as silent. Consider the so-called "silent" <b>'s in *subtle* and *bomb*. We could say that the <b>'s in these two words are silent, and let the matter rest. But by doing so, we would lose an important difference between these two cases. The form *subtle* occurs only with the <b> corresponding to zero, but <b> in *bombard* and *bombardier* corresponds to /b/. It is not sufficient, therefore, to say that the second <b> in *bomb* is silent; more exactly, it is silent before word junctures and before certain suffixes (compare *bombing, bombs, bombed*), and otherwise pronounced /b/. This is one of the forms of orthographic patterning that almost all traditional treatments of spelling overlook. Its full implications are explored in Chapter 8.

Distinguishing Simple and Compound Consonant Units

Another inherent feature in the orthography is the distinction between functionally simple and functionally compound consonant units. One of the most general, although not entirely regular, spelling-to-sound rules is that the vowel spellings <a, e, i, o, u> are mapped into one form before a single consonant unit that is followed by a vowel and into another form in all other environments. In the vocabulary of the direct letter-to-sound school, these forms are the *free* and *checked* pronunciations of the vowels, as shown in the examples below.

Free pronunciation		Checked pronunciation
<a>	/e/	/æ/
	*a*nal	*a*nnals
	*a*che	r*a*tchet
<e>	/i/	/ɛ/
	f*e*tal	f*e*ttle
	*e*ther	h*e*dge
<i/y>	/ai/	/ɪ/
	h*y*po	h*i*ppo
	wr*i*the	wh*i*ttle
<o>	/o/	/a/
	ph*o*nograph	s*o*nnet
	k*o*sher	n*o*xious
<u>	/(j)u/	/ʌ/
	s*u*per	s*u*pper
	t*u*be	l*u*xury

To apply this rule, simple and compound consonant units must be differentiated—a task that cannot be done by appeal only to the number of letters involved. The digraph <sh>, for example, is composed of two letters, yet it functions as a simple unit, as in *kosher*. On the other hand, <x> is a single letter, yet it functions as a compound unit, as in *luxury* and *noxious*. What is needed is a consistent criterion for classing consonant units as simple or compound. Although the classifications of <x, ch, th, ph, rh> may be intuitively obvious, those of <ck, dg, tch> are not. First, the rule mentioned above (and, as will be shown soon, almost all spelling-to-sound rules) should be based not on letters or graphemes as such, but rather on functional spelling units. Second, functionally simple and functionally compound units must be distinguished.

Graphemic Alternations

A feature of the graphemic system that has arisen partly from scribal necessity and partly from pedantry is the alternation of various letters according to their graphemic environments. In such cases, two different letters that correspond to the same sound occur in complementary (or near-complementary) distribution. The functionally simple vowel spellings <i> and <y>, for example, alternate according to word position, not only as single units (*try–tried*), but also as parts of vowel digraphs (*tray–paid*). The letters <u> and <w> also alternate under the identical conditions. Other types of alternations include <er> and <re> (*racer–acre*), <el> and <le> (*angle–angel*), <ity> and <ety> (*sanity–anxiety*), and the various spelling changes that occur with suffixation. These are discussed in a closing section of this chapter.

SELECTION OF UNITS

The Grapheme–Phoneme Parallel

The description of spelling-to-sound relationships begins with certain units on the spelling or graphic level, and ends (for convenience) not with actual speech sounds, but with phonemes. Traditional studies in this area have generally employed the term *grapheme* as parallel to *phoneme,* and various attempts have been made to formalize graphemics or to elaborate on the grapheme–phoneme parallel.[1] The linguist W. Nelson Francis attempted to organize the alphabet and the pronunciation marks similarly to traditional phonemic classes, with graphemes and allographs in parallel to phonemes and allophones:

> Borrowing some ideas and methods from phonemics and morphemics, for instance, we could conclude that each of the various letters has two or more different shapes, which seem to be in complementary distribution or free variation. This in turn suggests that each different shape can be called an **allograph,** and a family of allographs a **grapheme.** . . . Taking inventory of the segmental graphemes of standard English writing or printing, we find that there are thirty-seven of them, which can be classified in two groups:
>
> (a) Twenty-six LETTERS OF THE ALPHABET <abc . . . z>
> (b) Eleven MARKS OF PUNCTUATION <, ; : . ? ! ' – — " (>
>
> In addition we must include SPACE, a sort of zero grapheme.[2]

Even with this description, the graphemic and phonemic systems are far from parallel. Although various single graphemes can be mapped (through intermediate levels) into single phonemes, there are also grapheme clusters that operate as single units, as explained in the opening section of this chapter. Since one cannot deduce the behavior of these clusters from the behavior of their constituents, it must be concluded that units higher than the grapheme exist on the graphic level (e.g., <ch> and <th>). An adequate description of English graphics should therefore describe such units. To meet this need, Robert A. Hall has differentiated between simple and compound graphemes:

> The compound graphemes of English include a great many sequences of vowel letters, graphic diphthongs such as *ae, ai, au, ea, ei, eo, . . . eu, ie, oa, oi, ou, ue,*

in addition to double vowel letters like ee or oo. There are also certain combinations of consonant letters which function as single units and hence must be considered as compound graphemes: e.g. *ch, gh, ph, rh, sh, th, ng;* and again, all the double consonant letters such as *bb, dd,* etc.[3]

Even this division, does not create a workable parallel between grapheme and phoneme. Certain graphemes function solely as *markers;* that is, they do not themselves enter into correspondences but mark correspondences for other graphemes or grapheme clusters, or morpheme properties. Final <e> performs at least 13 different marking functions (see the "Markers" section later in this chapter). For example, it indicates vowel correspondences as in *mate* and *cute* (cf. *mat* and *cut*); it marks consonant correspondences, as in *trace, change,* and *bathe* (cf. *bath*); and it preserves graphotactical[4] patterns, as in *have, toe,* and *glue.* The phonemic level has no parallel to this.

One other major difference between graphemes and phonemes is that phonemes are language-dependent, functionally defined units, while graphemes are not necessarily language-dependent or functionally defined. Almost all speech communities that use the Roman alphabet have the same graphemic system, according to current definitions of graphemics; yet their phonemic systems are vastly different. Furthermore, a new grapheme can be added at will to the graphemic system, regardless of whether it contrasts functionally with existing graphemes. The Anglo-Norman scribes reintroduced <q> into English orthography. Yet this grapheme performed the same function as <k>, which remained in the English writing system.[5] The parallel situation does not exist on the phonemic level; in fact, the opposite is true. A new phoneme comes into existence only when a new contrast appears.

The term *grapheme* refers to letter classes. The individual letters (as written, typed, or in any other way produced) are called *graphs,* and each graph is classed under 1 of the 26 graphemes in the current alphabet. The decision to label two graphs as the same or different depends in no way upon whether they function as the same or different form. Both <q> and <k>, for example, correspond only to /k/ (or are silent); yet <k> and <q> are not classed as members of the same grapheme. The difference between these two graphs therefore cannot depend upon the relationship of spelling to sound or upon any other language-related feature, but only upon the graphic features of the two forms. This process of classification is vastly different from the process by which two *phones* (sounds) are assigned to phonemes. Form is also considered in classing graphs into grapheme patterns, but both form and function are essential for classing phones as members of phoneme classes.

Levels of Analysis

In a theoretical model for mapping spelling into sound, graphemic words are divided into their morphemic constituents, and then these are related to intermediate (morphophonemic) units by an ordered set of rules. Other rules then relate the morphophonemic units to phonemic forms. All rules that are based upon nongraphemic features are applied in an ordered sequence on the morphophonemic level, yielding various sublevels of intermediate forms for each word. The final morphophonemic form is then mapped automatically onto the phonemic level. Although the intermediate level is not strictly a morphophonemic level, it is labeled as such here. Its primary function is to separate graphemically dependent rules from grammatically and phonologically dependent ones. For now the reader need only be aware that graphemes are not formally mapped directly into phonemes, but into an intermediate level. As much as possible, I will continue to speak of grapheme–phoneme (or letter–sound) correspondences.

Types of Graphemic Units

In the remainder of this book, both *letter* and *grapheme* refer to one of the alphabetic characters <a> through <z>, and the phrase *graphemic level* is used as a general reference for the spelling level. The actual language-dependent units on the graphemic level that are significant for the prediction of sound are called *functional units* and are divided into two classes: *relational units* and *markers*. A relational unit is either a single letter (e.g., <x>) that relates to one or more phonemes (including a zero phoneme, or silence), or a string of two or more letters that has a phonemic correspondent (including zero) that cannot be predicted from the behavior of the unit's separate letters (e.g., <ch> as in *chair*). A marker is a letter whose primary function is to indicate the phonemic correspondence of a relational unit or to preserve a graphotactical or morphological pattern (e.g., <u> in *guide*, <e> in *face*), and which has no pronunciation. A silent letter can be either a relational unit or a marker, depending on what functions it serves within a word. Furthermore, a relational unit can serve a marking function, such as the <i> in *city*, which marks <c> → /s/. But since <i> maps into a sound other than zero or silence, it is classed as a relational unit in this word.

Relational Units

The same letter or letter cluster can be part of more than one relational unit. Thus <gn> in *cognac* and *poignant* is a single relational unit that corresponds to the phonemic cluster /nj/, while <gn> in *sign* and *malign* is not a relational unit, but rather a combination of two relational units that correspond separately to the morphophonemes /g/ and /n/. (Further rules map /g/ either into /ø/ [silence] or into /g/, depending upon allomorphic considerations; cf. *signal* and *malignant.*) The selection of relational units is based upon function and composition. Any string of letters that corresponds to a nonzero phoneme is a potential relational unit. However, only those strings whose phonemic correspondences cannot be predicted by general rules that operate on smaller units contained in the string are classed as relational units. The digraph <ch> in *chair*, for example, is a relational unit, since the phoneme /č/ cannot be predicted from general rules based upon <c> and <h> separately. Geminate consonant clusters, however, are not single relational units, since their phonemic forms can be obtained from rules that operate on their separate constituents. (The leveling of clusters such as /ff/ to /f/ can be accounted for by a general phonotactical rule.)

An especially difficult case for determining relational units is <ng>. From a linguistic standpoint, it could be treated as a sequence of two relational units in words like *long* and *thing*. By mapping <ng> first into /ng/, a general rule could then be applied to shift /n/ to /ŋ/ before velar stops (/k/ and /g/), and then a different rule used to level a final, unpronounceable cluster to its first element. However, because of the prevalence of words with final <ng> in English and the practicality, especially for spelling, of having a functional unit that corresponds directly to /ŋ/ in words like *ring* and *strong*, <ng> is treated as a single relational unit except in words like *stronger*, where the <g> is also pronounced.

Another problematic case is the sequence <cch> as found in Italian borrowings (e.g., *finocchio, radicchio, zucchini*), as well as in the Latin borrowings *bacchanal* and *saccharin*. In Italian spelling, <ch> occurs only before <e> or <i> when a /k/ is represented, since <c> in this position is pronounced /č/, as in *cello* and *ciao*. The sequence <cch> in Italian represents a long consonant, in contrast to <ch>, which represents a short or normal length, and could be treated as a pseudogeminate like <ck>, <dg>, and <tch>. However, in some <cch> words borrowed into English, the vowel before <cch> is free (e.g., *finocchio, radicchio*). Therefore, <cch> here is treated as <c> + <ch> rather than as a separate functional unit, and the free vowels before <cch> are treated as exceptions to the general vowel pattern (see Chapter 6).

Some other potential consonant functional units are <dj>, which occurs in a few less common borrowings from Arabic (e.g., *djinni*, "genie"); and <dh>, which occurs in Hindi, Sanskrit, and Arabic borrowings (*dhoti, sandhi, dhow*) and in one English word, *edh*, which is a variant spelling for *eth* and is pronounced /εð/. Neither spelling occurs with sufficient frequency, however, to be included even as a minor unit.

Consonant relational units are classed as functionally simple or functionally compound. For English spelling, <tch, dg, ck, wh, x, gn, pph, rrh> are function-ally compound; all the rest, including <ch, th, sh, ph>, functionally simple. The simple–compound distinction is needed for an accurate statement of a number of rules, as explained earlier. In the sequence vowel + consonant + final <e>, for example, the vowel is generally mapped into its free alternate if the consonant is a functionally simple unit (or this type of unit plus <l> or <r>), and into its checked alternate if the consonant is a functionally compound unit or a cluster. Consider these examples:

Free alternate	Checked alternate
b*a*ke	*a*xe
*a*che	b*a*dge
conc*e*de	*e*dge
cl*o*the	h*o*dge

Vowel units are classed as primary (<a, e, i, y, o, u> plus <æ, œ>) or sec-ondary (<ai, ay, ea, ee>, etc.). Examples of markers are the final <e> in *mate* and *peace,* the <u> in *guest,* and the <k> in *trafficking,* all of which indicate the pro-nunciation of a preceding letter. The sequence <ue> in *plague, brogue,* and many other words is composed of two markers. The <u> after <g> marks the corre-spondence <g> → /g/ rather than <g> → / ĵ/.[6] Since <u> generally does not ap-pear in final position in English words, a final <e> is added, as in *continue* and *blue* (compare the alternations <ou>–<ow> and <au>–<aw>; see Chapter 9). A geminate consonant cluster also performs a marking function, since it regularly indicates the checked correspondence of the preceding vowel.

The strongest evidence for a separate class of markers in English orthography is found in orthographic alternation patterns. For example, final <e> as a marker for the pronunciation of a preceding <c> or <g> is dropped before a suffix that begins with a letter that will perform the same function as the <e>. Therefore, *notice* drops the final <e> before <ing> (*noticing*), since <i> also marks the cor-respondence <c> → /s/, but retains the <e> before <able>, since *noticable* would have <c> → /k/. Similarly, the <e> added to an otherwise terminal <u> is dropped before any suffix, since the only function of the <e> is to avoid having word-final <u> (e.g., *argue–arguing*).

Relational units are classed as consonants or vowels, depending upon the class of the phonemes into which they are mapped (glides are classed as consonants). Some relational units are classed as both consonants and vowels—for example, <u> in *language* (consonant) and *during* (vowel). Within these classes, major and minor patterns are distinguished on the basis of range of patterning and frequency of occurrence. Thus <ch> is classed as a major consonant unit, but <kh> (*khaki*) is classed as a minor unit. Although the major–minor classification may appear arbitrary, it distinguishes frequently occurring, productive patterns from infrequent patterns that generally occur in only a small number of borrowings.

In some treatments of spelling, forms like <gu> (*guard*), <ti> (*nation*), <di> (*soldier*), and <a . . . e> (*bake*) are adopted as basic spelling units.[7] Although such a course has not been adopted here, it is interesting and informative nevertheless to extend this treatment to some of its logical conclusions. In the units just mentioned, so-called "silent" letters are always included as parts of other spelling units, regardless of the functions that they perform. Therefore the <b> in *debt* and the final <e> in *peace* would fall into the same basket, since they are both silent—the units presumably being <bt> and <ce>. This treatment unfortunately obscures a basic difference between these two silent letters: namely, that the <e> at the end of *peace* marks the correspondence <c> → /s/, while the <b> in *debt* is a functionless scribal insertion. The <e> at the end of *peace* is part of the general pattern of markers of English orthography; the <b> in *debt,* on the other hand, is an unproductive, isolated occurrence.

Furthermore, consider the traditional enumeration of spelling units as reflected in such words as *clothe* and *pace.* Both words have, by the traditional treatment, a silent <e> that must be attached to another letter; yet it is not clear which unit either <e> should be attached to, since in each word it marks two separate patterns. In *clothe* <e> marks the correspondences <o> → /o/ and <th> → /ð/, whereas in *pace* it marks <a> → /e/ and <c> → /s/. If we take the traditionalist approach, we are faced with a dilemma here: Are the units <o> + <the> and <a> + <ce>, or <o . . . e> + <th> and <a . . . e> + <c>? Or shall we take a fine razor and split <e> into two parts so that both alternatives can be taken? If we do not treat <e> as a member of a class of markers that is separate from the class of relational units, no satisfactory solution is possible.

The last of the major problems inherent in the traditional view is that an unnecessarily large number of basic units is created by the merger of markers with relational units. Besides all the geminate consonant clusters, the following, among others, must also be recognized as basic units:

<the>	*breathe*	<ce>	*trace*
<dge>	*edge*	<lle>	*belle*
<le>	*able*	<gne>	*cologne*
<re>	*acre*	<ffe>	*giraffe*
<ye>	*bye*	<aoh>	*pharaoh*
<ge>	*change*	<ah>	*pariah*
<xe>	*axe*	<eh>	*vehement*
<ve>	*love*		

All the units above must be classed as basic units in the traditional view, but their behavior can be predicted from the behavior of their components. The final <e> in the clusters shown above is a marker whose various functions are explained later in this chapter. Geminate clusters (*belle, giraffe*) can be handled by considering each consonant separately and leveling the resulting clusters by a single phonotactic rule. The letter <h> in *pharaoh* and *pariah* is a marker, while in *vehement* it is deleted by a phonotactic rule (compare *vehicle–vehicular*).

Given this introduction, the consonant and vowel relational units are shown below. (Units followed by an asterisk are discussed in the following paragraphs.)

Major relational units

Consonants		Vowels	
Simple	Compound	Primary	Secondary
<b> <gh> <n> <s> <w>*	<ck>*	<a>	<ai>/<ay> <ie>
<c> <h> <ng> <sh> <y>*	<dg>	<e>	<au>/<aw> <oa>
<ch> <j> <p> <t> <z>	<tch>	<i>/<y> <ea>	<oi>/<oy>
<d> <k> <ph> <th>	<wh>	<o>	<ee> <oo>
<f> <l> <q> <u>*	<x>	<u>	<ei>/<ey> <ou>/<ow>
<g> <m> <r> <v>			<eu>/<ew> <ui>/<uy>

Minor relational units

Consonants		Vowels (Secondary)
Simple	Compound	
<kh>	<gn>	<aa>
<rh>	<pph>	<ae>
<sch>	<rrh>	<eau>
		<eo>
		<ieu>/<iew>
		<oe>
		<ue>
		<ye>

Notes

<u> is a consonant unit when it corresponds to /w/, as in *quick, language,* and *assuage.* It may also be a vowel unit, or part of a vowel unit (<ou>), or a marker (*guest, plague*).

<w> is a consonant unit when it corresponds to /w/ (e.g., *warm, beware*). It also appears as part of a vowel unit (<ow>, <aw>), but never as a vowel unit by itself, except in the Welsh borrowing *crwth* (a Celtic musical instrument).

<y> is a consonant unit when it corresponds to /j/ (e.g., *yes, beyond*). It also appears as a vowel unit, and as part of a vowel unit (e.g., *cycle, boy*).

<ck> is a consonant unit in words such as *rack* and *tack.* In instances like *picnicking,* however, <k> is a marker. Although <ck> in this form could be treated as a replacement for <c>, the marker solution is preferred because it parallels other spelling changes with suffixation.

MARKERS

The primary functions of markers, as just mentioned, are to indicate the correspondences of other letters and to preserve graphotactical or morphological patterns. For example, <v> does not normally occur in final position in English; where it would, a final <e> has been added (e.g., *have, love*). Various relational units also serve as markers, but since they also correspond to sounds, they are classed as relational units rather than as markers. In the following discussion, the various types of markers that occur in English are listed and summarized.

Final <e>

1. In the word-final pattern VCe, where V is a stressed, single-letter vowel spelling and C is a simple (consonant) functional unit, <e> generally indicates the free pronunciation of V. Thus we have *mate–mat, mete–met, site–sit, note–not,* and *cute–cut.* For reasons obscured by time, this function of final <e> also applies to monosyllables ending in <aste>: *baste, chaste, haste, paste,* and *waste* (but not *caste*). Notice, however, that <e> is not used to mark the free vowel pronunciations in *cold, wild, find,* or *hall,* or in other forms that have free vowels before final <ld, nd, ll>. For numerous VCe spellings where V does not carry the primary word stress, <e> nevertheless marks a free pronunciation: *evacuate, inchoate, create.*

In words such as *able, ruble,* and *noble,* final <e> might also be treated as a marker for a free vowel. However, this treatment leaves <l> corresponding to /əl/, which is illogical. Furthermore, since most final <le> forms are reversals of an earlier <el>, and all are pronounced either as syllabic /l/ or as schwa + /l/, final <le> could be treated as a complex unit similar to <wh> rather than as <l> + marker <e>. But this would create a unique vowel–consonant basic unit, so instead we will live with <l> and <e> as separate units, knowing that their sound correspondences are out of order.

2. In words such as *create, intermediate,* and *heroine,* final <e> shows the preceding vowel to be a separate vowel spelling, as opposed to the second element in a secondary vowel spelling. (A dieresis is also available for this marking function and is occasionally used, as in *naïve* and *coöperate.* However, the dieresis is employed less and less in American typesetting and is almost never used in words such as *idea.*) For verbs and a small number of adjectives that end in <ate> (e.g., *create, nauseate*), the <a> has its free pronunciation, therefore giving two marking functions to <e>. In most nouns and adjectives, however, <ate> is pronounced as an unstressed /ɪt/ or /ət/; compare, for example, *inebriate* (verb) and *inebriate* (noun).

3. For a few words, a final, silent <e> after <l> is retained before <able> to signal the presence of a syllable that might otherwise be elided: *handleable* (cf. *handling*), *settleable* (cf. *settling*).

4. Related to the separate vowel cases are words such as *morale* and *rationale,* where <e> marks the preceding vowel as stressed (cf. *moral, rational*). Some French borrowings that end in <ale> (e.g., *internationale*) retain a final <e>, even though in English the final vowel tends not to be stressed.

5. In *pharmaceutical,* <e> marks the soft pronunciation of <c>. Without the <e>, <c> would be followed by <u> and therefore would be pronounced as in *cute.* The assumed suffixation process here begins with the base form *pharmacy,* to which the suffix *-utical* is added. (But note *pharmacology.*) For *face, race, rice, fleece,* and dozens of other forms that end in <ce>, <e> also marks the soft pronunciation of <c>. In adding suffixes that do not begin with <i, y, e>, the <e> is retained as a marker (e.g., *trace–traceable–tracing*).[7] This marking function is highly regular, with no common exceptions.

6. Parallel to the soft-<c> marking functions is the soft-<g> marking function, as in *age, change, huge,* and *bulge,* as well as in personal names such as *Sargeant* and *George.* For words that end in <nge>, such as *change,* the final <e> also shows that <ng> is not a digraph corresponding to the velar nasal, as in *hang.* In adding suffixes that do not begin with <i, y, e>, <e> is retained as a marker (e.g., *change–changeable–changing*). After <dg>, <e> is a graphemic or *graphotactical* marker, since <dg> does not occur in final position.

7. After what would otherwise be a final <th>, <e> marks a voiced (as opposed to a voiceless) consonantal pronunciation. Compare *bath–bathe, breath–breathe, cloth–clothe, sheath–sheathe, teeth–teethe,* and *wreath–wreathe.* (*Lath–lathe* alternate in pronunciation as do the preceding examples, but lack a semantic association.) Although the majority of the <the> forms are verbs, not all are (cf. *lathe, lithe, withe*).

8. After a number of words that would otherwise end in nonmorphemic <s>, <e> has been added to avoid the appearance of a final inflectional <s>, as in *moose, goose,* and *mouse.* After voiced consonants + <s>, <e> also marks the correspondence <s> → /s/ in contrast to <s> → /z/ (cf. *hearse–hers, tense–tens, sparse–spars*). A nonmorphemic <s> is generally avoided in final position in nouns, adjectives (by analogy to nouns), and verbs under the following conditions:

a. When preceded by a consonant:

collapse	*dense*
eclipse	*sense*
else	*hearse*
false	*coarse*

b. When preceded by a compound vowel:

goose	*praise*
moose	*raise*
house	*noise*
mouse	*poise*

The only true exceptions to these restrictions are the singular nouns *summons* and *lens,* and words ending in <ous>. *Summons,* an Anglo-French adoption, had variant spellings in <nce> and <nse>. Through analogy (both spelling and pronunciation) with the identical form, *summons* became the standard spelling. *Lens* is a late 17th-century Latin adoption for which the variant spelling *lense* now occurs. The suffix <ous>, if spelled <ouse>, would be pronounced /aus/ as in *mouse* and *house.* Apparent exceptions are words such as *hydraulics, mathematics, mumps,* and *billiards,* which function as both singulars and plurals. In these, however, the <s> can be classed as a morphemic unit. The <e> marker is not added where <s> is preceded by a simple vowel spelling, but here <e> cannot be added because it would mark an incorrect pronunciation for the simple vowels. Compare *us–use, his–rise, locus–recluse, tennis–improvise.*

Related to the marking of nonmorphemic <s> is the placement of a final <e> after final <z>, as in *adze, bronze, freeze,* and *ooze.* Since <z> has limited distribution in English spelling, and final <z> is restricted to a small group of words (e.g., *quiz, topaz, whiz*), the actual function that final <e> serves here is not obvious. It may be to show that <z> is voiced (cf. *chintz, quartz, waltz*) or simply to avoid having <z> in final position. (Note that *adz* exists without the final <e>, but this is not the preferred spelling.)

9. After final <ch>, <e> marks a /š/ pronunciation as opposed to /č/: *cache, gauche, mustache, niche* (British English), *pastiche* (but *avalanche*) versus

teach, rich, much. This is one of a number of patterns inherited from French that apply only to French borrowings.

10. English spelling has an aversion to two-letter words beyond a core of function words: *am, an, as, at, be, do, go, he, in, me, no, of, on, or, so, to, we, ye.* Where two-letter words might otherwise exist, either the final consonant is doubled (i.e., geminated) or a final <e> is added (e.g., *awe, owe,* and *toe*).[9] With suffixation, <e> after a final <o> is not dropped, either in monosyllabics or in multisyllabics: *canoeing, hoeing, shoeing, toeing.* Bucking this pattern are *ax* (which is also spelled *axe*) and *ox* (which is never spelled *oxe*). On the addition of <e> after <o>, the 1852 edition of Noah Webster's dictionary had the following explanation:

> Woe.—This word takes the final *e,* like *doe, foe, hoe, sloe, toe,* and all similar nouns of one syllable. The termination in *o* belongs among monosyllables, to the other parts of speech, as *potato, tomato,* etc.[10]

11. After what would otherwise be a final <v> or <u>, an <e> is added. This practice developed during the late Middle English period, partly because of the graphical identity of <u> and <v>. Examples include *love, glue, have, plague, glove,* and *continue.*

12. Markers are used to discriminate words under two circumstances. In the first, words with different pronunciations but potentially the same spellings are sometimes differentiated, usually with the addition of an <e> marker, as in two examples discussed in item 4 above (*moral–morale, rational–rationale*). In *dyeing, holey,* and *singeing,* a final <e> that normally would be dropped is retained to differentiate these words from *dying, holy,* and *singing.*

The second circumstance involves the addition of a marker, once again usually <e>, to differentiate homophones (e.g., *aid–aide, bell–belle, main–Maine*). Sometimes a final consonant is doubled and an <e> added, although almost all such cases are French borrowings (e.g., *grippe*) or were influenced by French spelling (e.g., *steppe*).

Finally, a vast number of French borrowings end in a silent <e> that might be treated as a marker of Frenchness. Most of these words have retained their main word stress on the final syllable, as it is in French (e.g., *cocaine, caffeine, questionnaire*), but a few have shifted to first-syllable stress (e.g., *etiquette, vaudeville*). To treat these <e>'s as markers is probably justifiable, but looks can be deceiving. *Dilettante* could pass itself off as French, but it is Italian, as is *gazette* (although borrowed through French). For now these marks of foreignness will be left out of the official marker category, pending a more thorough analysis of their orthographic and phonological habits.

13. A final, silent <e> is used to dress words in the garb of earlier periods. Thus *olde* and *shoppe* are faux Middle English or early Modern English, in contrast to the modern forms *old* and *shop*. Only a few other words are commonly costumed this way, generally for business establishments or for housing development names, as already explained in Chapter 3 (e.g., *Towne Court*).

Consonant Doubling (Gemination)

1. A geminate consonant cluster regularly marks a checked correspondent for a preceding vowel. Compare, for example, *anal–annals, fetal–fetter, hypo–hippo, rotor–rotter* ("blackguard"), *super–supper*. Exceptions to this pattern are rare, consisting mostly of recent pronunciation shifts (e.g., *collate*) and borrowings.

2. To limit the stock of two-letter words to high-frequency function words, gemination of the final consonant has been used for words ending in a consonant, thus giving *add, odd, inn, egg, ebb,* and *yegg* ("safecracker")—the only examples of these geminates in word-final position except for proper nouns (e.g., *Ann*).

3. Consonant gemination is often used to distinguish one-syllable personal names from their homonyms: *Denn–den, Matt–mat, Webb–web*.

The Letter <u>

Where <g> pronounced as in *gopher* would otherwise be followed by a vowel that would signal a soft pronunciation as in *gym*, a <u> is sometimes added (e.g., *baguette, guess, guide, guild, guilt, Guinness, guise, plague, Portuguese*). This spelling has not been extended, however, to a group of Scandinavian words that have hard <g> before <e> or <i>, such as *gear, get,* and *give*. Similarly, the hard pronunciation of <c> is preserved by <u> in *biscuit* and *circuit*.

The Letter <k>

A <k> is inserted between a final <c> and a suffix beginning with <i, y>, or <e> to mark the correspondence <c> → /k/. Thus we have *picnic–picnicking, traffic–trafficking, panic–panicky, shellac–shellacked*.

The Sequence <al>

The cluster <al> is inserted between a final adjectival <ic> and the adverbial <ly>, if an adjective in <ical> does not exist (e.g., *basic–basically, rustic–rusti-*

cally, scenic–scenically). Generally, the <al> is mapped into zero in such forms. Spelling pronunciations, however, have introduced forms in which the <al> is pronounced.

Diacritics

A small array of diacritics is available for marking letter–sound correspondences, but they find less favor among authors, editors, and printers with each passing year. A cedilla under a <c> preserves a soft pronunciation in environments that otherwise would signal a hard pronunciation (e.g., *façade*). A dieresis marks the second letter of a sequence of two vowels as an independent vowel (e.g., *coöperation*) or a final <e> as pronounced (e.g., *Brontë*). For Spanish borrowings, a tilde marks <n> → /nj/ (e.g., *señor*); for Portuguese, it marks a nasalized vowel (e.g., *irmã*). Also available but restricted in use are the acute and grave accents, the macron, and a few lesser-known marks such as the haček (Czech for "little hook").

Other Markers

Postvocalic <h> before a consonant or juncture could be classed as a marker, even though no clear marking function can be determined from the few existing occurrences of this form: *ah, hurrah, oh, pharaoh, pariah, hallelujah.* (The alternative is to class <ah, oh, aoh> as relational units.) For the interjections *ah, bah,* and *oh,* <h> may have been added as a marker of glottal stoppage, that is, as an intensifier. In *pharaoh* and *hallelujah,* <h> corresponds to the final consonant in the Hebrew reflexes of these words and therefore marks them as foreign. This may also be the function of the final <h> in *pariah,* a Tamil borrowing for which <h> has no historical justification, and *shah,* a Persian borrowing. A few German borrowings (e.g., *ohm*) also have a postvocalic <h> that could be classed as a foreign word marker. In *prohibition* and *vehement,* the <h> pronunciation is deleted by a general morphophonemic rule.

GRAPHEMIC ALTERNATIONS

<i> and <y>

Vocalic <i> and <y> (which can be considered as members of the same functional unit) occur in complementary distribution: <y> in final position and before other vowels, and <i> elsewhere. There are, however, numerous exceptions to this pattern. A considerable number of Greek and Latin borrowings retain <y> in medial position (e.g., *asylum, rhythm*). In addition, some medial <y>'s have resulted from added final <e>'s (e.g., *rye* and *bye*), and from scribal pedantry, as in *rhyme,* which was converted from the earlier *rime* on the mistaken analogy with Latin *rhythm.* Initial <y> (vowel) occurs in the archaic form *ycleped* and in the chemical names *yttrium* and *ytterbium,* while final <i> occurs in several distinct patterns. One is the plural of Latin borrowings whose singulars end in <us>, such as *alumni, fungi, magi,* and *stimuli* (*alibi* and *quasi* are singular in Latin). Similarly, it occurs as the plural of Italian borrowings whose singulars (used in Italian only) end in <o>, such as *broccoli, confetti, ravioli,* and *spaghetti* (Italian singulars *broccolo, confetto, raviolo,* and *spaghetto*). *Macaroni,* another Italian borrowing, is singular in Italian.

Most of the remaining words ending in <i> are also borrowings: *alkali, charivari, houri,* and *potpourri* are French; *anti* is Greek; *ski* is Norwegian; *chili* is Mexican; *haki* is Urdu; *mufti* is Arabic; *yogi* is Hindustani; and *rabbi* is Hebrew (borrowed via Greek and late Latin). One of the few American English exemplars is *taxi,* an early 20th-century coining. Others include the shortened forms *hi-fi* and *sci-fi,* both of which are 1950s inventions. Many of these words had alternate spellings with final <y> or <ee>, but apparently a desire to retain the foreign appearance favored the spellings with final <i>.

The alternation of <i> and <y> occurs with suffixation in the following cases:

1. When <ing> is added to words ending in <ie>, <e> is dropped and <i> is changed to <y> (e.g., *die–dying, tie–tying*).
2. When a suffix not beginning with <i> is added to a base ending in <y>, <y> changes to <i> (e.g., *icy–iciest, mercy–merciless*).
3. A few words that end in vowel + <y> irregularly change <y> to <i> before some suffixes (e.g., *day–daily, lay–laid*).
4. Before a suffix beginning with <i>, <y> does not change (e.g., *boyish, copyist*).

The letters <i> and <y> also alternate as parts of the compound vowel units <ai, ay, ei, ey>, and <oi, oy>. The <y> alternate appears before vowels and word junctures, and the <i> alternate appears in all other cases. Exceptions to this pattern are the following:

geyser: An Icelandic borrowing, taken from the name of a hot spring in Iceland.
moiety: A Middle English adoption of Old French *moite, moitie.*

oyster: A Middle English adoption of Old French *oistre, uistre*. Judging from the *OED* entries for this word, <oy> was the only spelling commonly employed.

paranoia: A late 19th-century Latin adoption. The <oia> spelling was probably retained because of its similarity to other medical terms ending in <ia> (e.g, *megalomania, malaria, anemia, dementia,* and *hysteria*).

sequoia: A Latinization (in botanical terms generally) from *Sequoyah,* a Cherokee Indian name.

<u> and <w>

As consonant spellings, <u> and <w> are for the most part in complementary distribution, <u> appearing for <w> in the environments <gu> and <qu> (initial and medial), <ju> and <nu> (medial), and <pu> and <cu> (initial). In all other cases <w> occurs, except for the three forms *suave, suede,* and *suite.* Exceptions to most of these exist, as the reader by now must suspect for just about any pattern presented. The most common spelling for /kw/ is <qu>, but some French and Spanish borrowings occur with <cu> (*cuirass, cuisine, Ecuador*). For /gw/, <gu> is the only spelling evidenced. Across morpheme boundaries, exceptions can be found for all medial patterns (e.g., *awkward, ragweed*). Listed below are the <u> spellings for <w> that are found in the larger vocabulary of English, except for <qu>, which is too common to list.

<cu>	<gu>	<su>
cuesta	*anguish*	*assuage*
cuirass	*bilingual*	*consuetude*
cuisine	*consanguinity*	*desuetude*
cuisse	*distinguish*	*dissuade*
<ju>	*extinguish*	*mansuetude*
marijuana	*Guam*	*persuade*
	Guatemala	*persuasion*
<nu>	*inguinal*	*suasion*
ennui	*Jaguar*	*suave*
	language	*suede*
<pu>	*languish*	*suite*
pueblo	*languid*	
puissance	*lingual*	

linguist
linguistics
Nicaragua
penguin
saguaro[11]
sanguine
unguent
Uruguay

The spellings <u> and <w> also alternate as the second parts of the compound vowel spellings that begin with <a, e, o>. The <w> variant generally appears before another vowel spelling or <y> and in morpheme-final positions, while the <u> variant occurs in all other positions. This pattern, however, is far from regular.

EXAMPLES OF REGULAR SPELLINGS

<au>	<aw>	<eu>	<ew>	<ou>	<ow>
auction	*awe*	*Eucharist*	*ewe*	*ounce*	*coward*
audit	*draw*	*eulogy*	*ewer*	*oust*	*however*
augur	*gnaw*	*feud*	*brewer*	*out*	*power*
applaud	*saw*	*neuter*	*shrew*	*compound*	*allow*
fault	*straw*	*pneumatic*	*flew*	*south*	*cow*
trauma	*thaw*	*rheumatism*	*threw*	*trousers*	*vow*

Exceptions

1. In initial and medial position before a consonant (usually <d, k, l>, or <n>), <aw> can occur:

awkward   *bawd*
awl   *scrawl*
awning

2. In medial position before a consonant (usually before <d, n>, or <t>), <ew> can occur:

newt   *lewd*
pewter   *shrewd*
hewn

3. In final position, <ou> can occur:

> *bayou*   *bijou*
> *caribou*   *thou*
> *you*

4. In initial and medial position before a consonant (usually <d, l>, or <n>), <ow> can occur:

> *owl*   *drowse*
> *own*   *fowl*
> *crowd*   *town*

The letter <u> in final position in English orthography is rare. Besides the examples given above, the only other examples are mostly French borrowings:

> *adieu*   *aperçu*   *beau*   *bureau*
> *chateau*   *fichu*   *impromptu*   *lieu*
> *menu*   *parvenu*   *perdu*   *plateau*
> *portmanteau*   *purlieu*   *rondeau*   *tableau*
> *trousseau*

The non-French words with final <u> (excluding <ou>, which has been covered earlier) are few: *flu,* a shortening of *influenza; gnu,* a modification of a Bushman word (also once spelled *gnoo*); *kudu* (a large African antelope), which, like *gnu,* first appeared in G. Forster's *Voyage around the World* (1777); *kudzu,* a Japanese borrowing for a similarly borrowed vine of uncontrollable growth propensities; *tabu,* a variant of *taboo,* which (like *tatoo, taro,* and *kava*) derives from one of the Polynesian languages and was brought to the English-speaking world in Captain Cook's journals (1768–1779); and *virtu,* an early 18th-century Italian borrowing.[12]

<ous>–<os> and <ity>–<ety>

The ending <ous> becomes <os> before <ity>: *viscous–viscosity, curious–curiosity, monstrous–monstrosity.* The ending <ity> becomes <ety> after <i>: *anxiety, propriety, society.*

<er>–<re> and <el>–<le>

Parallel in kind to, but far less regular than, the <u>–<w> and <i>–<y> cases are the alternations of the endings <er>–<re> and <el>–<le>. In American English,

<er> is preferred except after a vowel and when the wrong pronunciation of <c> or <g> would be indicated. Thus we have *meter, center,* and *winter,* but *lyre, pyre, acre,* and *ogre.* Where this pattern is broken, irregular pronunciations can result, as in *eager, meager, dagger, tiger,* and *anger.*[13] Recent French borrowings form a special class of irregularities (e.g., *macabre, timbre*), as do British English spellings such as *metre* ("metric unit"), *fibre, theatre,* and *centre.*[14]

For unstressed, final <el> and <le>, small patches of sanity can be found in a sea of chaos. The <el> spelling occurs in only about 150 common words, while <le> occurs in about 800, but among the latter are 350 that end in either <able> or <ible>. Another 75 of the <le> words are accounted for by <gle> and <cle> words that could not be spelled <gel> or <cel> without signaling different pronunciations of <g> and <c>. (Compare the pronunciations of <g> and <c> in *angle* and *angel, parcel* and *particle.*) The remaining <el> and <le> spellings, although exhibiting occasional patterning, cannot be justified by any reasonable orthographic principles. The <el> spelling, for reasons yet to be determined, occurs after doubled <m> (*pommel, pummel*), <n> (*channel, fennel*), <r> (*barrel, quarrel*), and <s> (*tassel, vessel, mussel*). The <le> spelling occurs after doubled <b> (*bubble, cobble*), <d> (*cuddle, toddle*), <f> (*baffle, sniffle*), <g> (*giggle, toggle*), <p> (*ripple, supple*), <t> (*kettle, tattle*), and <z> (*dazzle, frazzle*). The spelling <le> also occurs after <ss> in a single word, *tussle.* Since the number of words for each doubled consonant group is small, and no general principles are involved except for <gg>, the patterns that exist may be accidental.

Another limited case of graphemic alternation is found in the suffixes <ity> and <ety>. The former is the preferred spelling, occurring in over 300 common words. It alternates to <ety> after <i> to avoid the sequence <ii>: *anxiety, sobriety, variety.* The ending <ety> also occurs in words that end in <e>: *nicety, entirety, subtlety.*

Spelling Change

Finally, certain spelling changes that occur with suffixation create graphemic alternations. Some of these changes have been discussed above, particularly for <i> and <y>. Additional changes involve those consonants that can double at the ends of words. These have single–double alternates, as in *run–running* and *tip–tipping.* Similarly, final <e> alternates with zero when suffixes starting with vowels are added: *take–taking, trade–tradable.* But this change is blocked where different pronunciations of <c> and <g> would be signaled: *trace–traceable, change–changeable.* The <k> inserted in *trafficking* and related forms gives the appearance of a <c>–<ck> alternation, as do the <s>–<es> and <d>–<ed> alternations in *cats–watches* and *blazed–blasted.*

LOOKING AHEAD

With full comprehension of this graphemic base, you are ready to explore the history of English orthography and then to engage the spelling–sound basics of the following chapters. Chapter 6 is for enrichment, sketching the history of English spelling from its origins under Latin and Irish tutelage to modern-day American practices. Chapter 7 returns to some issues raised already and introduces a few new ones as a prelude to discussing consonant and vowel patterns in Chapters 8 and 9.

NOTES

1. The earliest mention of the grapheme–phoneme parallel that I can find is in Saussure (1916/1959), 23, 30. Saussure saw four features in the letters (he did not use the term *grapheme*) that parallel features in the phonemic system. Pulgram (1951) upped the count of parallel features to nine. For a summary of linguistic writings on the grapheme–phoneme parallel, see McLaughlin (1963). On the word *grapheme,* see Henderson (1985).
2. Francis (1958), 436.
3. Hall (1961), 14.
4. The term *graphotactical* applies to the sequence or patterning of graphemes (i.e., letters).
5. Latin <q> occurred before <v> as a spelling for /kw/ in some early Old English manuscripts (see the entry for the letter <q> in the *OED*), but <cw> was a more common spelling for Old English /kw/. After the Norman Conquest, <q> was reintroduced into English orthography by Anglo-Norman scribes; by the end of the 13th century, <qu> had replaced both <cw> and <kw> as a spelling for /kw/. For a full discussion of the Anglo-Norman influence on English orthography, see Scragg (1974).
6. For *plague, vague, rogue, vogue,* and *fugue,* <ue> serves the further function of marking a free vowel in the first syllable. Since <e> by itself at the end would indicate a /ǰ/ pronunciation of <g>, <u> is added as at the beginning of *guest.*
7. See, for example, Hall (1961), 17–22.
8. The letter <e> performs two marking functions simultaneously in *trace:* It marks the correspondences <a> → /e/ and <c> → /s/.
9. The exceptions, for the most part, form a lexicon of orthographic marginalia: imitative terms (*do, re, mi,* etc.); back-formations (*ad, Ed,* etc.); interjections (*ah, oh,* etc.); and *ax, ox, pi,* and a few others.
10. Webster (1852), 81.
11. The <gu> in *saguaro* is sometimes pronounced /gw/ and sometimes /w/.
12. Cook (1955–1974); Forster (1777).
13. About two dozen words have final <ger> where <g> corresponds to its hard (/g/) rather than its soft (/ǰ/) pronunciation.
14. The <re> spelling in *timbre* ("sound quality") differentiates it from *timber* ("wood").

CHAPTER 6

Origins and Evolutions

> Upon the history of the English language,
> darkness thickens as we tread back the course of
> time. The subject of our inquiry becomes, at
> every step, more difficult and less worthy.
> —GOOLD BROWN (1851), 56

Principle 4 in Chapter 1 is that "Etymology is honored"; this implies that some part of the history of words may be carried in their spellings. This chapter discusses the history of English orthography, and then sketches some of the major developments that have brought English orthography from the nascent system seen in the earliest Old English records to the more complicated pastiche of today. Although a good chronological treatment exists of the spelling of English words,[1] it is just that—a history in chronological order of the spellings of English words. No treatment exists of the development of the orthographic system as a system, nor does any treatment deal adequately with orthographic change.[2] Equally important is the issue of orthographic authority: What agencies led the changes that occurred, or maintained stability when further change might have taken place?

TERMINOLOGY AND EXAMPLES

First, let us review some terminology. As explained briefly in a note to Chapter 4, the phrase *Old English* refers to the language as spoken and written from the earliest records (the late seventh and early eighth centuries) to about 1100 when An-glo-Norman scribes, as a result of the Norman Conquest of 1066, were firmly es-tablished in England and many of the phonological changes of the past two cen-turies became evident in manuscript spellings. The next period, called *Middle English*, extends past the death of Chaucer in 1400 to about 1500, when the speech of London became the de facto standard for English speakers. The con-figurations of the language from that point on are all referred to as *Modern Eng-lish*, and no one seems to worry about how long we can go on applying this label or what the next language period might be called: *Postmodern English* or *New Modern English*? In each period, the earlier portion is referred to as *early* (e.g., early Middle English, early Modern English) and the latter portion as *late* (e.g., late Old English). (No one to my knowledge, however, has referred to present-day English as late Modern English.) The abbreviations found in the etymology notes in dictionaries for these three periods are OE, ME, and MnE, with e (early) and l (late) prefixed to indicate early and late segments (e.g., eMnE, lOE). These terms are not abbreviated here, however.

With these preliminaries, we can now turn to the central issue of this chapter, which is not "How and why has spelling changed?", but "How and why has the relationship between spelling and sound changed?" The former question, which borders on the antiquarian, calls for a chronicling of changes to the spellings of words, with some accounting of the forces that brought about these changes. What I want to present, in contrast, is an account of how the spelling–sound sys-tem changed. How these two approaches differ will become more obvious short-ly. To illustrate what readers of English manuscripts and early printed pages con-fronted in the past, some samples of English writing and printing are presented in Figures 6.1 through 6.3.

Shown in Figure 6.1 is a manuscript page with transcription of a homily com-posed near the last decade of the 10th century by AElfric, abbot of Eynsham, but copied by a scribe at Worcester in the third quarter of the 11th century. Notice the distinct forms of <s, g, w, r>, and the three characters not found in the present-day alphabet: <Æ> ~ <æ> (ash), <Ð> ~ <ð> (eth), and <þ> (thorn).

Figure 6.2 shows the opening lines from Geoffrey Chaucer's *The Canterbury Tales*, composed about 1387. This introduction to the stories told by a motley group of fictional pilgrims over 600 years ago represents the London variety of East Midland speech, rendered into a late Middle English orthography. Almost all the function words (e.g., *at, from, of*) are spelled as they are today, as are some of the content words (e.g., *twenty*). But distinct differences between Middle and Modern English are also evidenced: The letter <y> is deployed in a number of places where Modern English has <i> (e.g., *nyne, nyght, pilgrymage, ryde, veyne*); final <e> is retained at the ends of words that within 200 years drop both

SE HÆLEND CRIST

syþþan he to þisum life com and mann
wearþ geweaxen, þa ða he wæs þrittig
wintra eald on þære mcnniscnesse,
þa began he wundra to wyrcenne
and geceas þa twelf leorningcnihtas
þa þe we apostolas hataþ. Pa wæron
mid him æfre syððan and he hym tæhte
ealne þone wisdom þe on halgum
bocum stent and þurh hy ealne cristendom astealde. Pa cwædon hy to þam
hælende: 'Leof, tæce us hu we magon
us gebiddan.' Pa andwyrde se hælend
and þus cwæð: 'Gebiddaþ eow mid þysum
wordum to minum fæder and to eowrum
fæder, gode ælmihtigum :

PATER NOSTER QUI ES IN CELIS

ÐU URE FÆDER

þe eart on heofenu(m) seo þin nama
gehalgod. Cume ðin rice. Seo ðin wylla on eorðan swa swa on heofenum. Syle us
to-dæg urne dæghwamlican hlaf. And forgyf us ure gyltas, swa swa we forgyfað ðam
þe wið us agyltaþ. And ne læd þu na us on costnunge ; ac alys us fram yfele. Sy hit swa !'

Figure 6.1. Except from Ælfric's Pater Noster Homily (Bodleian, Hatton 113) (right), with a transcription (left). From Kaiser (1961), facing p. xxxii. Copyright 1961 by Rolf Kaiser.

the pronunciation of this sound and its spelling (e.g., *roote, seeke, soote*); <ee>, <e>, or <e . . . e> spell modern <ea> (e.g., *eek*, "each"; also *breeth, redy, seeke, swete*); and <l> is irregularly doubled at the ends of monosyllables (<alle>, but also <al> and <ful>). Some morphological differences also exist, such as the <en> form of verbs (*holpen, longen, maken, seken, wenden, wolden*) and *hem* for Modern English *them*. Still, the modern shape of English orthography can be discerned from this literate East Midland hand.

In Figure 6.3 is an extract from John Hart's work on orthography, published in London in 1569. Although this passage is nearly modern, <u> and <v> are still

THE CANTERBURY TALES

Fragment I (Group A)

General Prologue

Here bygynneth the Book of the Tales of Caunterbury.

Whan that Aprill with his shoures soote
The droghte of March hath perced to the
    roote,
And bathed every veyne in swich licour
Of which vertu engendred is the flour;
Whan Zephirus eek with his sweete breeth   5
Inspired hath in every holt and heeth
The tendre croppes, and the yonge sonne
Hath in the Ram his halve cours yronne,
And smale foweles maken melodye,
That slepen al the nyght with open ye   10
(So priketh hem nature in hir corages);
Thanne longen folk to goon on pilgrimages,
And palmeres for to seken straunge strondes,
To ferne halwes, kowthe in sondry londes;
And specially from every shires ende   15
Of Engelond to Caunterbury they wende,
The hooly blisful martir for to seke,
That hem hath holpen whan that they were
    seeke.
    Bifil that in that seson on a day,
In Southwerk at the Tabard as I lay   20
Redy to wenden on my pilgrymage
To Caunterbury with ful devout corage,
At nyght was come into that hostelrye
Wel nyne and twenty in a compaignye,
Of sondry folk, by aventure yfalle   25
In felaweshipe, and pilgrimes were they alle,
That toward Caunterbury wolden ryde.
The chambres and the stables weren wyde,
And wel we weren esed atte beste.
And shortly, whan the sonne was to reste,   30
So hadde I spoken with hem everichon
That I was of hir felaweshipe anon,
And made forward erly for to ryse,

To take oure wey ther as I yow devyse.
    But nathelees, whil I have tyme and
        space,   35
Er that I ferther in this tale pace,
Me thynketh it acordaunt to resoun
To telle yow al the condicioun
Of ech of hem, so as it semed me,
And whiche they weren, and of what de-
    gree,   40
And eek in what array that they were inne;
And at a knyght than wol I first bigynne.
    A KNYGHT ther was, and that a worthy man,
That fro the tyme that he first bigan
To riden out, he loved chivalrie,   45
Trouthe and honour, fredom and curteisie.
Ful worthy was he in his lordes werre,
And therto hadde he riden, no man ferre,
As wel in cristendom as in hethenesse,
And evere honoured for his worthynesse.   50
At Alisaundre he was whan it was wonne.
Ful ofte tyme he hadde the bord bigonne
Aboven alle nacions in Pruce;
In Lettow hadde he reysed and in Ruce,
No Cristen man so ofte of his degree.   55
In Gernade at the seege eek hadde he be
Of Algezir, and riden in Belmarye.
At Lyeys was he and at Satalye,
Whan they were wonne; and in the Grete See
At many a noble armee hadde he be.   60
At mortal batailles hadde he been fiftene,
And foughten for oure feith at Tramyssene
In lystes thries, and ay slayn his foo.
This ilke worthy knyght hadde been also
Somtyme with the lord of Palatye   65
Agayn another hethen in Turkye.

Figure 6.2. Opening of the General Prologue to *The Canterbury Tales*. From Chaucer (c. 1387/1957), 17. Copyright 1957 by Houghton Mifflin Company. Used with permission.

Orthographie is a Greeke woorde signifying true writing, which is when it is framed with reason to make vs certayne wyth what letters euery member of our speach ought to bee written. By which definition wee ought to vse an order in writing, which nothing cared for vnto this day, our predecessors and we haue ben (as it were) drouned in a maner of negligence, to bee contented with such maner of writing as they and we now, haue found from age to age.

Figure 6.3. Introduction to John Hart's *An Orthographie*, published in London in 1569. From Hart (1569/1955), I, 168–169. Copyright 1955 by Almqvist & Wiksell. Reprinted by permission.

used interchangeably; <ie> occurs for <y> at the end of *Orthographie*; and final <e> appears often where modern use has removed it. In addition, *maner* is still spelled with a single <n>, as it was in the French from which it was borrowed, and a small number of other words that have <ee> or <o> today are spelled differently (*speach, ben, woorde*). What is striking, nevertheless, is that less than 100 years after the introduction of printing into England and less than 150 years after the reintroduction of English as the language of Parliament, the orthography is so regular.

HOW ORTHOGRAPHY CHANGES

The shapes of letters may change for a variety of reasons, none of which is related to the translation from spelling to sound: to save parchment, to distinguish one letter from another that is graphically similar, to exhibit new aesthetics, and so on. Orthographic change—that is, change in the patterns that account for spelling–sound relationships or for graphotactical patterning—can occur only through borrowings, sound change, or direct scribal intervention.[3] Furthermore, any of these changes can be benign in the sense that they introduce no changes in the patterning per se, but only in the words now classed under a particular pattern or in the initial or terminal symbols that define a pattern.

Sound Change without Spelling Change

Consider what is called the *Great Vowel Shift*, a major transformation of the late Middle English long vowels.[4] Those long vowels that could be shifted higher were. In addition, the vowels spelled earlier with <ea> and <ee>, which were phonemically distinct, merged. Thus, for example, the <a> in *make*, which at the beginning of the 16th century was pronounced somewhat like <o> in General American English *mock*, became by the late 15th century something close to what we hear in American today.

The two highest vowels in Middle English, /i:/ and /u:/,[5] which were pronounced somewhat like the vowels in modern *bead* and *food*, became the diphthongs /aɪ/ and /ou/, as in modern *high* and *grouse*. Thus Middle English *hous*, which was pronounced /hu:s/ at the end of the Middle English period, became /haus/ in early Modern English. Similarly, Middle English *mis* shifted in pronunciation from /mi:s/ to /maɪs/. Since this change was (almost) totally regular, its only impact on the spelling–sound system was to change terminal symbols: Where formerly the rule was "*X* in environment *Y* is mapped into *Z*," now it became "*X* in environment *Y* is mapped into *P*." Notice that for the most part, the Great Vowel Shift involved a change only of phonology, not of spelling. Functional spelling units that represented long vowels continued to be written the same, although their phonemic values had changed.

A similarly dramatic change occurred over almost a 1,000-year period as final inflectional endings on English words were first leveled to a small number of sounds and finally, for most of them, to /ə/ spelled <e>. That is, final inflectional /a/, /e/, /u/, and various other sounds and sound sequences, all unstressed, slowly merged over time, with subsequent spelling change. By the time printing began in England at the end of the third quarter of the 15th century, this final schwa was disappearing, but printers found it convenient to have the flexibility to keep or discard the final-<e> spelling as a means of line justification. More important, because of the vowel lengthenings and shortenings that had occurred at the end of the Old English period and through early Middle English, a final <e> after a single consonant signaled, for most words, a long vowel in the preceding syllable.

In some words, a final <e> was added to show a preceding long vowel pronunciation, as, for example, in *paste, haste*, and *waste*, where an irregular shortening process had left <a> representing both a long and a short vowel before the final consonant cluster <st> (e.g., *past–paste*). (For *paste, haste*, and *waste*, spellings with final <e> appeared along with <aa, ai>, and <ay> spellings until perhaps the 16th century, when the <a . . . e> spelling became established.) Through these processes—the leveling of final inflections to schwa, lengthening of vowels in open syllables, disappearance of the final inflectional schwa—final <e> acquired its most noticeable marking function. Its extension to words that did not regularly end in <e> indicates an acceptance by orthoepists, lexicographers, and writers of this marking pattern.

Sound Change with Spelling Change

Sometimes sound change has been followed by spelling change, thus leading to orthographic simplification. For example, in Old English the initial clusters /hl/, /hr/, and /hn/ existed, as in *hloh*, "laugh"; *hraefn*, "raven"; and *hnutu*, "nut." Before the end of the Old English period, these initial clusters were leveled to /l, r, and n/. This sound change begins to be reflected in spelling as early as the second half of the 10th century. One <h> cluster that was rarely leveled in initial position was <hw>, as in Old English *hwaet*, "what." Although the subsequent history of what was initial /hw/ in Old English is quite complex, the effect of the reversal of initial <hw> to <wh> (which occurred as early as 1200) had an awkward effect on the orthography, because where the initial cluster /hw/ is retained, the correspondence of <wh> to /hw/ is not order-preserving; that is, the spelling sequence reverses the order of the sound units. This is an anomaly, however, because no other major correspondence does this.

Scribal Change without Sound Change

A rather benign change occurred in the first half of the 19th century with the U.S. respelling of British <ou> as <o> in such words as *humor* and *honor*, and the reversal of <re> to <er> in such words as *center* and *theater*. This change began in the late 18th century under the urgings of Noah Webster and became established within the next 25 years. Since <or> and <er> spellings already occurred in U.S. English with the same correspondences as in *humor* and *center*, no new correspondences were created. Furthermore, since final <re> was retained in words that had <c> or <g> before <re> (e.g., *acre*, *ogre*), and final <our> continued to exist in words such as *glamour*, no correspondences were lost.

Sometimes scribal changes have made spelling–sound patterns more predictable. One example was the adoption by Anglo-Norman scribes, beginning in the late 12th century, of <ch> for <c> when <c> represented the phonemic antecedent of Modern English /č/. Before this adoption, <c> represented both a velar stop (/k/ as in Old English *cyning*, "king," and *cynn*, "kin") and what at one time was a palatal allophone of /k/, but that with vowel changes in Old English became a separate phoneme (e.g., Old English *cirice*, "church"). Before the substitution of <ch> for <c> → /č/, <c> before <e, i>, or <y> could be either /k/ or /č/. After the substitution, no ambiguity remained—at least not until about 1500, when sound changes in French and scribal tampering upset the regularity of the pattern.

Another example is the extension of single consonants to doubled consonants (geminates) to mark a preceding vowel as short. Through the same lengthenings and shortenings mentioned before, vowels in syllables that terminated with a consonant (closed syllables) were short, while those in syllables that terminated with a vowel (open syllables) were long. This process had its complexities, however, since it applied mostly to one- and two-syllable words, and the consonants or consonant clusters that led to a closed syllable are not easily described for the two syllable words. Nevertheless, where a geminate consonant spelling occurred between vowels in early Middle English, it always marked a closed syllable. Geminate consonant spellings originally marked long consonants in Old English; these contrasted phonemically with corresponding short consonants. In addition, vowels before long consonants were almost always short. By the end of the Old English period, however, no phonemic contrast remained between long and short consonants, so the geminate spellings were dropped at the ends of most words, since a single-consonant spelling also marked a short vowel in this position. In medial position they were retained, because ambiguity could occur in the pronunciation of the preceding vowel if the geminates were leveled to single-letter spellings.

By the 13th century a few words were respelled with doubled consonants to show a preceding short vowel (e.g., *ladder*), and in the 15th and 16th centuries this process was extended to a larger number of words (e.g., *manner, saddle, scatter, hallow*). *Manner*, for example, first appeared in English in the first half of the 13th century, spelled *manere*, as it was in French. By the late 16th century writers such as Shakespeare spelled the word with doubled <n>, and by the middle of the 17th century *manner* was the established spelling. In addition to the extension of medial geminate consonants, single-letter final consonants were regularly doubled by the mid-17th century before a vowel-initial suffix (e.g., *-ing*) to signal that a preceding single-letter, stressed spelling represented a short (checked) vowel.

A last example of scribal change that affected the orthography occurred during the Renaissance. Hundreds of words were respelled to reflect real or imagined classical origins. Thus, for example, the earlier *dette, dout,* and *sutile* were respelled with <b>'s to parade their Latin ancestry. The main effect of this scribal pedantry was to create irregular spelling–sound correspondences. For a few words, however, later spelling pronunciations eliminated the irregularity. One was *subject*, a 14th-century French borrowing, which was spelled without a <b> initially (*sugettes, soget, sugget*). By the end of the 14th century <b> spellings occurred, although it is doubtful that they had a pronounced /b/ at that time. In early Modern English, however, <b> became pronounced, thereby removing this word from the silent-<b> list. Among dozens of other examples of classical restorations that became pronounced are *perfect* (Middle English *perfit*), *hymn* (Middle English *ymne*), *humble* (Middle English *umble*), *fault* (Middle English *faute*), and *falcon* (Middle English *facoun*).

The Impact of Borrowings

So far I have stressed changes that resulted in simplifications to the orthography or were benign, with the exception of some of the neoclassical respellings that occurred during the Renaissance. Now the other shoe drops, with a few examples of changes that complicated English orthography. The first involves the importation of initial-<g> words, primarily from the Scandinavian countries during the Middle English period. With a few exceptions, late Middle English had evolved a pattern in which initial <g> before <e, i, y> was mapped to /j̆/ and otherwise to /g/. However, a rash of Scandinavian borrowings such as *get, gear, gift, geld,* and *girth* provided exceptions to this pattern, because <g> before <e, i, y> in these words was hard rather than soft. (Late 19th-century borrowings such as *geezer, gefilte,* and *geisha* added to the exception pool.) With native words affected by Scandinavian pronunciation (e.g., *give*), or words that for reasons unknown evolved a spelling with initial hard <g> before <e, i, y> (e.g., *gird, girdle*), the existence of a <g> pattern became questionable.[6]

Borrowings are often responsible for new functional units, although rarely do these units assume a major functional load in the English lexicon. For example, <kh> spellings from Hindi (e.g., *khaddar, khaki*) and Turkish (e.g., *khedive*) have brought a new functional unit, <kh>, which corresponds invariably to /k/. Other borrowings (e.g., Yiddish *tchotchke,* "trinket") have yielded graphotactical changes, because <tch> normally occurs only after single-letter short vowel spellings. Similarly, a group of coinings with doubled <v> (*navvy, divvy, revved*) have changed a prohibition against geminate <v>.

Borrowings can also create variations on existing spelling–sound patterns. By the early Modern English period, for example, <i> in stressed syllables had a short pronunciation as in *trip* and *river,* and a long pronunciation as in *strive* and *sublime.* These were generally predictable, but exceptions existed as in *triple* and *give.* With the importation of French words such as *police, marine, sardine,* and *caprice,* an additional correspondence was added for <i>.

Mechanisms of Change: A Summary

We have seen how borrowings without spelling change can create new functional units, new correspondences, or exceptions to existing correspondences. Similarly, examples of sound change have been given—with or without subsequent spelling change—that affected terminal symbols only, created irregularities for patterns, or created new patterns. Sound changes can also merge sounds, as occurred in early Modern English with the sounds originally spelled <ea> and <ee>. Since no spelling change occurred, only initial symbols in spelling–sound patterns were affected. However, from a spelling perspective, a single sound now had two different spellings based upon features that were no longer evident in the words involved.

But scribal change can also occur, even without sound change or borrowing.

During the early Middle English period, Anglo-Norman scribes introduced a number of French spelling conventions for English, dramatically altering spelling–sound patterns. In the 15th and 16th centuries, neoclassical respellings again altered the orthographic landscape; and in the United States at the end of the 18th century and the beginning of the 19th century, further scribal changes occurred, this time to distinguish U.S. spellings from their British companions. To explain how these various changes affected the structure of the orthographic system, we switch to a chronological account of the development of English orthography. With this as a base, we return in several concluding sections to broader questions about the origins of the current orthography, and to the development of some of the major patterns.

EVOLUTION OF ENGLISH SPELLING

The Runic Alphabet

The Germanic peoples who settled in Britain in the fifth century brought with them the *runic alphabet*, or *futhark*, as it is called after its first six letters, which correspond roughly to the Old English letters <f, u, þ, a, r, k>. This alphabet, which is believed to be derived from a similar North Italic system, consisted originally of 24 characters called *runes*, but was increased to over 30 in the course of the Old English period. From the form of surviving runic inscriptions, it appears that the Germanic invaders of Britain restricted their alphabet mainly to ornamental purposes.[7] Surviving Anglo-Saxon runic inscriptions are found primarily on knives, swordhilts, coins, and burial monuments. The earliest, the Caiston-by-Norwich bone, may be as early as the 4th or 5th century,[8] but the dating of an inscribed piece is notoriously difficult and at best can only be approximate.[9] The longest runic inscriptions in England, carved in the Ruthwell Cross and the Franks casket, date from after the introduction of Christianity and the establishment of an English orthography based on the Latin alphabet. Use of the runic alphabet declined after the Danish invasions of the middle of the ninth century, and disappeared altogether by the 11th century.[10]

Old English Orthography

Christianity came to Britain in the fourth century with its acceptance as the official religion of the Roman Empire. Germanic invaders, however, stalled its spread in Britain beyond the Celtic and Irish domains until the missionary efforts that began at the end of the sixth century with the landing of Augustine on the

Isle of Thanet. An early stronghold of English Christianity was Northumbria, and it was from the monasteries of this region that the earliest extant Old English documents were transcribed or composed in the Latin alphabet (Caedmon's *Hymn*, Bede's *Death-Song* and *Ecclesiastical History*, and *The Leiden Riddle*). Irish influence in early Old English calligraphy is undeniable.

Irish-English script (called *insular script*) was based on a combination of uncials and minuscules, and was derived from the insular half-uncial hand (see Figure 6.1).[11] Most distinctive were the forms for <e, f, g, r, s>, which were similar to the modern Irish forms for these letters. In this respect the Irish influence was evident. But in the deployment of the letters for Old English sounds, Irish influence is minimal. The Latin sound–spelling correspondences were the bases for the earliest Old English writings. In a short time, nevertheless, native innovations entered into the system.

Two runic symbols, thorn (þ) and wynn (ᚹ), replaced Latin <th> and <uu>; a new character, eth (ð), was created[12]; and <y, æ>, and <h> were given functions quite different from those that they performed for the Latin language. The lack of Irish influence beyond the letter forms was due primarily to the nascent state of Old English orthography during the early Old English period. The earliest Old Irish manuscripts, which date from the late eighth and early ninth centuries (and were probably written on the Continent), show limited orthographic regularity. There was thus little that the Old English scribes could learn from their Old Irish counterparts, apart from how to write the individual letters. On how to represent spirants and the front-rounded vowels—problems for which Latin orthography could offer no solutions—Old Irish orthography was equally impotent, so the English were forced to devise their own solutions.

Among the single-letter spellings used in Old English, <j> and <v> did not exist, and <q, x, z> occurred rarely. The letter <k> was used more often than these three were, but not as frequently as <c> to represent /k/. The digraph <th> was the most common spelling for the allophones /θ/ and /ð/ in the earliest texts, although <d> occurred occasionally in medial and final positions for these functions.[13] The spellings <d> and <th> were used interchangeably in Old Irish, both for the voiced dental stop and for the interdental spirant. Later, medial <d> was modified to <ð>, and this symbol replaced both <th> and <d> as a means for expressing /θ/ and /ð/. In the 10th century, however, the runic thorn became established in initial position, while <ð> remained the primary choice for medial and final positions in a word.[14]

The earliest spellings for /w/ were <u> and <uu>. The runic wynn entered in late Old English, completely replacing these latter two. In the meantime, however, <uu> was carried to the Continent, from which it was reintroduced into English orthography in the 11th century. Geminates were used to represent long consonants; the vowels were represented by the single-letter spellings <a, æ, e, œ, i, o, u, y>, plus <ea, eo, io, ie>, which represented diphthongs of uncertain values. To represent Old English /y/ and /y:/, <ui> was used in the earliest texts, but was soon replaced by <y>.

The centers of authority for early Old English were the monasteries, where Latin texts were copied and new texts generated. Each kingdom—North and South Northumbria, Mercia, Kent, and Wessex—had its own center of authority. By the end of the ninth century, however, King Alfred had consolidated power from his home base of Wessex, beaten back the Danes who had invaded and devastated large areas of England, and begun to restore learning and literacy throughout England. The Benedictine reform movement also had its effect at this same time. Through a core group of scribes at the monastic center at Winchester in the second half of the 10th century, documents were copied in the dialect of Wessex and circulated throughout England for recopying, thus establishing the West Saxon dialect as a de facto standard.[15] Who these scribes were and how they were trained is not known.

Transition to Middle English

From 900 through the middle of the 11th century, West Saxon dominated as a literary dialect. Although the orthography was stable, it did not completely disguise sound changes and conflicting dialects. The most significant orthographic change in the Old English period was in the representation of vowels in unaccented syllables, especially in inflectional endings. In the early texts such vowels are represented by the same symbols used for the accented vowels, "but very soon *æ, e, i,* fall together in one sound, which was written *e.*"[16] The letter <o> was also substituted for unaccented <u>, and by late Old English the symbols <a, o, u> were used interchangeably. Fries calculates that "by 1100 only 16½ percent of these endings were still spelled with their historical vowel letters; 73 percent were spelled with e; and 11½ percent had *a, o, or u,* but not the letter with which they had formerly been spelled."[17] By the end of the Old English period, English may have had only a single unstressed vowel, /ə/.[18]

Anglo-Norman Influence

After the Norman Conquest (1066), two factors led to a major overhauling of the English orthography. One was the ascendancy of French as the official language of England, with the concomitant importation of French words into English and of French scribes into England. The other was the late Old English and early Middle English sound changes, which the orthography attempted to follow. At times these forces were inseparable, as for example, in the formation of the diphthong spellings <aw> and <ew>, where both French borrowings and the coalescence of /w/ with a preceding vowel in native words brought about the digraph vowel spelling.

We can no more determine which influence was more important than we can determine exactly when these influences began to decline and the influence of the classical revival and of printing began to arise. Nevertheless, the orthography underwent continual change from before the Norman invasion until the end of the 16th century, and the factors that brought about the changes themselves changed. At first the Anglo-Norman influence was unmistakable, yet of all the alterations due to this influence, few involved spellings that were unique to Norman orthography. Many, such as <w, qu, k, ph>, had once appeared in Old English orthography but had failed to establish themselves. Others, such as <sh>, were created especially for English. In addition, several minor influences were present, such as the tendency to avoid potentially ambiguous sequences of *minims* (short downstrokes) and the attempts to mark vowel quantity.

The years from the end of the Old English period to the middle of the 12th century were marked by a gradual decline of the West Saxon orthographic standard and the rise of sharply defined regional variations. From the middle of the 12th century, which marked the earliest establishment of Anglo-Norman orthographic changes, until the middle of the 15th century, the orthography, though marked by both interdialectal and intradialectal differences, moved toward a norm that was finally settled by the Chancery scribes in the 15th century (see below). At the beginning of this period orthographic changes attempted to follow sound changes, but by the end of the period the orthography had become fairly stable. The orthographic changes that appeared, however, were all in the direction of regular spelling–sound correspondences. Even the marking of vowel quality was achieved with some degree of success before the Great Vowel Shift, but the large influx of foreign words during and after this shift tended to obscure the degree of regularity that was achieved.

Middle English Scribal Changes

According to some writers, a series of orthographic changes were instituted in the 13th century to make handwritten documents easier to read.[19] In each case the major concern was to avoid a sequence of minims, since in the Carolingian script used at that time, such successions were difficult to read. A sequence of three minims, for example, could be read as <in, ni, m, iii, ui, iu>, or <w>. Some of the indicated changes, such as the use of <y> as a variant of <i>, resulted from similar Norman practices; others, such as the inversion of <hw>, were devised especially for English. In the latter change a more phonologically accurate spelling, <hw>, was sacrificed for a more legible one (<wh>). Thus, Old English *hwaet* (Modern English *what*) was respelled *whaet* in Middle English.

Several purely graphic changes also occurred at this time, and in each the avoidance of minim sequences was clearly a motivating factor. One such change was the addition of the dot over the lower-case <i>, which developed from a "faint sloping line" that Middle English scribes introduced to distinguish <i> from contiguous <m, n, u>, and to distinguish <ii> from <u>.[20] A second change involved the distribution of the curved and angular forms of <u> (<u> and <v>), which were used in Old English and Middle English indiscriminately for both consonant and vowel values. Middle English scribes tended to use <v> initially and <u> elsewhere, regardless of whether they represented consonants or vowels. However, when <u> would be adjacent to <m> or <n>, an exception was made for legibility through the substitution of <v>. Other changes brought <o> in place of <u> when adjacent to <m> or <n> (e.g., *ton, monkey, woman*), and <k> for <c> before <e, i, m, l>. In these changes the desire to increase legibility appeared to be the major concern. In all of them, however, alternative explanations are possible, and the evidence in favor of legibility as an explanatory factor is often no stronger than the evidence against this claim.

Development of the Chancery Standard

In the second half of the 15th century and in the 16th century, the advent of printing and the fringe benefits of the classical revival produced further changes in the orthography; however, these changes were aimed at showing the origins and morphological structures of words, rather than their pronunciations. Although the number of words affected by these influences was large, the overall effect on the orthography was small. With the passing of this period, the character and form of the orthography were all but settled. In the later years the functions of <u> and <i> were separated from those of <v> and <j>; final <e> gained a few more marking functions; and the endings <re> and <our> were forced to defend themselves against <er> and <or> (a battle that they won in England, but lost in America). In addition, a few stray words like *come* and *colonel* underwent graphical surgery, but for all practical purposes the 16th century fixed the appearance of English orthography.

By far the most important shift for English orthography in its last 700 years occurred during the first decades of the 15th century, when what M. L. Samuels has called the "Chancery Standard" developed.[21] According to John Hurt Fisher, this style of language—a formal, official language of government—developed as a consequence of the restoration of English after 1420 as the official language of Parliament.[22] By 1400 the spoken language of administration was English, but French and Latin remained as the written forms. A few petitions in English did occur before 1420 (2 before 1400 and 8 during the period 1400–1420), but in the period 1421–1430, 63 were recorded in English; the flood continued thereafter, with a proportional reduction in French and Latin petitions.[23]

During the four decades following 1420, the Chancery Standard was established by the Chancery clerks as a model for government use and was spread throughout England by professional scribes. It appeared first in petitions and responses, but it was quickly adopted for private correspondence and business, soon becoming the standard for licenses, pleas, writs, court records, transfers of property, bills, and other business records and transactions. These were the text genres that affected the lives of ordinary citizens—not literary writing such as plays, poems, and sermons, which were mainly for the elite in the 15th century, or the writing produced by the schools and the church, which was primarily Latin until after about 1525. Chancery English was based upon Wyclifite manuscripts written in the various Wyclif centers, plus the London-based writing of authors such as Chaucer and Gower, most of whom were for some time in their lives civil servants or closely involved with Chancery.

In spelling, the Chancery Standard introduced few new approaches. Instead it selected among competing spellings and thereby accelerated a movement toward regularization and standardization that would continue for almost 200 more years. The most important characteristics of Chancery spelling were (1) <gh> for "native" palatals (e.g., *high, though*); (2) <d> for the past tense; (3) <i> rather than <y> in words like *which*; (4) <u> in words like *shuld, such,* and *much*; (5) <i>–<y>, <u>–<v>, <u>–<w>, and <ou>–<ow> alternations close to those that occur today; and (6) final <e> to mark a free vowel. A few Chancery spellings failed to catch on, nevertheless. Examples include <o> before <n> in *land, stand,* and other words ending in <nd>; *eny* in place of *any*; *shew* for *show* (although *shew* is still occasionally used in England); and *on* or *oon* for *one*.

The Impact of the Renaissance

The 15th and 16th centuries marked the peak of the Renaissance and the beginning of the modern period. It was the time of Machiavelli and Tasso; of Leonardo, Michelangelo, and Raphael; of Luther and Calvin; of Rabelais and Montaigne; and of Erasmus. The study of "man" flourished, the classics were revived, and education became a property of the middle class. Few if any areas of human interest escaped renovation—art, religion, literature, and education were all affected. Mannerism and anti-Mannerism, the Reformation and the Counter-Reformation, Humanism, and the reform of Greek and Latin pronunciation all reflected the new focus on human beings and human endeavors. The Renaissance brought, along with an awakening nationalistic spirit, a new concern for education, encouraged by the intellectually liberated middle class. For centuries schools and education had been an ecclesiastical concern, geared primarily for those entering religious orders. Now, for the first time in England, control of learning was placed in secular hands, and education soon became an essential concern of the middle class.

One indication of the extension of education was the increase in the number of schools and the number of students attending one form of schooling or another. According to one study of schooling in six rural counties of England, the number of elementary and grammar schools increased from 35 in 1480 to 410 in 1660—almost a 12-fold increase during a period in which the total population increased by no more than a factor of 2.[24]

Interest in Spelling Reform

With the Renaissance came also a renewed interest in the English language. The first English grammars, the first English readers, and the first spelling reform tracts for English all appeared in the course of the 16th century.[25] Interest in orthography reached a new height, and while John Hart was arguing for reform in the direction of phonetic spelling, the remainder of the populace quietly accepted reforms based upon etymology and morphology.

> The history of English scientific and practical grammar may be said to begin with the Elizabethan phoneticians and spelling reformers. The movement which they represented was a natural outcome of the great intellectual awakening which marks the second half of the sixteenth century. . . . The English language, men felt, was an object of patriotic concern which could not decently be left to take care of itself in so fundamental a matter as orthography. In particular, however, the impulse to revise and regulate came more or less directly from across the channel, where a similar treatment of the French vernacular was actively underway.[26]

Before the development of the Chancery Standard, there was no evident concept of a standard language or a standard system of spelling. By the end of the 15th century, however, printers such as William Caxton (d. 1491) were asking what form of English was best for printing. By the reign of Henry VIII (1509–1547), the concept of standard English was established.

Classical Reforms

The flavor of the Renaissance was evident in the restoration of Latin spellings in thousands of English words, but other influences were also present. Printing was an established force by the middle of the 16th century, and the majority of the orthographic conventions of the early printers gained immediate acceptance. The runic thorn, for example, was not present in the Roman type stocks of the first printers of English, being replaced by <th>. Caxton's <gh> in *ghost* and *ghastly*, and the increased use of <z>, were also adopted and became permanent fixtures in the orthography. In addition, the mass production of books brought about a subtle change in the function of orthography. With limited production of handwritten documents, writing was intended in many instances for reading aloud. But with the rise of printing, the written appearance of words gained in importance. The graphic differentiation of homonyms and the graphic identity of allomorphs became essential. Such factors were also influential in French orthography, according to Pope:

> The works written in the vernacular in the older period had been destined to be sung or read aloud, but the great mass of legal documents were composed to be read, and thus spelling came to be regarded more and more as a matter for the eye, a tendency that was increased when printing multiplied the number of readers. It became therefore more and more usual to use spelling both to distinguish homonyms and to link together related words wherever possible.[27]

Classical influences worked on both ends of the spelling–sound relationship. On the one hand, reforms in Latin pronunciation occasionally led to a reform in the pronunciation of English words borrowed from Latin, without a corresponding change in the orthography. On the other hand, orthographic changes were made to display classical origins without changes initially in the pronunciation. The pronunciation reform came primarily in the relationships based on <s> and <x>. Dobson, whose two-volume text on early modern English pronunciation is the most authoritative on the subject, writes: "The English pronunciation of Latin . . . must . . . have used [z] for Latin intervocalic s. . . . But the 'reformed' pronunciation of the sixteenth century substituted [s] for [z] in the pronunciation of Latin s."[28] Thus, for example, *asylum* and *desolate* have <s> corresponding to /s/ where we would expect /z/. The extent of the reform of Latin pronunciation and its carryover into English have not been accurately evaluated. Dobson notes several exceptions to indicate that the reform was only partial in English.[29] Intervocalic /ks/ for <x> in words like *exit* and *exercise* is also attributed to an early 16th-century reform of Latin pronunciation.[30]

Both of these pronunciation reforms were unusual because they represented sound change by fiat—a phenomenon that must have appalled the neogrammarians. Latin, however, was the basis of all school curricula in England. Students were weaned on Lily's *Carmen Monitorium*, cut their baby teeth on Aesop and Terence, and reached maturity on Lily's *Grammar*, Horace's *Epistles*, and Donatus's *Figura*.[31] Latin was also used in religious and legal proceedings. The question of why more Latin influence was not present, or why under similar conditions other languages were not altered in a similar way, cannot be answered. We know only that the sound changes appeared to be derived from similar changes in Latin pronunciations and that Latin was a thriving concern at the time.

The spelling reform was restricted mostly to the replacement of existing spellings with those that more closely reflected the supposed classical origins of the words. In some cases, silent letters became pronounced, like the <b> in *subject* (cf. Middle English *suget*); the <c> in *perfect* (cf. Middle English *perfit*); and initial <h> in *hermit* and *hostage*, neither of which had initial <h> pronounced as /h/ in Latin or French. In a few cases the spelling change had no influence on pronunciation (e.g., <c> in *arctic*, <Th> in *Thomas*). Although the majority of the spelling reforms were established in the 16th century, many had their origins one or two centuries earlier, when spellings refashioned on classical models began to appear in Old French. This is particularly true of the respelling of Old French <a> as <ad>, as in *administer*, *admiral*, and *advert*, and of the addition of <h> to the beginnings of such words as *heir*, *heresy*, and *hermit*. From Old (and Middle) French they were borrowed into English, where, for the most part, the new spellings became pronounced. Although the enthusiasm for classical spellings soon disappeared in French, it remained in English.

The Great Vowel Shift

Toward the end of the Middle English period and into the early Modern English period, the long vowels of Middle English went through a dramatic change, shifting upward and to some degree forward in their pronunciation. The two long vowels that could not shift any further upward, /iː/ and /uː/, became diphthongs. Thus Middle English *hous*, pronounced /huːs/, shifted to the form we hear today, /haʊs/, and Middle English /bliːnd/ became Modern English /blaɪnd/. Exactly when these changes began, what stages they passed through, and when they were completed is still debated. Some of the changes may have begun as early as the

1200s, and some may not have been completed until the early 1700s. Nevertheless, the timing and mechanics are of less interest here than the impact on spelling–sound patterns.

The front vowels were changed as follows:

/iː/ → /aɪ/, as in *find, mice, nine*. Earlier <i> and <y> spellings were changed mostly to <i>, except at the ends of words. Some earlier <i> spellings were changed to <ei> and <ey>.

/eː/ → /i/, as in *sweet, see, mete*. The Middle English sound is called close (/eː/) to distinguish it from open *e*, /ɛː/. By Early Modern English it had a variety of spellings: <e> (*mete*), <ee> (*beet*), <ie> (*chief*), and <eo> (*people*), all of which remain today.

/ɛː/ → /i/, as in *sea, meat, team*. By the 15th century, open *e* was spelled <ea> and did not rhyme with close-*e*. However, by the end of the 17th century the two sounds had merged. In several words (*break, great, steak, yea*), for reasons unknown, /ɛː/ did not shift to /i/, and in others such as *bread, head,* and *thread*, it had apparently shifted to short /ɛ/ before the Great Vowel Shift.

/aː/ → /e/, as in *blame, nail, day*. Earlier /aː/, spelled <a, ai>, or <ay>, shifted regularly to /e/.

The changes in back vowels were of similar complexity:

/uː/ → /aʊ/, as in *house, mouse, south*. The spelling <ou>, imported with French words during Middle English, was regularly pronounced /uː/ in late Middle English. In a few words, /uː/ failed during the Great Vowel Shift to become a diphthong (*through, wound*); most others that have <ou> → /u/ today were borrowed after the end of the 15th century (*group, rouge, soup*).

/oː/ → /u/, as in *food, fool, shoot*. This sound was spelled <oo> or <o> in Middle English, and is called close *o*, in contrast to open *o*, which is described next. After the shift to /u/, a shortening to /ʊ/ occurred in a group of words (*book, foot, took,* etc.). In at least two words, *flood* and *blood*, /u/ both shortened and unrounded to /ʌ/. Other spellings for Modern English /u/ and /ju/ derive mostly from Middle English diphthong spellings: <eu, ew>, and <u> (*neutral, pewter, rude*).

/ɔː/ → /o/, as in *float, grow, road*. Although not distinguished from close *o* in Middle English spelling, by the mid-16th century the spelling <oa> was substituted for earlier <oo> and <o> spellings where /o/ was derived from earlier /ɔː/. This may have been based on analogy with <ea> to distinguish open from close vowels.

Although these changes were dramatic for pronunciation, their impact on spelling–sound patterning was less so. For example, <ou> continued to represent the vowels in *house, mouse,* and *south*; only the phonological character of the vowel changed. The merger of open *e* and close *e* simplified spelling–sound mappings while complicating mappings in the reverse direction—that is, sound–spelling. Although some might argue that English vowel patterns were nearly regular prior to the Great Vowel Shift, the evidence doesn't support this claim. With no mechanisms for distinguishing open and close *e* and open and close *o*, and with some long–short distinctions not made in the orthography (e.g., /a:/ and /a/), regularity was limited. Nevertheless, the Great Vowel Shift was the last major phonological change in English phonology, and with the vowel shortenings and unroundings that followed it, the modern vowel patterns were established.

Transition to Modern Times

Throughout the Middle English period, the orthography underwent continual renovation in the direction of more regular spelling–sound correspondences. In the 15th and 16th centuries, a classical flavoring, smacking of morphology and etymology, was added. The resulting product was then turned over to the early printers for trimming. The printers showed little bias toward phonology, morphology, or etymology; they simply strove for regularity, and where it did not exist, they selected one of the conflicting forms as a standard. Changes that came after this period were relatively minor, the most important being the functional separation of <u> from <v> and of <i> from <j>, the adoption of <(e)d> as the past-tense marker, and the replacement of final <ie> by <y>. Even more minor irregularities were ironed out by the lexicographers—the <our>–<or> and <re>–<er> conflicts; the addition of final <e> to words ending in <dg> and <g> to mark a /ǰ/ pronunciation; and the addition of silent final <e> to short words like *are*, *come*, and *woe*.

The separation of <u> from <v> and <i> from <j> was advocated as early as 1551 by the orthoepist John Hart, but did not become established in England until after 1630. It occurs much earlier in Spanish and Italian.[32] The past tense and participle marker <(e)d> appears as early as the 14th century, replacing <t> spellings in some words. It did not become firmly established until the 19th century, however.

The digraph <ie> and occasionally the single-letter spelling <i> were the regular endings for such words as *already*, *necessarily*, and *facility* until the last quarter of the 17th century, when <y> was substituted. Orthoepists such as Mulcaster (1582) and Hume (c. 1617) used <ie> regularly. Butler (1634) had *usually* and *woorthily* alongside *excellenci*, *faciliti*, and *eleganci*.[33]

Some other orthographic irregularities were settled with the help of such lexicographers as Nathaniel Bailey, Samuel Johnson, and Noah Webster, although it is doubtful that these men were as influential in directing the orthography as is normally assumed. Webster, for example, advocated massive spelling reform in the early 19th century, but by 1840 he had recanted on most of his proposals.[34] The doubling of final <l> before suffixes is still unsettled, and the <re>–<er> and <our>–<or> controversies were settled differently on the two sides of the Atlantic Ocean.

The amount of orthographic change that has occurred since 1600 is small, and the amount that has taken place since 1700 is minuscule. Alterations in spelling–sound correspondences brought about by borrowings and sound change since 1600, however, are much greater. The sound changes affected primarily the checked vowels and the fricatives. While English orthography at the beginning of the Modern English period was attempting to mark vowel quantity with the succeeding consonants, classical and Romantic borrowings with no such marking system were being imported by the thousands. Fries estimates, on the basis of the entry cards used in the compilation of Middle English and early Modern English dictionaries, that the English vocabulary increased by over 275 percent in the years from 1475 to 1700 (from 45,000 entries to 125,000).[35] Whatever regularity was achieved in the spelling of English words in the Middle English period was soon obscured by borrowings after the orthography was fixed.

DEVELOPMENT OF MAJOR ORTHOGRAPHIC PATTERNS

I have just sketched some of the direct causes of the orthographic changes that led from the earliest Old English system to the present one. No single body legislated these developments, no national orthographic character guided them, and no single principle served as their blueprint. As explained above, the present set of patterns derives from an underlying native orthography, over which, at various times, foreign patterns have been overlaid. Where functional units took on the different sounds that a morpheme assumes in its various guises, morpheme identity was preserved with sound change, as in, *breath–breathe* (both vowel and consonant spellings), *athlete–athletic*, and *divine–divinity*. But an equal number of cases exist where sound change across forms of the same morpheme was accompanied by spelling change: *wife–wives*, *provide–provision* (consonants), *glass–glaze* (consonants), *space–spatial*, *mother–maternal*, *see–sight*, *take–took*. How interactions among sound change, scribal change, and borrowings combined to yield specific orthographic patterns is discussed next, followed by a discussion of orthographic authority.

The <ch> Pattern

In modern English, <ch> has three pronunciations—/č/, /š/, and /k/—with little within the spellings of the words to assist the reader in choosing among them for an unknown word. The initial stage in the development of this pattern resulted in the French spelling <ch> replacing Old English <c> for what became modern /č/. Many French words that were borrowed from the early 1200s until about 1500 followed this pattern (these words are shown here in their Modern English spellings): *chapel, change, champion, challenge, chair, chief,* and more. But by 1500, /č/ in French, which for purposes of this explanation is best represented as /tš/, had lost its initial /t/, thus becoming /š/; therefore, French <ch> words borrowed after this time had the mapping <ch> → /š/.[36] An alternative spelling, <sh>, was available but was never substituted, thus leaving *champagne, chef, chaperon, sachet,* and many more words with <ch> → /š/.

Further complicating the earlier regularity was a tendency to respell words borrowed from Latin or Greek according to their classical patterns. Thus earlier *cristen, qwere, cronakle,* and *collor* were respelled in the 16th century as *christen, choir, chronicle,* and *choler.* This introduced the /k/ pronunciation for <ch>, which was then reinforced with subsequent borrowings from Greek and Latin, or with words patterned after these languages (such as *chromium* and *chlorine*).

The <c> Pattern

The letter <c> in word-initial position has two common pronunciations: a fricative, /s/, which occurs when <c> is followed by any spelling for a mid- or high-front vowel (usually <e, i>, or <y>); and a stop, /k/, otherwise.[37] This pattern holds for <c> in other positions, but is complicated by the palatalization of /s/ to /š/ in certain phonological environments (e.g., *ocean, social, gracious*).[38] Behind the simplicity and regularity of this pattern, however, is a complicated mixture of sound changes, lexical borrowings, and changes in scribal practice that involved spellings not only for /s/ and /k/, but for /č/ as well. How these processes interacted to produce the existing <c> pattern demonstrates how intentional change (i.e., scribal modifications) can combine with random change (i.e., sound change and lexical borrowing) to produce a highly regular pattern. In other circumstances, such as with some vowel pronunciations, similar changes have yielded less orderly results.

By the time of the earliest English writings, the letter <c> represented two phonemically distinct sounds, as described above in the section on scribal changes: /k/ as in present-day *king,* and a phonemically distinct palatalized form before most occurrences of front vowels. This latter sound has evolved into modern /č/ as in *church*. The evolution of /k/ and /č/ began in prehistoric Old English with the development of allophones for /k/: a palatal form before front vowels, and a velar form otherwise.[39] After this change, a process called *i*-umlauting led to the change of back vowels to front vowels when the back vowels were followed by a high-front vowel (/i/) or glide (/j/) in the following syllable. These latter sounds were either lost or changed into /e/ before the historic period of English, so that by the time of the first English records, the palatal and velar allophones of /k/ had become separate phonemes.

Thus Old English *cennan* (*beget*) had a velar /k/, while *cest* (*chest*) had a palatal /k/, which developed into Modern English /č/. Although the functional load for this phonemic opposition (particularly in early Old English) was initially quite low, with late Old English and early Middle English sound shifts, and with a heavy importation of loan words into Middle English and early Modern English, its functional load increased markedly.

At the same time that <c> was used in Old English for the velar and palatal /k/ phonemes, the sound /s/ was spelled almost exclusively with the letter <s> (e.g., Old English *mys, lys, sinder*; Modern English *mice, lice, cinder*).[40] The letter <k>, although known to Old English scribes, was infrequently used until after the Norman Conquest. When it was used, nevertheless, it represented the velar /k/ phoneme almost without exception.[41]

Had the writing of Middle English not been dominated so fully by Anglo-Norman scribes, and had French and Latin words not been imported wholesale into Middle English, the subsequent histories of <c, k>, and <s> might have been no more than a continuation of the Old English practices. But the Norman Conquest brought not only a new view of how native words should be written, but an influx of French and Latin words of such magnitude that many of their spellings became the dominant models for English.

One of the earliest spelling changes made by Anglo-Norman scribes was to substitute <k> for <c> to represent the velar /k/ phoneme before front vowel spellings. By this change such Old English forms as *cent, cyng*, and *seoce* were rewritten as *kent, kyng*, and *seoke* in Middle English. In addition, by at least as early as 1160, <ch> assumed the duties of <c> when it represented the palatal /k/ phoneme, which by the Middle English period is assumed to have completed its shift to /č/.[42]

With this realignment, <c> in native words had only one sound, /k/, as in *callen* (*call*) and *cole* (*coal*). But in Latin and French, a sequence of sound changes paralleling those in English for /k/ produced a second major pronunciation for <c>: Late Latin /k/ before /e/ and /i/ palatalized, giving /č/ in Italian and /ts/ in French. Thus <c> in Old French, as in Old English, represented both a velar stop and a phonemically distinct palatalized or affricated derivative of this stop.[43] By the end of the 13th century, French (and Latin) /ts/ was reduced to /s/, thus giving the correspondence <c> → /s/ in a large number of words that were later borrowed into English: *cease, ceiling, cement, cider, circle, civic*. By analogy, <c> then replaced certain <s> spellings in the 15th and 16th centuries in English (e.g., *ice, mice, lice, cinder*). The resulting pattern for <c> pronunciations gives /s/ in Modern English for <c> before <e, i>, or <y>, and /k/ otherwise. As stated earlier, this pattern is obscured somewhat in medial position for those occurrences of /s/ that palatalize to /š/ (e.g., *ocean, special*). Nevertheless, the basic correspondences for <c> are almost totally predictable.

Primary Vowel Patterns

The story of the development of the primary vowel patterns—the free–checked (long–short) alternates of the primary vowel spellings <a, e, i, o, u>, is an orthographic soap opera, sustained over almost 1,000 years. Vowels were lengthened and shortened, and then the long ones were raised or became diphthongs; new vowels were imported; spellings changed; allophones developed and then became separate phonemes; and other phonemes merged. A complete, detailed history of this evolution is a sure cure for insomnia and is not attempted here. Instead, two of the developments are briefly traced. The first is for <i>, which traveled the simplest route from Old English to Modern English and still retains a reasonable approximation to what it represented in King Alfred's time. The second is for <u>, which is more typical of the evolution of the three primary vowel patterns not sketched here. To begin, recall that Modern English <i> in stressed syllables most often represents either /ɪ/ as in *sit* or /aɪ/ as in *site*. Similarly, <u> represents either /ʌ/ as in *cut* or /ju/ as in *cute* (or /ɪu/ as in *fume*, or /u/ as in *rude*).

<i>

In Old English the spelling <i> represented a short vowel, /i/ (*sittan*), and a corresponding long form, /i:/ (*fif*). Through a series of shortenings and lengthenings that started apparently before the close of the Old English period and stretched through the early Middle English period, /i:/ in disyllabic words shortened to /i/ in syllables that were terminated by a consonant (closed syllables). This led eventually to Modern English contrasts such as *wife–women* (*wife–wimman*) and *five–fifteen* (*fyve–fiftene*). In parallel with these shortenings, vowels that terminated syllables in disyllabic words (open syllables) as well as vowels before certain consonant clusters (e.g., /ld, mb, nd/) lengthened, leading to the Modern English free vowels in words such as *blind* and *wild*.

In late Middle English or early Modern English, /i/ shifted to /ɪ/, thus switching a quantity contrast to one based on muscle tension (free–checked). Then with the Great Vowel Shift, /i:/ shifted to a diphthong, /aɪ/, thus completing the migration from Old English /i/ ~ /i:/ to Modern English /ɪ/~ /aɪ/.

\<u>

As with \<i>, \<u> in Old English represented both a short and a long vowel—/u/ and /u:/, as in *hnutu* ("nut") and *mus* ("mouse"). Before the end of the early Middle English period, the quantitative contrast of /u/ and /u:/ shifted to a tense–lax contrast, /ʊ/ and /u:/. Long (lax) \<u> (/u:/) was respelled by the end of the 13th thirteenth century with the Anglo-Norman digraph \<ou>, and during the Great Vowel Shift this changed to the diphthong /aʊ/, thereby escaping from the orbit of the Modern English free and checked vowels. Meanwhile, back in Middle English, French borrowings with \<u> → /y:/, a long, high-front rounded vowel that did not exist in English at the end of the early Middle English period, were pronounced by Middle English speakers with a diphthong /ɪʊ/ (e.g., *fume*), thus creating the correspondence \<u> → /ɪʊ/. At that point \<u> had three different pronunciations, /ʊ/, /u:/, and /ɪʊ/. In early Modern English /ʊ/ developed the positional allophones [ʊ] and [ʌ], which in time became separate phonemes, as in *bush, bushel,* and *put* versus *fun, luck,* and *rut.*

This latter separation produced two modern reflexes of Middle English short /u/, of which /ʌ/ was designated by orthoepists and philologists as the short (i.e., checked) form. Long (i.e., free) /u/ descended directly from late Middle English /ɪʊ/, but has three different Modern English realizations: /ɪu/ after labial or labiodental consonants (e.g., *bugle, fume, pure*); /ju/ after /h/ and /k/ and in initial position (e.g., *humor, cube, use*); and /u/ after /r/ (e.g., *rude, rumor*).

Completing the creation of one major part of the free–checked pattern, the final-\<e> component, was the sequence of changes for final inflectional endings described above in "How Orthography Changes." Together, these changes account across all five primary vowel spellings for such contrastive pairs as *mat–mate, met–mete, sit–site, pop–pope,* and *cut–cute.*

Gemination

Geminate consonants, with the exception of the Spanish borrowings *llama* and *llano* and the proper name *Lloyd,* occur only in medial and final position, with the latter restricted to a small number of geminates. Consonant gemination developed from Old English spellings for long consonants, which in the earliest records contrasted with short consonants. After consonant length was no longer phonemically significant, spellings with doubled consonants, because of Old English syllable structure, came to indicate short vowels. In time, gemination was extended to borrowed terms, but not consistently. Since Old English vowels before single final consonants were almost always short, gemination in final position was abandoned except for <ss, ff, ll>.

With the exception of a few recent French borrowings (e.g., *chauffeur*), geminate consonants occur only after single-letter checked vowel spellings. Therefore, <u, w, h, y>, which spell sounds that do not occur postvocalically, do not geminate; nor do <q> and <j>, because they are not used postvocalically. Digraphs and trigraphs do not geminate, although in the 15th century <tch> replaced earlier <cch> as a doubling of <ch>, and although <pph> (*sapphire*) can be classed as a doubling of <ph> and <rrh> (*myrrh*) as a doubling of <rh>. In parallel with <tch> are <dg>, a replacement for doubled <g> when it represented / ǰ/, and <ck>, a replacement for <kk>.[44]

The spellings <tch> and <dg> reveal considerable linguistic sophistication on the part of 15th-century scribes. The sound /č/ is phonetically a complex sound that begins with the articulatory system positioned for /t/, but ends with it positioned for /š/. In the IPA (see Chapter 4), /tš/ is the preferred representation for this sound, and /dž/ is preferred for / ǰ/, which is the voiced parallel of /č/. The graphemic representations <tch> and <dg> can therefore be mapped into /ttš/ and /ddž/, respectively; these level to /tš/ and /dž/, which are /č/ and / ǰ/. Doubling of the initial element is also present in <pph> and <rrh>, although the phonological relationship is lacking for <pph>. Together, these five geminate replacements are labeled *pseudogeminates*.

To complete the gemination summary, <x> does not double because it already (through its representation of two sounds) signals that a preceding vowel is checked, and <v> was not allowed to double in earlier periods because of potential confusion with <w>. Even when printing became common, the stricture against <vv> remained. Nevertheless, a few geminate <v> words have been admitted in the past two centuries (e.g., *chivvy, divvy, navvy, savvy*).

THE SHIFTING CENTER OF ORTHOGRAPHIC AUTHORITY

So far, the reader who has followed at least the spirit of the presentation has seen snippets of changes, strewn across a landscape of scribes, writers, printers, and lexicographers, who meddled with or ignored the spellings of English words as they chose. As stated earlier in this chapter, spelling–sound patterns change because either sounds change, or spellings change, or words borrowed into English carry with them new patterns or cause alterations to existing ones. Patterns emerged not because of the carefully renderings of the logical positivists of the scribal trade, but because of peculiar interactions of these particular types of alterations, usually extended over long periods of time. This may sound like magic—the deities of the scribal trade conspiring to make orthographic concoctions.

There is, however, a more logical view, which begins with the inadequacy of the 26 letters of the Roman alphabet to represent the 40-plus phonemes of English that existed at any period in the language's history. Different solutions were tried at different times. In the earliest records, a number of digraphs appear for the spirants and fricatives not found in Latin. Occasionally a vowel letter was doubled to show length, and in time letters were borrowed from runic writing or new ones created. As words were borrowed with alternative spellings, or as scribes from other language communities came to the task of writing English, foreign approaches were often applied to native problems. As sounds changed, other solutions became possible, such as the use of geminate consonants and silent final <e> as markers.

Still, this does not explain why scribes and writers in one era were willing to alter spellings, but those in another era were not. Or why words imported into English sometimes retained their native spellings and sometimes did not. One possible starting point is to assume that since alphabets are primarily phonologically based, it is only natural that those in charge of the orthography would try to keep the flow from spelling to sound transparent or obvious. This position suffers from two problems. First, it is not true for English, since during certain periods spelling did change with sound change (e.g., leveling of initial /h/ clusters), while at other times nearly the same changes (e.g., leveling of initial /wr/, /gn/, and /kn/ clusters) resulted in no spelling change. Second, no central authority has ever been empowered to look after English orthography. Nevertheless, throughout its history, periods of greater and lesser orthographic authority have existed, although the centers for scribal practice have varied and the attitudes or philosophies held by those most influential for the orthography have also varied.

LOOKING BACK

This tale of the unfurling of English orthography from its humble and inchoate origins in the seventh and eighth centuries up to the modern period is admittedly not a smooth narrative. A few leading actors and a few stages have been introduced, a few patterns have been traced the full length of the cloth, and the notion of authority has been dangled for a brief time. But much more remains to be explored. Dialects, for example, can be discerned in spellings almost up to the introduction of printing in England, but have not been covered fully here. Some are important—especially since the majority of the extant Old English records are written in West Saxon; yet modern English derives from a different dialect, Mercian, for which only a limited set of documents survive.

The critical elements of this tale concern two issues. First, how did etymology and tradition eventually obtain prominent positions in orthographic reform? Second, how did sound change, borrowings, and scribal license combine to produce the main patterns of the current orthography—the free–checked vowel spellings, the hard and soft pronunciations of <c> and <g>, the <i>~<y> and <u>~<w> alternations, the use of pseudogeminates, and the wide use of markers? Much more remains to be said on these topics, but thanks to the work of a distinguished group of philologists, linguists, and historians, a substantial base already exists for the needed explorations.

LOOKING AHEAD

From here we turn to the meat-and-potatoes section of the text—the patterns and rules that link spelling to sound. The next chapter lays down the basics of this process, centered on the question of regularity. The two following chapters present the patterns and rules for consonant and vowel spellings, respectively.

NOTES

1. Scragg (1974).
2. In contrast to the situation for orthography, an ambitious work on the history of punctuation has recently been published (Parkes, 1993).
3. I use the term *scribal* here to refer to any individual or agency who had authority over orthography. Until the end of the 15th century, scribes were the most influential. Then came printers, orthoepists, lexicographers, and such agencies as the English Chancery or the U.S. Board on Geographic Names.
4. To avoid complications that would add little to understanding the issues discussed here, I do not present a complete phonemic accounting of the phonology of any period in the history of English, except for what has been presented in Chapter 4 for Modern English. It is helpful to know, however, that until the Great Vowel Shift, English had a phonemic contrast between what are reconstructed to be quantitatively long and short vowels.
5. The representation /i:/ is for a long vowel, in contrast to the short form /i/. This indicates a phonemic contrast presumably based upon length of articulation, although evidence for this being the sole distinguishing feature is lacking.

6. In a few cases, a <u> was inserted between an initial <g> and a following <e> or <i> when the <g> had a hard pronunciation (e.g., Old English *gest*, Modern English *guest*).
7. For an overview of the runic alphabet, see Hogg (1992). Fuller treatments on the topic of runes can be found in Page (1973) and Parsons (1995). On the question of whether the Germanic peoples believed runes to be magical, see especially Page (1964).
8. Hogg (1992), 79.
9. Page (1990) discusses some of the difficulties in dating inscriptions.
10. Blair (1956, 305–311) summarizes the extant runic inscriptions in England.
11. See Campbell (1959), 12, n. 1.
12. Opinions differ on the origins of this letter. Hogg (1992, 75) summarizes the situation thusly: "The origin of eth, like its name, is more obscure, and although it is sometimes said to be a borrowing from Irish scribal tradition, this is not certain." The name "eth," according to Robinson (1973), derives from Modern Icelandic and was not the name used in Old English for this letter.
13. I assume here that the voicing of the medial spirants /f, s, θ/ occurred in prehistoric Old English.
14. Hogg (1992), 76.
15. A number of studies have explored the standardization of the West Saxon dialect. See especially Gneuss (1972) and Hofstetter (1988).
16. Campbell (1959), 19.
17. Fries (1963), 164. The particular endings that Fries mentions are the dative plural <um>, weak noun and weak adjective <an>, past plural <on>, nominative and accusative <as>, and genitive plural <a>. He does not describe, however, the corpus upon which these figures are based.
18. Hogg (1992).
19. See, for example, Strang (1970), 230.
20. Pyles (1964).
21. Samuels (1963).
22. Fisher (1977); see also Fisher (1996).
23. Fisher (1977).
24. Jordan (1961), cited in Martin (1994), 336.
25. The earliest extant comments on the English language are contained in William of Malmesbury's *De Ponifibus*, written about 1125. A passage from Malmesbury was cited in Higden's *Polychronicon*, and in turn was translated into English by John of Trevisa in 1387 (see Craigie, 1946, 115). The first English grammar was Bullokar's *Bref Grammar*, published in 1586. *The Cambridge Bibliography of English Literature* (Bateson, 1941–1957, I, 376) lists the *A.B.C. both in Latyn and Englishe* (c. 1538) as the earliest extant English reading book. On early spelling reform tracts, see Chapter 11.
26. Kittredge (1906), 1–2.
27. Pope (1934), 282. On the transition to silent reading, and on a variety of other issues related to the reading of handwritten documents, see Saenger (1998).
28. Dobson (1957), II, 929.
29. Dobson (1957), II, 929.

30. Dobson (1957), II, 929.
31. A discussion of the curricula and books of the English Renaissance schools can be found in Woodward (1967), 268–322.
32. See the entry for the letter <i> in the *OED*.
33. See Mulcaster (1582/1970), Hume (c. 1617/1865), Butler (1634/1910).
34. Malone (1925).
35. Fries (1963), 168. A more recent estimate made by Robert E. Lewis, editor of the *Middle English Dictionary*, places the Middle English vocabulary at around 56,000 words (R. E. Lewis, personal communication, February 28, 1999).
36. As pointed out in Chapter 4, the affricates /č/ and /ǰ/ can be treated as stop + fricative sequences: /tš/ and /dž/.
37. In a few Italian borrowings such as *cello* and *ciao*, initial <c> is pronounced /č/. These are ignored here.
38. In general, /s/ palatalizes to /š/ before a high-front vowel or glide, but only when the primary word stress falls on the immediately preceding vowel. The /s/ that palatalizes is generally spelled <c> (*ocean*, *social*) or <t> (*nation*, *rational*). This latter spelling is a Renaissance replacement for an earlier <c> or <s>.
39. On this series of sound changes, see Penzl (1947) and Vachek (1959).
40. However, /s/ in the cluster /ks/ was usually spelled with the <x>, while /ts/ in Biblical names and occasional English words was spelled with the <z> (Campbell, 1959).
41. The runic alphabet differentiated the velar and palatal variants of /k/, but Old English scribes failed to adopt similar mechanisms.
42. Mossé (1968).
43. The use of <c> for the cluster /ts/ occurs in a few Middle English words but was not widely used (Mossé, 1968).
44. The geminate cluster <kk> occurs only in (1) inflectional forms of *trek* and *yak* (e.g., *trekked*, *yakked*), (2) rare borrowings such as Japanese *tekka* ("tuna") and Australian *yakka* ("work"), and (3) a few informal or imitative terms such as *tekkie*.

CHAPTER 7

Discovering Regularity

I abhor such . . . rackers of orthography as to
speak dout, fine, when he should say dou*b*t; det,
when he should pronounce de*b*t,—d, e, b, t, not
d, e, t. . . .
—HOLOFERNES, in *Love's Labor's Lost*
(Shakespeare, 1598/1952), V.i. 20–25

According to Principle 5 in Chapter 1, "Regularity is based on more than
phonology." What regularity is for an orthography, and what the features are that
determine it, are the concerns of this chapter. A craving for order has characterized the human mind as far back in time as human thoughts can be traced. Hes-
iod's Greek cosmogony placed the beginning of all things in the formless, impen-
etrable darkness of chaos, from which order rather violently evolved. Ancient
and modern astronomers have labored over the cosmic confusion, imposing order with cycles and epicycles, circles and ellipses, and black holes and space cur-
vatures; still, evidence of disorder remains, and there are many sleepless nights
on account of it. Our task here is to explore regularity in spelling-to-sound patterns, made necessary by the need in the following chapters to label some patterns as regular and others as irregular. If you are willing to accept that some reasonable scheme has been adopted for this task and have little interest in the details, you may want to plunge right into consonant correspondences, which are
presented in the next chapter.

THE IDEA OF REGULARITY

For the linguist, order is judged by the elusive measure of regularity. The most prized trophy of any philological foray is a demonstration of order rescued from the debris of irregularity. Jakob Grimm, a 19th-century German philologist (and folklorist), suggested a set of rules to relate the sounds of various Indo-European languages, and thereby brought a semblance of order out of many centuries of chaos.[1] But he still left a marginal mess for other 19th- and early 20th-century philologists to clean up. The concept advanced by Noam Chomsky in the 1950s of a finite set of generative patterns for deriving an infinite set of sentences imposed a higher degree of theoretical regularity on language capabilities than had existed previously.[2] But what is regular in one system may be irregular in another, and what one analyst sees as order, another sees as disorder. This results not so much from the complexity of language as it does from the elusiveness of the concept of *regularity*.

Linguistic Definitions of Regularity

Attempts to define *linguistic regularity* have appealed either to the internal structure of the linguist's description or to the assumed language-processing habits of the native speaker. Zellig Harris, a 20th-century linguist, defined *descriptive linguistics* as a search for regularities, but only hinted at how one separated the regular from the irregular: "Descriptive linguistics, as the term has come to be used, is a particular field of inquiry which deals not with the whole of speech activities, but with the regularities in certain features of speech. These regularities are in the distributional relations among the features of speech in question, i.e. the occurrence of these features relatively to each other within utterances."[3]

Earlier, the European linguist Otto Jespersen had invoked human language processing for defining *formulas* and *free expressions*—concepts that were linked to the classes of regular and irregular. Formulas are whole units, such as *How do you do?*, retrieved intact from memory rather than being generated by productive rules or habits from their components; free expressions are the results of applying a rule or series of rules, and, according to Jespersen, "always show a regular formation."[4] That this dichotomy might create some difficulty for the analyst was admitted by Jespersen, but somehow he felt that careful scrutiny would solve all: "It follows that the distinction between them [free expressions] and formulas cannot always be discovered except through a fairly close analysis."[5]

But if we accept that free expressions are generated anew in each case by the speaker, then it is not analysis that is required, but experimentation. Somehow we must lift the cranial carapace, expose the mental activities to view, and observe whether units are being switched directly from memory to output channels or whether there is a more complex shuffling and joining of separate building blocks into wholes. Analysis can lead to hypotheses about which utterances could be free expressions, but direct observation of production itself is necessary to be strictly in line with Jespersen's classification.

Even Leonard Bloomfield, the father of modern linguistics and a follower of behaviorism, brushed dangerously close to the cerebral cortex in defining regular and irregular forms: "We may say that any form which a speaker can utter without having heard it, is regular in its immediate constitution and embodies regular functions of its constituents, and any form which a speaker can utter only after he has heard it from other speakers, is irregular."[6] As examples of the application of this definition, Bloomfield cited the formation of the regular plural *foxes* and the irregular plural *oxen*. Bloomfield no doubt meant by "can utter" the phrase "has the capability to utter," but even this is an extension of the linguist's analysis to the mind of the speaker (an accusation that would have elevated Bloomfield's blood pressure). A native speaker of a language cannot utter (or does not have the capability to utter) the plural of any noun until other speakers are heard producing the plural, if we assume that "utter" implies "produce with certainty of correctness" and not just "produce." Given that we know one irregular noun plural, then we must admit the possibility that others occur. We may assume that native speakers will tend to make plurals of unfamiliar nouns based upon the regular rules for generating plurals. However, we cannot assert that native speakers will respond this way without making inferences about language-processing strategies.[7]

If we insist that "can utter" means only "possesses a rule for uttering," then we face the dilemma of deciding which rules a native speaker possesses. To claim that the native speaker possesses all rules that the linguist can describe as regular vitiates the original definition, because now regular forms are those that the analyst calls regular, and the speaker is removed from the loop. On the other hand, claiming that the only plural forms that a native speaker can't utter are those not heard previously from other speakers leads to contradictions, at least for Bloomfield. The alternation of /f/ to /v/ in plurals such as *knife* and *wife* should become regular because the speaker can possess a rule for this alternation, if we assume that information is available on when to apply it (just as native speakers must learn when to apply—or not to apply—the noun plural rule, because exceptions exist). But Bloomfield calls this specific alternation "irregular."[8]

Charles Hockett, like other structural linguists, has appealed to linguistic description in terms of frequency: "An alternation is *regular* if it is what occurs most frequently under stated conditions, any other alternation which occasionally occurs under the same conditions then being *irregular*."[9] There are two problems in attempting to apply this definition. First, what constitutes a legitimate "stated condition"? Second, what does one count to arrive at "frequently"? On this latter problem, observe the Modern English pronunciations of the words *hideous, idiot*, and *perfidious*, in which the pronunciation of the <d> has not changed to the sound heard at the beginning of *judge*, as it has in *cordial, soldier*, and *residual*. (This particular change, called *palatalization*, is explained in Chapter 8.) The simplest rule to cover these words is to assign the *hideous, idiot* types to the regular class and the *cordial, soldier* types to the irregular class. This is justified on the basis of frequency: a small number of irregular forms and several handfuls of regular forms.

On the other hand, if all the palatalizations that occur in English are included in the tally, a different separation of regular and irregular results. Words such as *atrocious, abrasion*, and *bastion* have undergone a similar set of pronunciation changes. In the company of these forms, *cordial* and *soldier* represent the regular result, whereas *hideous, idiot*, and so on represent the irregular. Even if the connection between the <s>, <z> and the <t>, <d> palatalizations is rejected, the combined frequencies of the <t>, <d> palatalizations would still leave *cordial* and *soldier* as regular forms. From the linguist's vantage point, the more general solution is preferred; it is assumed that such blanket coverage can be justified by more than aesthetic appeal. This appears to be the situation here, where an articulatory link between the two groups of palatalizations exists.

More recent linguistics texts have often finessed this issue by assuming that linguistic rules derive from underlying psychological mechanisms and that "language has its own system of rules whose workings need not reflect particular conventions of logic or common sense."[10] Besides reflecting a questionable assumption about language competence, this legerdemain leaves unanswered how linguists are to choose among competing interpretations, how development occurs as a speaker moves from one rule to another, and what level of functioning should be considered in creating rules. It also, of course, does not help in defining regularity.

REGULAR AND IRREGULAR WORDS

Exactly what a *regular* word is seldom finds discussion in educational tracts, yet educators have had no reluctance in making rather exact estimates of the number of regularly spelled words in the English language.[11] One problem in classifying words as regularly or irregularly spelled is to decide on whether regularity is defined by reading or spelling, or both. Doubled consonants in *ebb, butt*, and *watt* are regular for reading. They are pronounced the same as single consonants in these positions. Yet for spelling they are irregular, because <b, d, n, t> typically do not double at the end of words. (The appeal here is to frequency: <b, d, n, t> do not double at the end of any other nonproper nouns in the Thorndike 20,000-word list.) *Dove, glove, love, shove* and *cove, rove,* and so on are irregular for reading, because the pronunciation of <o> before <v> cannot be predicted. At best, the irregular group can be reduced to *dove, glove, love, shove,* and a few others, because these words disobey the final-<e> pattern (see Chapter 6). Yet, for spelling, a set of rules exists:

1. /ʌ/ before /v/ is spelled <o>; /o/ before/v/ is spelled < o>.
2. <v> (which spells /v/) does not double, thereby making *navvy, flivver,* and *divvy* irregular.
3. Where <v> would otherwise occur in final position in a word, an <e> is placed after it.

Oyster is another example of reading regularity and spelling disaster. The digraphs <oi> and <oy> are both pronounced /ɔi/, so that in reading no irregularity is aroused by the <oy> in *oyster*; for spelling, <oy> is irregular, because <oi> almost invariably occurs before consonants and <oy> in all other positions.

Second on the problem list is the criterion for regularity. Is frequency alone sufficient, and if so, what is to be counted? Or should predictability be considered, and if so, what constitutes legitimate predictability? Let us assume first that frequency of occurrence is a primary factor. The unit <ch> has three major pronunciations in English: /č/ as in *choose,* /š/ as in *chef,* and /k/ as in *echo.* In the Thorndike 20,000-word list, approximately 62 percent of the <ch> spellings are pronounced /č/, 26 percent /k/, and 12 percent /š/. Does this imply that 62 percent of the <ch> spellings are regular and 38 percent are irregular? How does a reader know, in looking at a word with a <ch> spelling, whether the word is regular or irregular? Shouldn't a /š/ pronunciation at only 12 percent be more irregular than a /k/ pronunciation at 26 percent? Furthermore, and more crucial to the regularity decision, should types or tokens be considered in evaluating regularity? The figures cited above are obtained by assigning equal weight to every unique word that contains <ch>, regardless of that word's popularity (i.e., frequency of occurrence) in present-day English. Should special weight be given to the more frequently occurring words?

This argument could be crucial in some instances, such as the pronunciations of medial <ch>, if we assume that frequency could share equal importance with position. The most frequent pronunciation for <ch> in total occurrences is /č/, but in medial position this pronunciation trails the /š/ pronunciation by many percentage points. However, the medial <ch > → /š/ words are considerably rarer than the medial <ch> → /č/ words (*cliche, crochet, sachet* vs. *achieve, archer, merchant*).

On the other hand, if regularity is to be judged by predictability, then the basis of prediction—Hockett's "stated conditions"—becomes the stumbling block. In the <ch> words, for example, a familiar orthographic bromide assigns the French words to /š/, the Greek words to /k/, and the unadulterated English forms to /č/.[12] But how is a child to know a word's original citizenship, faced for the first time by one of these formidable letter strings? For the trained etymologist, this may be a basis for predicting pronunciation, but for the average reader it is not. Language origin is therefore inadmissible evidence for operational predictability. However, more is said on this topic later in this chapter.

What about syllable divisions? One of America's dictionaries once gave as a guide to the perplexed reader the following advice: "*b* is usually silent after *m* in the same syllable, as in *bomb, climb, thumb*, etc."[13] How is one who has not seen or heard such words as *bomber, bombard, thimble*, and *amber* to syllabify these forms correctly from their spellings? There is no rule in the speaker's intuition that would select /bám ər/ over /bámb ər/ but /ǽm bər/ over /ǽmb ər/. Furthermore, English phonology is notorious for its ambulatory syllable boundaries. In *keeper*, for example, the syllable break, if it occurs, can be before the /p/ or after it. (Most often in fast speech, the /p/ in *keeper* is an interlude linking the nucleus of the first syllable with the nucleus of the second, without break.)[14]

Prediction rules based on syllable breaks simply cannot be applied to many English words. (This is not to say that some syllable boundaries cannot be predicted from spelling. If consonant clusters between vowels cannot be word-initial or word-final, for example, they must be split between the preceding and succeeding syllables, as in *grandpa*.) Stress, another candidate for a predictor, is an extremely complex factor to assess. There are certain preferred stress patterns in English, so that by frequency alone stress can be predicted with some calculable (and high) probability of success. To predict stress exactly, however, where no stress-fixing prefixes or suffixes occur (such as <ity>), requires in many situations a complete knowledge of a word's etymology; this has already been rejected as a predictor.

This does not leave much for us to go on, if we assume that the ground rules require (at least for reading) that sound be predicted from the graphemic form of the word, in the absence of any knowledge based on that particular word as a whole. This means that rules for prediction must not include lists of words to which the particular rules apply (or do not apply). Such rules may state that a letter in a particular word position has a particular pronunciation, or that a letter has one pronunciation before certain letters and another before all others, but not that letter <x> in word *y* is to be pronounced as /z/. There is a dilemma even here, however. Consider the rules for the letter <f>. In all its occurrences in English words, except for one (*of*), <f> is pronounced /f/. (The geminate <ff> can be handled by a general rule for leveling geminate clusters.) The rule for pronouncing <f>, therefore, is "<f> → /f/ except in *of* and its compounds, where <f> → /v/." But now a word list is included, and we no longer have, by the arguments adduced above, a legitimate predictor of pronunciation. We cannot predict the pronunciation of <f> until we check whether we are dealing with *of* or one of its compounds. The path out of this entanglement is to have two ordered rules—the first stating that <f> in *of* maps to /v/, the second covering everything else. Reality is not altered, but if we assume prior elimination of exceptions, all sorts of things can be made to appear regular.

FURTHER IDEAS ABOUT WORD FREQUENCY

In the discussion just completed, the notion of regularity has been discussed, and a strict reliance on frequency of occurrence has been rejected. The argument advanced has been, in brief, that the English spelling–sound system is based upon a variety of patterns (some resulting from changes in English phonology and some from borrowings and alternative scribal practices), and that the discovery of these patterns requires an understanding of the history of English orthography and phonology as well as an appreciation of present-day speech. Therefore, frequency by itself is not a sufficient basis for establishing patterning or regularity. Nevertheless, frequency does have a role in defining patterns, but it is not obvious what should be counted: the number of different words that a grapheme–phoneme pattern occurs in, regardless of the popularity of those words in print; or just the total number of appearances for a pattern in running text, regardless of how many different words are involved. The former is called *type frequency* because it is based on a count of unique words or *types*, while the latter is called *token frequency* because it takes into account repeated occurrences of words in running text.

If type frequency is to be used, then a method for defining types needs to be established. Are all words that contain a particular spelling–sound pattern to be counted as types, or only those that are basic forms or roots? Table 7.1 summarizes the type frequency counts just discussed for <ch>. The unit <ch> is (ultimately) mapped into /č/ in 57.2 percent of the words spelled with <ch>, into /k/ in 31.3 percent, into /š/ in 10.0 percent, and into /ø, h/, or /ǰ/ in 1.6 percent. How-

TABLE 7.1. Type Frequency Counts for Pronunciations of <ch>

	Initial	Medial	Final	Total
		Word position		
/č/	157	67	63	287
/k/	58	87	12	157
/š/	37	13	0	50
/ø/	0	3	0	3
/h/	3	0	0	3
/ǰ/	0	0	2	2
Total	255	170	77	502

ever, among the 28 words that have <ch> → /k/ in initial position, five are variants of *character*, four are variants of *chemical*, two are variants of *chaos*, and two are variants of *chimera*. That is, only 19 of 28 initial exemplars are base forms, and among these 4 are proper names. For medial position, the reduction is even more dramatic: Only 22 of 74 exemplars are base forms (excluding proper names). Thus type counts raise two issues: to count or not to count variants, and to count or not to count proper names.

Variants are problematic within themselves. If only base forms are desired, elimination of inflected forms (e.g., *boys, running, jumped*) presents no difficulties. But is *chemist* close enough to *chemical*, and *chaotically* to *chaos*, to be eliminated? Also, how should we treat words that appear similar but have different roots, such as *bombard* and *bombastic*? For token counts, the proper-name issue is relevant but not the variant issue, because all occurrences will be counted regardless of whether they are variants of other terms or not. However, a new issue arises with token counts: reliability of sampling. For the high-frequency words, a million-word corpus is adequate, but the majority of the words that occur in an English dictionary occur eight or fewer times in such a corpus.[15] Repeated samples of a million words, drawn from similar publications, are likely to give frequency distributions with large standard deviations for these infrequently occurring words. In the absence of larger data bases to use for frequency counts, we have limited data for differentiating the token counts of the majority of the English vocabulary.

The larger issue related to token counts is their role in defining spelling–sound patterns. What is argued here is that type counts, not token counts, are important. Different words reflect the productivity of a pattern; in contrast, token counts are artifacts of language structure and language usage. Patterns in function words (e.g., *the, of, in*) will have abnormally high frequencies of occurrence because of the frequent occurrence of function words in English syntax. For a content word, frequency of usage depends on how common the word's referent is in everyday life and the degree to which that word is rendered into print.

Among the consonant patterns, <f> → /v/ occurs in only one word, *of*, but that word is among the most frequently occurring in English print. Note, however, that the pattern has not been extended to any other words, nor have spelling pronunciations of <f> → /v/ occurred with other English words. The consequence of invoking token frequency in defining patterns would be to establish <f> → /v/ as the most common mapping for <f> in final position, because the summed frequency of the 34 <f> → /f/ words (e.g., *beef, belief, roof*) is not as large as the frequency of occurrence of the single word *of*. There may be a psychological argument to be made in favor of this solution, but not a linguistic one.

Although type counts are important for establishing spelling–sound patterns, they are not the only evidence that is considered. This can be seen from considerations of the <g> patterns. In a small number of words, <g> is ultimately pronounced /ž/. These are all French borrowings, such as *camouflage, protégé, regime*, and *rouge*. For the remaining two mappings, /g/ and /ǰ/, a basic rule appears to apply: /ǰ/ before <e, i>, or <y>; otherwise /g/. However, a relatively large number of exceptions exist, and most of these exceptions are common words: *geese, get, gift, girder, give, tiger*. In initial position before <i>, more words have /g/ than /ǰ/, thus casting some doubt on the validity of this component of the pattern. But when the parallel patterning for <c> is considered, both are seen to have one pronunciation before spellings for mid- or high-front vowels or glides, and another pronunciation otherwise.[16] Given the two identical patterns, the exceptions, regardless of their frequencies of occurrence, are less significant.

THE IMPACT OF RELATIONAL-UNIT FREQUENCY

Closely related to type and token frequency is relational-unit frequency. In the original corpus used for this book, the most frequently occurring relational unit is <t> (4,989), and the least frequently occurring is <rh> (21).[17] Among the consonant units, six (<dg, gh, rh, tch, wh, y>) occur fewer than 100 times each. Twelve others occur from 100 to 999 times each, and the remainder occur 1,000 to 4,989 times each. Distribution by position also varies widely. Among the consonants, <dg, j, q, rh, wh> do not occur in word-final position, and <h> and <z> rarely do. The unit <wh> has 93.8 percent of its occurrences in initial position, while <x> has only 1.7 percent of its occurrences in this position. (The frequencies of occurrence of consonant relational units are shown in Table 8.2.)

The implications for spelling–sound patterning is that patterns that involve frequently occurring relational units can be described with a higher probability of accuracy than those that occur infrequently. The 436 examples of <ch> provide a sufficient corpus to discern what patterning exists and to predict what might occur in new words created or imported into the lexicon. In contrast, the small number of exemplars for <gh>, particularly in initial position (6), make generalizing hazardous.[18] Also affected by this range of distributions is any attempt to use frequency of occurrence of specific correspondences as a criterion for establishing patterns. Although frequency of occurrence should not be ignored, it must be used with extreme caution when only a small number of exemplars are available.

A DEEPER LOOK AT ETYMOLOGY

Etymology is important for discovering spelling–sound patterns and for understanding exceptions to general patterns, but it has just been declared to be inadmissible evidence for defining spelling–sound regularity. Is this justified? With many patterns an etymological formulation is tempting, but, as explained earlier, two objections stand in the way of such a practice here. First, etymology, unlike membership in Scottish clans, is not always determinable from a word's dress. Second, etymology is not always reliable. Each word has its own history. Sound change either in the language of origin or in English, scribal intervention, and phonological assimilation can alter etymological alignments.

Stress patterns in modern English illustrate these problems. In general, words of Germanic origin (including words retained from Old English) have the main word stress on the root syllable (which is usually the first), while words borrowed from French tend to have more even stress, the main word stress generally falling on the final syllable. However, many French borrowings of the Middle English and early Modern English periods assimilated to the Germanic pattern. Thus *college*, *palace*, and *universe* have first-syllable stress in English but last-syllable stress in modern French (*collège*, *palace*, *univers*). These contrast with more recent French borrowings, such as *brigade* and *patrol*, which have retained last-syllable stress. A rule based upon language of origin will be incomplete without taking into account the date of borrowing. But even that addition will not guarantee an accurate set of classifications, because some words were borrowed long enough ago to undergo assimilation but did not, either through analogy with later borrowings or for other reasons.

Consonant clusters in certain French borrowings provide an illustration of how sound change in the language of origin creates a problem in the use of etymology. As described in Chapter 6, French consonant clusters went through a leveling process in the late Middle French or early Modern French period, such that clusters like /t š/ (= /č/) and /dž/ (= /ǰ/) were leveled to /š/ and /ž/. Words borrowed from French before this change had <ch> pronounced / č/ and <g> pronounced /ǰ/; after the sound change, these spellings were pronounced /š/ and /ž/. *Chief, challenge,* and *duchess* represent the earlier pronunciations in modern English, while *chef, cliché, cortege,* and *massage* represent the modern French patterns. Among the <ch> and <g> words in Modern English are a number of *doublets*—that is, pairs that have the same root but different pronunciations. *Chief* and *chef* are in this class, as are *regime* and *regimen,* and *genre* and *gender.*

In an unrelated sound change, French final /t/ was dropped in modern French, giving *cadet* (with <t> pronounced) alongside *chalet* (with silent <t>). Other common silent-<t> words from French include *ballet, beret, bouquet, buffet, crochet, debut, depot,* and *ragout.* Once again, a rule based on etymology will need to specify specific time periods as well as to account for exceptions.

Pronunciations for <ch> are further complicated by classical borrowings that retain <ch> → /k/, such as *mechanic, chorus,* and *chemistry.* Here, however, the etymological case is further blurred by immigration paths and respellings. For example, *chimera* and *machine* are both from Latin; *chimera,* which retains <ch> → /k/, was borrowed directly in the late 14th century, while *machine,* which has <ch> → /š/, was borrowed via Middle French. But *mechanic,* which was borrowed via the same route as *machine* and has the same Greek root, retained <ch> → /k/. To add further complications, *choir,* which derives ultimately from Latin *chorus,* was borrowed via Middle French into Middle English and was spelled *quer.* In early Modern English it was respelled *choir.*

As a final note on the complexities of etymology, consider the various mappings for <c> that have been featured earlier. In general, <c> is mapped into /s/ before spellings for mid- and high-front vowels and glides. Most of these words are French borrowings, but because of the extension in the 15th and 16th centuries of the French spelling <c> to native English words such as *cinder* and *ice* (Middle English *sinder* and *is*), this pattern now applies also to words derived from Middle and Old English.

REGULARITY IN THE SPELLING–SOUND SYSTEM

Most accounts of English spelling–sound correspondences have been satisfied to present a catalog of patterns without attending to the overall characteristics of the system.[19] This may serve some interests, but it fails to provide a framework for understanding how the various components relate to each other. To treat English spelling–sound correspondences as a system, therefore, is a major goal here. In the remaining parts of this chapter, the nature of this system is discussed; this provides a gateway to the next chapters, which delve into specific correspondences. Based on the discussion just completed, I use *regular* and *irregular* in a loose sense, meaning either obviously patterned or unpatterned, or high-frequency and low-frequency, without careful enumeration of what objects are to be counted to arrive at such statistics.

Types of Correspondences

Regular spelling–sound correspondences can be classed first as either *invariant* or *variant*. The unit <f>, for example, corresponds regularly to /f/. In fact, this correspondence is so regular that only one exception, *of*, occurs among the 20,000 most common English words. Several other consonant spelling units are also invariant or nearly so (e.g., <ck, m, y, z>). The primary vowel spellings, which are described in Chapter 9, are rarely invariant, though not irregular in most cases. Variant correspondences are further classed as *predictable* (or nearly so) and *unpredictable*. Only variant, unpredictable correspondences are irregular.

Variant Correspondences

Variant correspondences are those correspondences that are still regular, but that relate the same spelling to two or more pronunciations, depending upon graphemic, phonological, or grammatical features. Initial <c>, as an example, corresponds to /s/ when it occurs before <e, i, y>; otherwise it corresponds to /k/.[20] The spelling <k> corresponds to zero in initial position before <n>, as in *knee*, *know*, and *knife*. In all other positions, <k> corresponds to /k/. This is graphemic conditioning from the letter–sound standpoint. As will be shown later, the silent initial <k> is explained more adequately by phonotactical rules. (The cluster /kn/ does not occur within a single morpheme in English. Where such prohibited consonant clusters would otherwise occur in morpheme-initial or morpheme-final position, the consonant farthest from the syllable nucleus is usually dropped. Thus we have *knee, gnat, ptarmigan, pneumonia, psychology, damn*, and *bomb*.)

Prediction Based on Word Position or Stress

Position alone may determine the correspondence of a spelling unit. For example, initial <gh> always corresponds to /g/ (e.g., *ghost, gherkin, ghoul*), but medial and final <gh> have pronunciations besides /g/, as is too often pointed out in spelling reform tracts. Stress may also be a conditioning factor for regular, variant correspondences. The most prominent role that stress plays in spelling–sound correspondences is in the pronunciation of unstressed vowels. Although the reduction of unstressed vowels to schwa is not entirely regular, it can still be predicted in many cases. The patterns, however, are highly complex and beyond the scope of this book. A more interesting example of stress conditioning occurs in the correspondences for intervocalic <x>, which corresponds to either /ks/ or /gz/, depending upon the position of the main word stress. If the main stress is on the vowel preceding <x>, the pronunciation is generally /ks/, as in *execute*; otherwise, the pronunciation is /gz/, as in *examine* and *exist*. Although this rule is similar to Verner's Law[21] for the voicing of the Germanic voiceless fricatives, it is not a case of pure phonological conditioning. Words like *accede* and *accept* have the identical phonetic environments for /gz/, yet have /ks/.[22]

Another class of correspondences in which stress is important consists of the palatalizations of /sj, zj, tj, dj/ to /š, ž, č, ǰ/, respectively. This form of palatalization occurs when /sj, zj, dj, tj/ are followed by an unstressed vowel, as in *social*, *treasure*, *bastion*, and *cordial* (see Chapter 4).

The retention or deletion of medial /h/ in most cases also depends upon the position of the main word stress. Compare *prohibit* with *prohibition* and *vehicular* with *vehicle*. In each pair, the first member, which has the stress on the vowel following <h>, has a fully pronounced /h/, while the second member, with an unstressed vowel after <h>, has no /h/. This rule also holds for *vehement*, *shepherd*, *philharmonic*, *annihilate*, *rehabilitate*, and *nihilism*, all of which generally have a silent /h/. (Some forms like these may have /h/ occasionally preserved by overcorrect pronunciations.)

Prediction Based on Morphemic Features

Morpheme Boundaries

The spelling <ph> regularly corresponds to /f/, as in *phase*, *sphere*, and *morpheme*. In *shepherd*, however, <ph> does not correspond to /f/, but to /p/. One way to explain this is to say that *shepherd* is an exception to the more general rule of <ph> → /f/. But if this is done, then the same process must be repeated when we are faced with *uphill*, *topheavy*, and every other form in which <ph> occurs across a morpheme boundary. The most satisfactory procedure is to say that <ph> corresponds to /f/ when it lies within a single graphemic morpheme, and that across morpheme boundaries <ph> is treated as the separate graphemes <p> and <h>. Therefore, morpheme boundaries must be considered in mapping spelling into sound. That this factor is not unique to <ph> can be seen from the following examples.

1. Within morphemes, geminate consonant clusters (as in *letter*, *add*, and *canned*) are pronounced as single consonants. Across morpheme boundaries, however, both graphemic consonants may correspond to separate phonemes, as in *midday*.

2. All the digraph and trigraph spellings are subject to the same morpheme boundary problem as <ph> (e.g., *hothead*, *changeable*).

3. The spelling <n>, before spellings in the same morpheme that correspond to /g/ or /k/, corresponds to /ŋ/ (e.g., *congress*, *finger*, *anchor*). Across morpheme boundaries, this generally does not hold (e.g., *ingrain*, *ingratiate*).

4. Many word-final clusters contain silent letters—for example, <gm, gn, mb> (*paradigm*, *sign*, *bomb*). Before certain morpheme boundaries, the silent letter remains silent, as in *paradigms*, *signer*, and *bombing*; before others, it is pronounced, as in *paradigmatic*, *signal*, and *bombard*. As long as the morpheme boundary is recognized, the correct pronunciation can be predicted. If the morpheme boundary is not recognized, then the latter three forms would be thrown together with *stigma*, *ignite*, and *bamboo*. It is not sufficient to state, for example, that <gn> and <gm> in final position correspond to /n/ and /m/, but in medial position to /gn/ and /gm/. Such rules fail in cases like *autumns*, *designing*, and *signer*. There is no way to avoid reference to morphemes in this case, unless one simply enumerates the words for each pronunciation. A regular pattern is present in these forms, the most important aspect of which is the preservation of morpheme identity. The alternations of /g/ and zero in these examples, along with the alternations of the vowels preceding <g>, are predictable. The direct spelling-to-sound approach once again breaks down when morpheme identity becomes important.

Morpheme Identification

In some cases the discrimination of a morphemic spelling from an identical, nonmorphemic spelling is necessary for the prediction of sound from spelling. Consider the following two word lists:

boys	*melodious*
judges	*stylus*
cats	*apropos*
man's	*careless*

The pronunciation of final <s> in any word from the left-hand column can be predicted by the following rules, if we assume that the base mapping for this <s> is /z/ (these rules must be applied in the order shown here):

1. If the final sound of the base word is a sibilant (/s, z, č, ǰ, s, ž/), insert /ɪ/ or /ə/ before /z/.
2. Match the voicing of the added ending to that of the sound before it. That is, if the sound before the added /z/ is unvoiced, change /z/ to /s/; otherwise leave as /z/.

These rules, however, apply only to <s> when it is one of the following morphemes:

1. Regular noun plural.
2. Third-person singular, present indicative marker for the verb.
3. Singular or plural possessive marker.
4. Any of the contractions like *John's* (from *John is*).

The past-tense marker <(e)d> functions similarly. In all of these cases, nevertheless, the direct spelling-to-sound approach fails unless it is based upon morpheme identity, and if so, the approach is no longer a direct spelling-to-sound approach.

Form Class

The digraph <ng>, as in *sing* and *singing*, represents the voiced velar nasal stop, corresponding to the voiced velar stop /g/ and the voiceless velar stop /k/. However, the pronunciation of any form ending in <nger> or <ngest> cannot be predicted unless the morphemic identities or <er> and <est> are known. If these are the comparative and superlative endings, then <ng> is pronounced /ŋg/, as in *stronger*; in most other cases the /ŋg/ cluster is leveled to /ŋ/, just as it is in word-final position. (Note, however, that if the base forms ends in <nge>, this rule does not apply: *changer, arranger, avenger*.) Morphemic identity is also important for predicting the pronunciation of word-final <ate>. In adjectives and nouns this ending is generally pronounced /ɪt/ (e.g., *duplicate, frigate, syndicate*), while in verbs it is usually pronounced /et/ (e.g., *deflate, duplicate, integrate*). A final example of where form class identity is necessary for correct pronunciation is in initial <th>. Function words beginning with this cluster have the voiced interdental spirant /ð/ (*the, then, this, those*), while content words have the voiceless spirant /θ/ (*theses, thin, thumb*).[23]

Phonotactical Influences

Consonant Clusters

The elision of sounds in consonant clusters can be predicted not only across morpheme boundaries, but also in initial and final position, as in *knee, gnat, bomb*, and *sing*. In all these cases, the correct pronunciation can be derived by first mapping all spelling units onto a prephonemic level, here represented by curly brackets {}, and then applying the rules for leveling non-English clusters to obtain the phonemic forms. Thus *knee, gnat, bomb*, and *sing* become first {kni, gnæt, bamb, sɪŋg}, and then the nonallowed clusters are leveled, giving /ni, næt, bam/, and /sɪŋ/.

Palatalization

To predict consonant cluster leveling is not the only reason for observing the arrangements of phonemes in English words. The palatalization of /sj, zj, tj, dj/ to /š, ž, č, ǰ/ as mentioned earlier, and the deletion of /j/ from the cluster /ju/, also depend upon this knowledge. In addition, many spelling-to-sound patterns that can be described only clumsily in direct spelling-to-sound terms are more adequately described in phonological terms. A preceding /w/, for example, tends to change /æ/ into /a/ when this vowel is not followed by a velar consonant (e.g., *swamp, assuage* (alternate pronunciation), *quadrant, swan, quality, quantum*; *wag, quack, twang, wax*). To describe this process in direct spelling-to-sound terms is difficult. The various spellings that correspond to /w/ and to /k, g, n/ must be enumerated, and even if this is done, the phonological nature of the /æ/ → /a/ shift is not revealed.

Different Forms of Irregularity

Irregular spelling-to-sound correspondences also show important differences. For example, *arcing* and *cello* both have irregular correspondences for <c>, but there is an important distinction between these two irregularities. *Arc*, from which *arcing* is derived, has the correct correspondence for <c>. When suffixes beginning with <e, i, y> are added to words ending in <c>, a <k> is normally inserted after the <c>, as in *picnicking* (cf. *picnic*) and *trafficked* (cf. *traffic*). The irregularity in *arcing*, therefore, is in the irregular formation of the derivative, which occurs for monosyllables ending in <c>. *Cello*, on the other hand, contains an aberrant correspondence for <c>, paralleled by only a few other Italian borrowings. More distinctions among irrregularities could be made, but these examples are sufficient for the purposes here.

LOOKING AHEAD

This completes the warm-up activities—the preliminaries to the full presentation of consonant and vowel patterns that follow in the next three chapters. Now you should understand the basic lexicon of grapheme, phoneme, and morpho-phoneme; possess a schema for both simple and complex mappings; and have an expectation that many exceptions to patterns will be presented, but that the majority of these will have at least a moderately interesting history. The consonant patterns are presented first (Chapter 8), followed by the primary and then the secondary vowel patterns (Chapter 9).

NOTES

1. Grimm (1819–1837).
2. Chomsky (1957).
3. Harris (1951), 5.
4. Jespersen (1924/1965), 24.
5. Jespersen (1924/1965), 20.
6. Bloomfield (1933), 274.
7. Everywhere else in Bloomfield's writings, regularity is defined in relation to the analyst's description—for example, "A set of forms that is not covered by a general statement, but has to be presented in the shape of a list, is said to be *irregular*" (1933, 213), and "Since the distribution of the three alternates [noun plural /-ĕz, -z, -s/] is regulated according to a linguistically recognizable characteristic of the accompanying forms, we say that the alternation is *regular*" (1933, 211).
8. Bloomfield (1933), 280.
9. Hockett (1958), 214.
10. O'Grady et al. (1989), 7. Similar attitudes can be found in other linguistics texts, such as Akmajian et al. (1990).
11. Wijk (1966), for example, claims that "the vast majority of English words, about 90–95 percent of the total vocabulary, do in fact follow certain regular patterns in regard to their spelling and pronunciation" (8). Spelling reformers no doubt view this educational cabalism with alarm.
12. This etymological determinism, however, is not strictly true. Most words borrowed from French before the French sound shift of / č/ to /š/ retain the <ch> → / č/ pattern, as pointed out earlier for *chief* and *chef*. In addition, *arch-*, ultimately from Greek, is pronounced /k/ in *archangel* but / č/ elsewhere (e.g., *arch*, *archbishop*, *archenemy*).
13. Bethel (1956), xi.
14. For more on this subject, see the first section of Venezky and Suraj (1993).
15. Kučera and Francis (1967).
16. The palatalizations that occur in words such as *ocean* are discussed later.

17. These counts are based upon relational units that occur alone. For consonants, this means not in a consonant cluster. If clusters are also counted, the count for <t> increases to 5,780, while that for <rh> remains at 21.
18. The *Random House* (see Chapter 2, note 1) contains 46 entries that start with <gh>, but when proper names, phrases, rare borrowings, and morphological cousins are removed, only five words remain: *ghastly, gherkin, ghetto, ghost,* and *ghoul.*
19. See, for example, Wijk (1966) and Scragg (1974).
20. More accurately, <c> corresponds to /s/ before spellings for mid- and high-front vowels: *cent, city, cycle, coelacanth.* Given the rarity of <oe> after <c>, however, this spelling is quietly ignored here. (Note, however, that the Itlaian borrowings *cello* and *concerto* are exceptions to the general pattern.)
21. Verner's Law, named after its discoverer, Karl Verner, a Danish linguist, accounts for cases where the Indo-European voiceless stops /p, t, k/ became /b, d, g/ in Germanic rather than /f, θ, h/.
22. The rule applies only to <x> between vowel spellings. When <x> is followed by a pronounced, voiceless consonant, it is always /ks/. Exceptions to the intervocalic <x> rule include *exile, exit,* and a few technical terms such as *exogamous,* which can be pronounced with either /ks/ or /gz/.
23. When <th> in a function word is followed by a consonant (e.g., *through*), it is voiceless.

CHAPTER 8

Consonant Patterns

Each word is in itself a small orchestra in which
the vowel is the voice and the consonant the
instrument, the accompaniment.
—VICTOR HUGO
(quoted in Barzun, 1991), 76

Principle 5, concerning regularity, continues to be explored in this chapter, which focuses on consonant letter–sound patterns. These vary from invariant ones such as <z> to the complex and partially unpredictable <s>. In between are mostly well-behaved patterns, but with occasional exceptions, due mostly to borrowings. Discussed here are several general consonant rules, plus the history, distribution, and letter–sound patterns for all of the consonant units.

FUNCTIONAL UNITS

The consonant functional units, as outlined in Chapter 5, consist of 22 single letters, 12 digraphs, and 4 trigraphs (see Table 8.1). Of these, 3 (<ck, dg, tch>) are frequently occurring geminate replacements, and 6 (<gn, kh, pph, rh, sch>, and two additional geminate replacements, <pph and rrh>) occur only in a limited number of borrowings. Among the others, some, such as <f, l, s> occur in clusters and in geminates; others, such as <wh, w, h, y>, have restricted distributions

TABLE 8.1. Consonant Spellings

Simple consonant units
<b, c, ch, d, f, g, gh, h, j, k, kh, l, m, n, ng, p, ph, q, r, rh, s, sch, sh, t, th, u, v, w, y, z>

Compound consonant units
<ck, dg, gn, pph, rrh, tch, wh, x>

---

because of both phonological and graphotactical constraints. A few, such as <q, k, j> are mainly scribally constrained. Not admitted into this pantheon of basic units are a few rare foreign spellings for which alternate interpretations are possible (e.g., <cz> as in *czar*, here treated as silent <c> + <z> → /z/), or for which only a few borrowings and no major patterns exist (e.g., <dj> as in *djinni*). In the discussion that follows, the distributional properties of the consonant functional units are discussed first, followed by their clustering properties, their gemination, and finally their correspondences to sound.

DISTRIBUTIONS

The distributions of single consonant units in a corpus of approximately 20,000 common words are shown in Table 8.2[1] These figures, which should be taken as approximations only, represent occurrences of consonant units outside of clusters. Thus the <z> in *quiz* is counted here, but not the <z> in *quartz*. The corpus (see the Preface) is composed of different word types, selected by frequency in printed texts, but without controls for either proper nouns or inflected forms. The count for initial <gh>, for example, includes *Ghent* as well as both *ghost* and *ghostly*. Frequencies below 10 are enumerated in the table footnotes.

From Table 8.2 the unequal distribution of consonant units is obvious. The units <ck, dg, ng, pph, rrh, tch, u> (as a consonant) do not occur in initial position, and <dg, j, kh, pph, q, rh>, as well as <u> (as a consonant), <w> (as a consonant), <wh>, and <y> (as a consonant) do not occur in final position.[2] The units <u, y, j, q, z> are the least frequently occurring single-letter consonant units (in the order listed, with <z> the least frequent), and <r, t, n, c> are the most frequently occurring single-letter units. Among the single-letter units, only <n> occurs more often in final position than it does in initial or medial position. (Included in the corpus are over 1,000 words that end in <ion>, plus hundreds that end in <an, en, ian>, or <on>.)

TABLE 8.2. Distributions of Single Consonant Units, Based on a Corpus of 19,697 Common Words

	Initial	Medial	Final	Total
\<b\>	747	575	76	1,398
\<c\>	1,487	1,407	377	3,271
\<ch\>	222	137	77	436
\<ck\>	0	101	132	233
\<d\>	1,186	1,108	661	2,955
\<dg\>	0	56	0	56
\<f\>	608	416	42	1,066
\<g\>	334	908	87	1,329
\<gh\>*	6	155	34	195
\<h\>	679	104	0	783
\<j\>	176	42	0	218
\<k\>	77	198	119	394
\<kh\>*	2	0	0	2
\<l\>	603	1,984	1,091	3,678
\<m\>	969	1,399	344	2,712
\<n\>	342	2,004	2,249	4,595
\<ng\>	0	196	376	572
\<p\>	954	663	195	1,812
\<ph\>	62	123	13	198
\<pph\>*	0	1	0	1
\<q\>	94	130	0	224
\<r\>	954	4,486	1,580	7,420
\<rh\>	21	0	0	21
\<rrh\>*	0	5	2	7
\<s\>	1,023	1,191	713	2,927
\<sh\>	161	90	183	434
\<t\>	570	3,675	744	4,989
\<tch\>	0	28	43	71
\<th\>	135	234	104	473
\<u\>	0	42	0	42
\<v\>*	353	1,181	5	1,539
\<w\>	346	101	0	447
\<wh\>*	90	0	0	90
\<y\>*	44	5	0	49
\<z\>*	30	272	5	307

*Notes:
\<gh\>: Initial \<gh\> occurs in *ghastly, Ghent, ghetto, ghost, ghostly, ghoul.*
\<kh\>: *khaki* and *khan* (*Chekhov* has \<k\> and \<h\> as separate units).
\<pph\>: *sapphire.*
\<rrh\>: *cirrhosis, diarrhea, hemorrhage, hemorrhoids, pyorrhea; catarrh, myrrh.*
\<v\>: All cases of final \<v\> are foreign proper names (*Slav, Yugoslav, Chekhov*), back-formations (e.g., *rev* for *revolve* or *revolution*), or loan words (e.g., *leitmotiv*).
\<wh\>: Compounds of the form *anywhere* and *elsewhere* are not counted.
\<y\>: Medial \<y\> occurs as a consonant in *beyond, Himalayas, lawyer, Maya, Sawyer.* (Compounds like *dooryard* are not counted.)
\<z\>: Final \<z\> occurs in *Agassiz, quiz, Suez, topaz,* and *whiz.*

GENERAL CONSONANT RULES

Silent Graphemes

As explained in Chapter 5, some relational units are mapped into zero in the spelling-to-sound mappings; for example, <b> in *debt, doubt, subtle* → /ø/. These are the true silent graphemes of English spelling and usually represent scribal pedantries or sounds that have been lost in the word pronunciations. Other silent graphemes are eliminated at a phonological level by rules that delete sounds from unpronounceable clusters (e.g., initial /gn/) or from sequences of the same consonant (e.g., /kk/). Unpronounceable sound clusters at the beginnings or ends of words generally drop the sound adjacent to juncture—that is, the first or last sound of the word. A partial list of clusters to which such a rule applies includes the following:

Initial clusters		Final clusters	
<bd>	*bdellium*	<mb>	*bomb, iamb*
<gn>	*gnostic, gnat*	<ng>	*sing*
<kn>	*knife, knee*		
<mn>	*mnemonic*		
<pn>	*pneumonia, pneumatic*		
<ps>	*psychology, psalm, psalter, pseudo-*		
<pt>	*ptarmigan, ptomaine, Ptolemy*		

Among the common exceptions are French borrowings ending in <gn> and <gm> (*sign, paradigm*). Implied here is an understanding of the allowable consonant clusters for English—a topic that has been discussed in Chapter 5. In general, English does not allow in initial position consonant sequences in which the place and manner of articulation are constant. Thus /pb, bp, td, dt/ do not occur initially. It is far easier, however, to enumerate what can occur rather than what cannot or does not occur. Where two different bilabial stops occur medially within certain words, the first stop assimilates to the second and is then leveled by a general geminate reduction rule. Only a small number of common words are affected by this rule (*clapboard, cupboard, raspberry, subpoena*), but it is highly regular.[3]

The problem is in defining the characteristics of the set of words to which the rule applies, since an equal number of compounds do not obey the rule: *scrapbook, shipboard, soapberry, soapbox,* and *soapbubble*. Words in this latter group, however, appear to be true compounds that can exist as separate (free) morphemes and that are occasionally written as such or as hyphenated forms.

The former group tends to have primary word stress on only one syllable with the other syllable unstressed, while the latter group tends to have level stress on the two syllables or primary stress on one syllable and secondary stress on the other.

Sequences of identical consonant phonemes are leveled to a single member of the sequence by the rule $/C_1 C_2/ \rightarrow /C_1/$, where $C_1 = C_2$. Thus we have *coffee*, *button*, *bullet*, and *dazzle* (among thousands of others). This rule cannot work on the spelling level because <cc> and <gg> may represent two different sounds, as in *accede* and *suggest*. Both of the rules just described can also be written on a morphophonemic level, but this is avoided until Chapter 10.

Gemination

The rule just described applies to doubled consonants, also called *geminates*. The letters that commonly geminate in medial position are the following:

<bb>	*cribbage, hobby*	<mm>	*common, mammal*
<cc>	*broccoli, moccasin*	<nn>	*funnel, dinner*
<dd>	*bladder, sudden*	<pp>	*supper, happen*
<ff>	*coffee, buffalo*	<rr>	*marriage, mirror*
<gg>	*luggage, beggar*	<ss>	*blossom, assess*
<ll>	*village, college*	<tt>	*shutter, button*
		<zz>	*blizzard, dizzy*

Of these, <cc> is restricted to representing /k/ and <gg> to /g/ as true geminates; otherwise they represent two different sounds, as in *accede*, or a single sound other than /k/ or /g/, as in *exaggerate*. Therefore, as a true geminate <cc> occurs only before spellings other than <e, i, y>.[4] The letter <z> is rare and <zz> is even rarer, occurring primarily in the ending <zzle> (e.g., *embezzle, fizzle, muzzle, puzzle*), in Italian borrowings (e.g., *mezzo, pizza, piazza*), and in a handful of other words (e.g., *blizzard, buzzard, gizzard*). (Although <ss> may replace <zz>, it is pronounced /z/ in only a small number of words: *dessert, dissolve, possess, scissors,* and a few others.)

In final position, as explained in Chapter 6, only <ff>, <ll>, and <ss> commonly occur. A few others, such as <rr> and <zz>, occur in a few words introduced through sound imitation (e.g., *burr, buzz*), homophone discrimination (e.g., *butt, putt*), or proper names (e.g., *watt, boycott*).

Consonant gemination also occurs when certain suffixes are added to words ending in a single consonant—for example, *run–running, forbid–forbidding, abet–abetted.* The orthographic rule is that words accented on the last syllable (including all monosyllables), when ending in a single, simple consonant spelling, preceded by a single vowel spelling, double the consonant before adding a suffix beginning with a vowel (including <y> by itself). Exceptions to this rule are plentiful, and usage is still unsettled on whether to double final <r>. For example, *inferable, referable*, and *transferable* are the preferred forms in both British and American usage, although the *Collegiate* gives *inferrible* as an alternative to *inferable*, an option not condoned by the *OED*.[5]

Usage varies on whether to double a final <l> after an unstressed single letter vowel: *traveled* or *travelled*. The nongemination of <v> and <th> has led to a large number of exceptions to the major pattern for the correspondences of the primary vowel spellings. *Cover, bevel, river, brother*, and *other*, for example, have vowel spellings corresponding to checked alternates in environments that indicate free alternates. To indicate the checked alternate, <v> and <th> would have to be geminated, but the graphotactical patterns of English exclude the doubling of these units. In *prison*, a slightly different problem exists. Although <ss>, which is needed to make the correspondence <i> → /ɪ/, is allowed, it generally corresponds to /s/ in medial position, as in *blossom, gossip*, and *lasso*, so it cannot be employed where <s> corresponds to /z/ (but see the exceptions just mentioned). The present use of <ss> is derived from Old French orthography, where intervocalic <ss> distinguished voiceless <s> from voiced <s> → /z/.

CONSONANT HISTORIES, DISTRIBUTIONS, AND CORRESPONDENCES

<b>

The second letter of the modern and classical Roman alphabets, <b> corresponds in position and (partially) in value to the Hebrew beth and the Greek beta. In Modern English it occurs in a limited group of initial and final clusters, the most common of which are initial <bl> and <br>, and final <lb, rb, mb>. It also occurs in medial geminates, <bb> and in the rare initial cluster <bd> (*bdellium*). The letter <b> regularly corresponds to /b/, as in *blooper, abate*, and *crab*. Three types of exceptions exist:

1. Silent <b>: *debt, doubt, subtle*.
2. Pre- or postjunctural deletion: *bdellium, bomb, crumb, iamb, lamb, rhomb, thumb*.
3. Medial cluster leveling: *subpoena*.

For *subtle* and *bdellium*, no amount of linguistic legerdemain will convert the
<b>'s to anything but mute, silent letters. The <b>'s in *debt*, *doubt*, and the vari-
ous words with final <mb>, in contrast, are pronounced in related words: *debit*,
indubitable, *bombard*, *crumble*, *iambic*, *rhombus*, and *thimble* (cf. *thumb*). In addition, hypercorrect pronunciations will occasionally yield /mb/ at the end of
lamb and *rhomb*. In *clapboard*, *cupboard*, *raspberry*, and *subpoena*, sequences
of two bilabial stops have been leveled to the second element (/b/ in *clapboard*,
cupboard, and *raspberry*, /p/ in *subpoena*).

##

The third letter of the modern and classical Roman alphabets, <c> is a derivative
of the Hebrew gimel and Greek gamma. It occurs primarily in initial and medial
positions by itself; in final position alone it is limited to the ending <ic> and to a
handful of other occurrences, primarily in borrowings (*arc*, *havoc*, *sumac*, etc.).
In clusters, it occurs mainly in initial <cl, cr, cu> (*cuisine*), and <sc>; in final
<rc> and <ct>; and as medial <cc>. The letter <c> corresponds to /s/ before <e>,
the ligature <œ>, and <i> and <y>.[6] Elsewhere it corresponds to /k/. As explained in Chapter 6, the /s/ may change to /š/ before a high-front vowel or glide
followed by another vowel, as in *ocean* and *social*. The /k/ and /s/ pronunciations
of <c> are commonly referred to in educational writing as the *hard* and *soft* pronunciations, respectively. Several types of exceptions exist:

1. In Italian, Czech, and a few other languages, <c> before <e> and <i>
   corresponds to /č/: *cello*, *ciao*, *Cinzano*, *concerto*.
2. The letter <c> is resolutely silent in *Connecticut* (second occurrence), *czar*, *Mackinac* (<c>, not <ck>) and *victual*. In *corpuscle* and
   muscle it is also silent, but regains its voice in the related forms *cor-
   puscular* and *muscular*.[7]
3. *Arcing*, *facade*, *sceptic*, and *soccer* represent different categories of
   exceptions to the general <c> rule. *Arc* has a regular <c> pronunciation. However, when <ing> is added, <k> is not added as it is in
   words of more than one syllable (compare *traffic–trafficking*). *Facade*, a mid-17th-century French borrowing, is spelled with a cedilla
   (<ç>) in French and sometimes in English to signal an exception to
   the general <c> rule. Most U.S. dictionaries give both spellings, although the form without the cedilla is almost always shown first.
       Sceptic (*sceptical*, *scepticism*) is a variant, generally preferred in
   British English, of *skeptic* (*skeptical*, *skepticism*). In French, initial
   <sc> before <e> (and <i> and <y>) is pronounced /s/. The modern

English pronunciation of *sceptic* probably resulted from direct association with the related Greek form. *Soccer* is a shortened form of
Association, the rule-standardizing organization for the sport, founded in England in 1863. The present name was spelled *socca, socker*,
or *soccer* at the end of the 19th century; although the last name has
become the standard spelling, it reflects little respect by sportsmen
for the orthographic patterning of English.

4. The sequence <cc> is generally /k/ or /ks/, according to the vowel
   that follows (see above), but several exceptions exist. These include
   Italian borrowings in which <cc> before <i> is /č/ (e.g., *cappuccino*,
   focaccia), and *flaccid*, where the first <c> is silent.

<ch>

The digraph <ch> is a French import into Middle English, first appearing around
the middle of the 12th century as a replacement for <c>, when it represented /č/.
It appears alone in all word positions and in a small number of clusters: initial
<chl> (*chlorine*) and <chr> (*chrome*), and final <lch> (*belch*) and <nch>
(*bench*). The most common pronunciation for <ch> is /č/, which occurs primarily in words derived from Old and Middle English (e.g., *child, chin, choose*) and
from Middle French (e.g., *chief, chime*). Later French borrowings have <ch> →
/š/ (*chef, chic, chiffon*), and some Latin and Greek borrowings have <ch> → /k/
(*chimera, chlorophyll, chorus, chrome*). Only a small number of reliable indica-
tors exist for <ch> correspondences. Before <l> and <r>, <ch> maps regularly to
<k> (*chloroform, chrome*), and in final position it is usually /č/, with a few clas-
sical exceptions (*epoch, eunuch, patriarch, stomach*). A few French borrowings,
such as *chassis*, have both /š/ and /č/ pronunciations of <ch>.

Exceptions to these patterns include a small group of silent spellings
(*drachm, fuchsia, yacht*) and Hebrew borrowings in which <ch> is a transliteration for a voiced velar fricative, /x/, sometimes realized in English as /h/—for example, *challah, Chanukah* (also spelled *Hanukah* or *Hannukah*), and *chutzpah*.
In *Greenwich* and *Norwich*, <ch> is commonly /ǰ/ but also can be /č/.

<ck>

A 15th-century replacement for <kk>, <ck> occurs only after single-letter
checked vowel spellings (e.g., *crack, chicken*), with the exception of a few proper nouns, such as the Greenwich Village street name *Bleecker*.[8] It forms no clusters and regularly corresponds to /k/.

\<d\>

The fourth letter of the modern and classical Roman alphabets, \<d\> corresponds to the Greek delta and Hebrew daleth. It occurs in all word positions by itself, and in a limited number of initial and final clusters: initial \<dr\> (*drop, drain*) and \<dw\> (*dwarf, dwell, dwindle*), and final \<dth\> (*breadth, width, hundredth*), \<ld\> (*bald, hold*), \<nd\> (*fund, diamond*), and \<rd\> (*cupboard, weird*). Of these, initial \<dw\> and final \<dth\> are rare. Other rare final clusters include \<dz\> (*adz*) and \<ldst\> (*wouldst*). The geminate cluster \<dd\> occurs medially in about 50 monomorphemic words (e.g., *addict, cheddar, saddle*); in final position it appears only in *add* and *odd*, and in a few personal name; (e.g., *Todd, Dodd*).

The most common pronunciation for \<d\> is /d/; however, the past-tense and participle endings \<ed\> and \<d\> map into /d/ after voiced sounds (*blamed, stayed*), into /ɪd/ after /t/ (*batted, blunted*), and into /t/ after voiceless sounds other than /t/ (*masked, refreshed*). Several sound changes involving /d/ complicate the spelling–sound tranquillity of \<d\>. In \<dj\> clusters (*adjacent, adjective, adjourn*, etc.), the sound sequence /d/ + /dž/ simplifies to /dž/, which is also written / ǰ/. Then, between /n/ and another consonant, /d/ is usually dropped (*handkerchief, grandmother, handsome*). Usage is unsettled, however, and words like *stands* and *landslide* may be heard as often with /d/ as without. The sound /d/ is always dropped from *Wednesday*, however.

The sequences /dɪ/ and /dj/, when followed by an unstressed vowel, tend to palatalize to / ǰ/ (*cordial, education, gradual*). Due to hypercorrect pronunciations promulgated in the 19th century, a few words such as *Indian* and *India* have either resisted palatalization or have been depalatalized. A similar process can be observed currently in *education*.

Assimilation has occurred in the phrase *used to* when it has the sense "accustomed." Here the /d/ has assimilated to /t/, but remains as /d/ when the sense is "utilized." Compare "The knife he used to cut the meat is broken" and "The knife he used to own was lost." The sound /d/ often also assimilates to /t/ in *width* and *breadth*.

\<dg\>

The digraph \<dg\> is a 15th-century replacement for \<gg\>, pronounced / ǰ/. Like \<ck\> and \<tch\>, it occurs almost always after a single-letter checked vowel spelling (e.g., *edge, fudge*). It forms no clusters and corresponds invariably to / ǰ/.

\<f\>

The sixth letter of the modern and classical Roman alphabets, \<f\> derives from the Hebrew vav via the Greek digamma, a letter that later disappeared from the Greek alphabet.[9] It shares the representation of /f/ with the less frequently occurring \<ph\>, and occurs in all word positions and in a small number of common clusters: initial \<fl\> and \<fr\>; final \<lf, rf\>, and \<ft\> (e.g., *flood, friend, calf, serf*, and *raft*). The geminate cluster \<ff\> occurs in medial and final positions (e.g., *coffee, staff*). Generally in final position \<ff\> occurs after a single-letter vowel spelling, while \<f\> occurs after digraph vowel spellings and consonants (*roof, elf*). Common exceptions to this pattern include *chef, clef, if, motif*, and *of*, plus the back-formation *decaf*.

Except in *of*, where \<f\> → /v/, \<f\> regularly corresponds to /f/.

\<g\>

The seventh letter of the modern and classical Roman alphabets, \<g\> is an inheritance during the Old English period of a form that the Romans derived from the Greek gamma. In Old English it represented at least four different fricative or stop phonemes. Today \<g\> occurs predominantly in initial and medial position in English words. A small number of words, almost all monosyllables, have final \<g\> (e.g., *bag, bug, frog*). This letter also occurs in the initial clusters \<gl, gn\>, and \<gr\> (e.g., *glide, gnat, grow*), and in the final clusters \<gm\> and \<gn\> (e.g., *paradigm, sign*). Rarer clusters include initial \<gu\> (*guano*), initial \<sgr\> (*sgrafitto*), and final \<rg\> (*Borg*).

The geminate cluster \<gg\> occurs primarily in medial position (e.g., *dagger*). Only *egg* and *yegg* ("safecracker") have final \<gg\>. Most \<gg\> occurrences are before final \<y\> or \<er\> where \<gg\> resulted from the doubling of final \<g\>: (*baggy, craggy, digger, foggy*, etc.). Because of a parallelism with \<c\>, \<g\> is treated as having two primary pronunciations: / ǰ / before \<e, i\>, or \<y\> and /g/ elsewhere. Numerous exceptions exist, however, including the following:

1. Many common words borrowed from Scandinavian languages have \<g\> → /g/ before \<e\> and \<i\>: *gear, get, gift, geld, gill, give*.
2. Most words that end in \<ger\> have \<g\> → /g/: *anger, auger, conquer, eager*.
3. Borrowings from a variety of languages other than Scandinavian also have \<g\> → /g/ before \<e, i\>, or \<y\>: *gecko* (Malay), *gefilte* (Yiddish), *geisha* (Japanese), *gestalt* (German), and *fungi* (Latin), which is also pronounced with /g/. In addition, some words derived from

Old and Middle English are also exceptions to the <e, i, y> pattern (e.g., *geese, gird, girl*).

4. In a small group of relatively recent French borrowings, <g> before <e> and <i> maps to /ž/: *bourgeois, camouflage, garage, sabotage.* Some of these have alternate <g> → /ǰ/ pronunciations, however.

5. In the oddity category are the British form *gaol* and the French borrowing *margarine*, which have /ǰ/ where /g/ is expected, and the Spanish borrowing *saguaro*, where <g> is sometimes silent.

Among the alternations for <g> are the cases with final /ŋg/ where /g/ is dropped before juncture but retained before the comparative and superlative endings: *strong–stronger–strongest* (vs. *bring–bringing*). The cluster /ŋg/ also occurs in a few other suffixed forms: *elongate, elongation, diphthongize, prolongate, prolongation, tingle.*

Word-initial <gn> maps to /n/ by one of the general consonant rules (*gnostic–agnostic*), and final <gm> and <gn> drop /g/ before a juncture but retain /g/ in certain suffixed forms (*sign–signify–signal, paradigm–paradigmatic*). The geminate cluster <gg> normally corresponds to /g/ except for *exaggerate*, where it corresponds to /ǰ/, and *suggest*, where it is /gǰ/.

<gh>

The digraph <gh> is an interloper in English orthography, the residue of sound change and printer experimentation, serving mainly as a benign target of spelling reform fulminations. It first occurred during the Middle English period as a replacement for the letter yogh, which originally represented palatal and gutteral fricatives, as in *night, high,* and *tough.* Today <gh> occurs almost exclusively in initial and final position, and in the final cluster <ght> (as in *night* and *sought*). But neither logic nor history can make much sense of its correspondences. William Caxton, the first English printer, was responsible for inserting an <h> after <g> in *ghost* and *ghoul,* and tried a number of others that failed to find favor in the following generations—for instance, *gherle, ghes, ghoot* (= *goat*). Among the other <gh> spellings, *ghetto* and *spaghetti* were borrowed from Italian, where <gh> is common; *gherkin, burgher,* and *dinghy* show respellings of earlier <g>; and most of the postvocalic <gh>'s are residues from when <gh> indicated a voiced velar fricative, which either became silent (*high, though, thought*) or merged with /f/ (*cough, enough, tough*). A few, however, such as *delight, haughty,* and *sprightly,* had <gh> inserted by analogy with other silent-<gh> spellings after <i> and <au>.

Among the <gh> oddities are *hough,* which has <gh> → /k/, and *hiccough,* which has <gh> → /p/. Otherwise, <gh> is mapped into /g/ in initial position and in *aghast, burgh(er), dinghy, sorghum,* and *spaghetti.* The remainder not mentioned here have silent <gh>.

<gn>

As a functional unit, <gn> occurs mostly in French borrowings of the last 300 years and corresponds to /nj/ (e.g., *lorgnette, mignon, vignette*). This unit might be treated as a sequence of silent <g> plus <n> → /nj/, but since /gn/ in French corresponds to a palatal nasal that is rendered in Modern English as /nj/, it is treated as a single functional unit in French (and Italian—e.g., *Bologna*) borrowings, paralleling Spanish <ñ> (e.g., *cañon*). (In Middle English this palatal nasal from Old French became either /nj/, as in *onion,* or /n/, as in *sign.*) In general, <gn> → /nj/ occurs only in medial environments such as <gnon> and <gnette>. Initial <gn> (e.g., *gnat* and *gnu*) is treated as a sequence of <g> + <n>, as is final <gn> (e.g., *align, consign, design, foreign*). In the latter group, <gn> requires this treatment because <g> corresponds to /g/ in <gn> compounds such as *signal* (cf. *sign*) and *assignation* (cf. *assign*). In the former group, <gn> is treated as a sequence of two units because *gnat, gnast, gnaw,* and so on had pronounced <g>'s in early Modern English.

<h>

The eighth letter of the modern and classical Roman alphabets, <h> derives from the Hebrew het via the Greek eta. The consonant spelling <h> occurs in all word positions, but in some medial positions and in all final positions it occurs only as a marker after a vowel. "It is intended to suggest stressed free vowels, as in the exclamations *ah!, oh!, hurrah!, bah!,* and in *shah, Yahweh.*"[10] The OED suggests that besides marking a free vowel, <h> also marks non-native words: "After a vowel, *h* is regularly silent, and such a vowel being usually long . . . the addition of *h* . . . is one of the expedients which we have for indicating a long vowel in foreign or dialect words."[11] It does not double, nor does it occur in initial clusters.

In mappings to sound, <h> corresponds either to /h/ or to silence—the former being the general case, the latter being restricted to the following:

1. Initial <h> in *heir, herb, honest, honor, hour,* and occasionally *hostler.*[12] Of these, *herb* regularly has /h/ in British English.
2. After a vowel in final position (e.g., *hurrah, pharaoh*) or before an-

other consonant (e.g., *ohm, fahrenheit*), <h> is silent, and can be viewed as a marker of a foreign vowel spelling (see Chapter 5).

3. After <x> (e.g., *exhaust, exhibit, exhort*), /h/ is generally lost, as it is in medial position in a small number of other words, such as *shepherd*.[13] There is also a slight tendency for intervocalic /h/ to be lost after a stressed vowel, as in *vehicle–vehicular*.

<j>

The 10th letter of the modern Roman alphabet, <j> did not exist in the older Roman alphabet. It began its existence in English as a variant of <i>, which in Old and Middle English represented both a vowel and a consonant. In Middle English a differentiated form of <i> developed to aid in discriminating <i> sequences, particularly in Roman numerals. In the 17th century <i> and <j> began to be differentiated for vowel and consonant representations. The letter <j> appears primarily in initial position before back vowel spellings, and occasionally in medial position before either back or front vowel spellings, as in *cajole, deject, majesty,* and *rajah*. In a number of cases where <j> appears before a front vowel spelling, a variant spelling with <g> exists—for example, *jest–gest, jingle–gingle,* and *serjeant–sergeant* (now differentiated in meaning). The Hebrew loan word *hallelujah* has the variant *(h)alleluia,* while the Spanish loan word *marijuana* has the variant *marihuana*. It does not appear in final position except in occasional borrowings (*raj*), and does not occur in initial or final clusters.

The letter <j> regularly corresponds to / ǰ / except in small groups of relatively recent borrowings: French <j> → /ž/ (*bijou, jabot, jacamar*), German, Hebrew, and Norwegian <j> → /j/ (*jaeger, Junker, hallelujah, fjord*), and Mexican Spanish <j> → /h/ (*jojoba, marijuana*).[14]

<k>

The 11th letter of the modern Roman alphabet and the 10th letter of the classical Roman alphabet, <k> derives from the Hebrew kaph via the Greek kappa. In late Latin, <k> was considered a supplementary letter to <c>, and was used primarily in borrowings that retained hard <c> before <e, i>, or <y>. It was little used in Old English, being introduced by Anglo-Norman scribes into Middle English for the same function it served in late Latin.

The letter <k> occurs in initial, medial, and final positions, but is limited to certain environments in each. In initial position it appears most commonly before <e> and <i> (both alone and in the cluster <sk>) and in the cluster <kn>. It does occur, however, in several recent borrowings before <a, o, u> (e.g., *kaffir, kangaroo, kosher, kulak*). In final position it appears commonly after the vowel spellings <ea, ee, oa, oo> (e.g., *beak, seek, soak,* and *took*), and in the clusters <lk, nk, rk, sk> (e.g., *milk, rank, hark,* and *ask*). One popular exception is the relatively recent creation *Amtrak*. Since <kk> is avoided in English orthography, <k> rarely occurs in final position after a stressed, single-letter vowel spelling, because in such positions it would double before suffixes that begin with a vowel. (The only common exceptions are *trek*, a mid-19th-century borrowing from African Dutch, and *yak*—both the shaggy fellow with horns and the verb necessitated by teenage talk on the telephone, the latter being a late 1940s coining.) In medial position it occurs chiefly before <e> and <i>. In words such as *snake* and *dike*, where the final <e> marks the correspondence of the preceding vowel, a <c> spelling for /k/ cannot be used because the final <e> would also mark the incorrect correspondence for <c>. The letter <k> regularly corresponds to /k/, the only exceptions being the initial cluster <kn>, where /kn/ was leveled to /n/ about the middle of the 17th century (e.g., *knee, knife, knowledge*).

<kh>

The spelling <kh> is a recent addition to the orthographic system, appearing in a small number of borrowings from Hindi (*khaddar, khaki*), Arabic (*khamsin, khan, sheikh*), and Turkish (*khedive*) It regularly corresponds to /k/.

<l>

The 12th letter of the modern Roman alphabet and the 11th letter of the classical Roman alphabet, <l> descends from the Hebrew lamed via the Greek lambda. It occurs in initial, medial, and final positions, as in *lamb, oleander,* and *coal,* and in a large number of monomorphemic clusters, the most common of which are as follows:

Initial clusters		Final clusters	
<pl>	*play*	<lp>	*pulp*
<bl>	*black*	<lt>	*malt*
<cl>	*climb*	<ld>	*hold*
<chl>	*chlorine*	<lk>	*bulk*
<gl>	*glaze*	<lf>	*half*
<fl>	*flower*	<lch>	*belch*
<sl>	*slip*	<lm>	*helm*
<spl>	*splash*	<rld>	*world*

Less common final clusters are <lb> (*bulb*), <ltz> (*waltz*), <lct> (*mulct*), and <lx> (*calx*). Except in combinations with <r>, <l> always occurs next to a vowel in a consonant cluster.

In general, the geminate cluster <ll> in final position appears only in one-syllable words, and then only after a single-letter vowel spelling (*ball, hill, hull,* etc.). At the end of multisyllabic words, <l> rather than <ll> is generally found. The exceptions to this pattern are either hyphenated compounds such as *half-full*, or words such as *appall, distill,* and *install*, which have alternate spellings with a single <l>. A small number of monosyllables end in a single <l> after a primary vowel spelling: *Al, el, gel, Mel, mil, nil, pal, Sal, Val.*

In mappings to sound, <l> corresponds to /l/, with these exceptions:

1. The first <l> in *colonel* corresponds to /r/. The spelling of this word is a double embarrassment, because the second <o> is no longer pronounced and the first <l> was a late 16th-century replacement for <r>, based on etymology.
2. In *could, should,* and *would,* and in a number of words after <a> or <o> and before <f, k, m>, or <n>, <l> is silent: *calf, folk, balm, Lincoln.* It tends to be lost before these consonants when preceded by /æ, a/, or /ɔ/, but too few words are involved to validate a rule.
3. Word-final <le> spellings after a consonant correspond to /əl/ or syllabic <l>.
4. In recent Spanish borrowings, <ll> is generally mapped to zero or to /j/, with compensatory lengthening of the preceding vowel (e.g., shift from /ɪ/ to /i/): *quesadilla, tortilla.*

<m>

The 13th letter of the modern Roman alphabet and the 12th letter of the classical Roman alphabet, <m> descends from the Hebrew mem via the Greek mu. It occurs commonly in initial, medial, and final positions: *moon, demon, bloom.* It also occurs in the initial cluster <sm> (*small, smooth*), and in these monomorphemic final clusters: <mp> (*limp*), <mph> (*nymph*), <lm> (*elm*), <rm> (*arm*), <sm> (*spasm*), and <thm> (*rhythm*).

In mappings to sound, <m> regularly corresponds to /m/ except in prejunctural positions after /ð/ and /z/, when it corresponds to syllabic <m> (e.g., *rhythm, schism, spasm*); in initial <mn>, where it is dropped (e.g., *mnemonic*); and in the oddity *comptroller*, where it corresponds to /n/ (and where the /p/ is usually silent). Altogether, these exceptions account for about a half-dozen occurrences of <m>.

<n>

The 14th letter of the modern Roman alphabet and the 13th letter of the classical Roman alphabet, <n> derives from the Hebrew nun via the Greek nu. It occurs in all word positions, although it is more frequently medial and final than initial. It also occurs in a small number of initial clusters: <sn> (*snow, snarl*), <shn>/<schn> (*shnook/schnook*), <kn> (*knee, knife*), and <gn> (*gnat, gnu*). In monomorphemic words it occurs in nine final clusters:

<nch>	*pinch, wrench*	<nth>	*labyrinth*
<nd>	*bend, wand*	<gn>	*sign, malign*
<nk>	*bank, drink*	<ln>	*kiln*
<nt>	*ant, aunt*	<rn>	*corn, torn*
<nx>	*larynx, pharynx*		

Before /k/ and /g/, which can be spelled <k> (*bank*), <c> (*uncle*), <ch> (*anchor*), <q> (*banquet*), <g> (*tongue*),[15] and <x> (*anxiety*), /n/ shifts to /ŋ/. The phonological process that accounts for this shift is called *assimilation*. In anticipation of the velar articulation of /g/ or /k/, /n/ shifts from its dental position to /ŋ/, which is the velar equivalent of /n/. This occurs in all environments except for stressed prefixes such as *con, in,* and *syn,* where both /n/ and /ŋ/ are common (e.g., *syncopate*), and with unstressed <un> (*unkempt, unknown,* etc.). Both /n/ and /ŋ/ can also occasionally occur when <con, in, syn> is unstressed (e.g., *congruence*). This should not be taken as a rule, but as a compromise in a phonetically unstable situation.[16] To map <n> directly to /ŋ/ would be cumbersome, since the sounds /g/ and /k/, as shown above, could be spelled <g, k, q, x>, or <c>. Rules for relating <c> to /k/ and <x> to /ks/ would have to be incorporated into this rule, along with the stress placement rules for *con, in,* and *syn*. Otherwise <n> corresponds to /n/, except in *kiln* and in the final cluster <mn>, where it is silent (but compare *autumn–autumnal, column–columnar, solemn–solemnity*).

<ng>

The digraph <ng> came into existence as a functional unit in words such as *long* and *thing* when the final /g/ was lost—a cluster leveling that occurred in the early Modern English period. As explained in Chapter 5, <ng> can be viewed from a linguistic standpoint as a sequence of <n> and <g>, which on the phonemic level became first /ng/ and then /ŋg/ and then /ŋ/ through general rules for shifting /n/ to /ŋ/ before velar stops, and then for leveling final, unpronounceable clusters.

<p>

The 16th letter of the modern Roman alphabet and the 15th letter of the classical Roman alphabet, <p> derives from the Hebrew pe via the Greek pi. It occurs in initial, medial, and final positions by itself, and in a variety of clusters—the most common of which are initial <pr, pl, sp>, and final <lp, rp, sp> (e.g., *program, plough, speed; help, harp, asp*). In the rare-cluster category is initial <pu>, for which only two exemplars occur in most modern dictionaries: *pueblo* and *puissance*. Less common clusters, which pattern quite differently from these, are initial <pn> (*pneumonia*), <ps> (*psychology*), and <pt> (*ptomaine*, and final <pt> (*receipt*) and <rps> (*corps*). The letter <p> regularly corresponds to /p/ except for (1) the unpronounceable initial clusters <pn, ps, pt>; (2) sequences of bilabial stops where <p> is the first element (e.g., *Campbell, cupboard*); and (3) a small group of borrowings and scribal tamperings (*corps, coup*, and *receipt*).[17] In all these exceptions, <p> is silent.

<ph>

The digraph <ph> was used in Latin and Old English writing to transliterate the Greek phi, as in *pharaoh*. Most modern <ph> spellings, however, are 15th- to 17th-century respellings of earlier <f> spellings (e.g., *pheasant, phantom, pharmacy*), or more recent technical terms (e.g., *pharyngeal, phenol*). This digraph is a relatively infrequent spelling in English, occurring mostly in initial and medial positions. Besides *graph* and its compounds, words with final <ph> are relatively rare, comprising a small number of Greek (*epitaph, lymph, nymph*), Latin (*triumph, sylph*), and Hebrew/Arabic (*caliph, Joseph, seraph*) borrowings. Clusters with <ph> are also relatively rare: <phl> (*phlange*), <phr> (*phrase*), <phw> (*phwack*), <phth> (*phthisic*), <sph> (*sphere*), <mph> (*nymph*), and <lph> (*sylph*). Most <ph> spellings either were derived from Greek or Latin or were created on a classical model to appear to be technical or scientific (e.g., *pheromone, pharynx, phosphate*). Some words with <ph> spellings have alternate spellings with <f>: *caliph–calif, phrenetic–frenetic, sulphur–sulfur*.

A few are from other languages (e.g., *pharaoh*—from Hebrew) or are recent creations spelled with <ph> to be distinctive (e.g., *phooey*). In *phthisic*, it is silent; in *nephew* in British speech, it is usually /v/; in *diphtheria, diphthong*, and *naphtha*, it is (or can be) /p/; otherwise <ph> corresponds to /f/.

<pph>

A totally marginal unit for English, <pph> appeared in the 17th century in *sapphire* (Middle English *saphir, safir*). Only two common words, *sapphire* and

Sappho (and their derivatives), contain this spelling. It is included here with great reluctance, only because of its relationship to <ck, dg, tch, rrh>. Like all the units just named, it is classed as a pseudogeminate; invariably, it corresponds to /f/. This unit might be treated as a combination of <p> + <ph>, however, this requires treating the first <p> as silent, and therefore is not identical to the analysis given for <ck, dg, rrh, tch>. *Sapphire* is a 12th century borrowing from Old French, perhaps of Persian origin. The <pph> spelling does not appear until the 17th century in English texts, however. The modern French spelling for this word is *saphir*.

<q>

The 17th letter of the modern Roman alphabet and the 16th letter of the classical Roman alphabet, <q> derives from the Hebrew koph via the Greek kappa. It was used in Old English almost exclusively in the combination <qu>, representing /kw/, but before the end of the Old English period this was replaced by the spellings <cu> and <cw>. After the Norman Conquest, <qu> was slowly reintroduced. The letter <q> rather than <qu> is treated as a functional unit, because the consonant correspondences <u> → /w/ (*quick*) and <u> → /ø/ (*liquor*) are the same as are found in such words as *guano*, *language*, and *suave*. Except for occasional borrowings (e.g., *Iraq*, *qintar*, *qoph*) and back-formations (e.g., *Shaq* for *Shaquille*), <q> appears with <u> whenever it occurs.[18] It also occurs in the initial cluster <squ> (*square*, *squirrel*, etc.). It regularly corresponds to /k/.

<r>

The 18th letter of the modern Roman alphabet and the 17th letter of the classical Roman alphabet, <r> derives from the Hebrew resh via the Greek rho. It occurs in initial, medial, and final positions and in a large number of clusters, the most common of which are the following:

Initial clusters

 	brace	<gr>	*grade*	<spr>	*spring*
<chr>	*chrome*	<phr>	*phrase*	<str>	*strong*
<cr>	*crash*	<pr>	*prize*	<thr>	*through*
<dr>	*drive*	<scr>	*screw*	<tr>	*train*
<fr>	*friend*	<shr>	*shred*	<wr>	*write*

Final clusters

<rb>	*orb*	<rf>	*scarf*	<rn>	*barn*
<rp>	*sharp*	<rth>	*fourth*	<rl>	*Carl*
<rd>	*ford*	<rsh>	*marsh*	(<rpt>	*excerpt*)
<rt>	*smart*	<rch>	*porch*	(<rst>	*first*)
<rg>	*Borg*	<rm>	*form*	<rld>	*world*

The list of final clusters is deceiving, however, in that the spellings for the /r/-colored vowel that is heard in *excerpt* and *first*, which include vowel + /r/, are treated as vowels; this removes final <rpt> and <rst>, because these occur only in words in which <r> is part of a vowel spelling. These are shown in parentheses above. In all cases where <r> represents a consonant, it corresponds to /r/.

<rh>

The digraph <rh> was used in Latin and then early Modern English writing for Greek *rho* in word-initial position. Therefore, most modern <rh> spellings, of which there are few, date from the end of the 14th century or later. This digraph, which invariably corresponds to /r/, occurs almost exclusively in initial position, and mostly in Greek and Latin borrowings (e.g., *rhapsody, rhetoric, rhinoceros, rhythm*). It also occurs in technical terms constructed from Greek and Latin components (e.g., *rhea, rhesus*). A few <rh> forms from other languages have nevertheless managed to penetrate the classical circle—for example, *rhebok* (Afrikaans), *rhumb* (Spanish), and *rhyme* (Old French).

<rrh>

A late 16th-century invention, <rrh> is included here as a functional unit with considerable hesitation. Like <pph, ck, dg, tch>, <rrh> appears only after single-letter vowel spellings, and then mostly in a small group of medical terms: *catarrh, cirrhosis, diarrhea, hemorrhage, hemorrhoids, pyorrhea*.[19] Like <pph>, it is treated as a pseudogeminate, although one could argue for an <r> + <rh> treatment. It invariably corresponds to /r/.[20]

<s>

The 19th letter of the modern Roman alphabet and the 18th letter of the classical Roman alphabet, <s> derives from the Hebrew *sin* (shin) via the Greek sigma. It occurs in initial, medial, and final positions by itself; in a large number of initial consonant clusters; and in four monomorphemic final clusters. The initial and final clusters are the following:

Initial clusters

<ps>	*psychology*	<sm>	*small*	<st>	*stand*
<sc>	*scare*	<sn>	*snow*	<sth>	*sthenic*
<sch>	*school*	*special* <str>		<str>	*strong*
<scl>	*sclerosis*	<sph>	*sphere*	<su>	*suede*
<scr>	*scream*	<spl>	*splash*	<sv>	*svelte*
<sk>	*ski*	<spr>	*spring*	<sw>	*swim*
<sl>	*slow*	<squ>	*squash*		

Final clusters

<sp>	*wasp*	<sk>	*ask*
<st>	*test*	(<rst>	*thirst*)

In initial position <s> corresponds to /s/, with only two common exceptions, *sure* and *sugar*, where it corresponds to /š/. The sound correspondences for <s> otherwise are the most difficult to predict among all the consonants. This difficulty results from two sound changes that have occurred over the last 900 years. In the first, voiceless /s/ became voiced, particularly when it stood between an unstressed and a stressed vowel. Compare, for example, the <s> pronunciations in *sign–design*, *serve–deserve*, and *sound–resound*. Similarly, /s/ at the end of *as*, *does*, *has*, *his*, *is*, and *was* has become voiced, as has the /s/ in the verb forms of such words as *close*, *house* and *use*, even though the adjective and noun forms have retained the voiceless /s/. (But note that <s> has remained voiceless in *bus*, *gas*, *this*, *thus*, *us*, and *yes*.)

The second change, palatalization, accounts for the /š/ pronunciations in such words as *sure*, *sugar*, *Sean*, and *tissue*, as well as the /ž/ pronunciations in *measure*, *pleasure*, and *treasure*, among others.[21] Further complicating the <s> picture is final, morphemic <s>, as in *dogs*, *girl's*, *jumps*, and *mayors*. After the sibilants /s, z, š, ž, č, ǰ/, as explained in Chapter 4, morphemic <s> corresponds to /ɪz/ (*judges*, *bushes*, *mazes*). After any voiced sounds except /z, ž/, and /ǰ/ it is /z/ (*girls*, *toys*, *Burr's*); otherwise it is /s/ (*cats*, *Cliff's*). Notice that nonmorphemic final <s> (or <se>) does not obey these rules: *nurse*, *manse*. (Final /s/ can occur after vowels also, as in *voice* and *loose*.) In initial and final clusters, nonmorphemic <s> is always voiceless (*scoop*, *skin*, *splash*, *best*, *mask*, etc.).

In final position, <s> is silent in a small group of French loan words (*corps*, *apropos, bourgeois, challis, chamois, chassis, debris, Illinois,*[22] *rendezvous, velours*), and in *aisle, isle,* and *island,* where its presence results from the classical pedantry of early modern English scribes (and, later, printers), plus confusion.[23] Otherwise, after any primary vowel except <e>, <s> → /s/ generally holds in final position (*canvas, serious, tennis,* etc.). The exceptions are the monosyllables just listed in which final <s> is voiced. After <e>, final <s> is almost always voiced (*diabetes, Socrates,* etc.). In medial position, dependable patterns are few. Generally a medial <s> after a voiceless consonant or <r> is voiceless (*balsa, false, rinse, nurse,* etc.).

<sch>

As an independent functional unit, <sch> dates from the 18th century and occurs mainly in a small number of German borrowings (*schnapps, schuss*); in a few words influenced by German pronunciations (*schistose*); in the transliteration of a number of Yiddish terms (*schlemiel, schlepp*); and in the British pronunciation of *schedule.* In all these cases <sch> corresponds to /š/. In *schism* <sch> corresponds to /s/, but given the lack of other exemplars of this correspondence, it merits no more than a passing mention. All other occurrences of <sch> can be decomposed into <s> → /s/ and <ch> → /k/ (*schema, school, schizoid, schooner,* etc.).

<sh>

The digraph <sh> appears in Middle English writing as early as 1200, but it was not established as a spelling for /š/ until the last quarter of the 15th century. It occurs in all word positions but in only two common clusters: <shr>, as in *shrimp* and *shrewd,* and <rsh>, as in *marsh* and *harsh.* It corresponds without exception to /š/.

<t>

The 20th letter of the modern Roman alphabet and the 19th letter of the classical Roman alphabet, <t> derives from the Hebrew taw via the Greek tau. It occurs in initial, medial, and final position as a single consonant, and in the following common monomorphemic initial and final clusters:

Initial clusters

<st>	*storm*	<tr>	*train*
<str>	*strip*	<tw>	*twenty*

Final clusters

<ct>	pact	<mpt>	attempt	(<rst>	first
<ft>	left	<nct>	distinct	<rt>	smart
<ght>	fought	<nt>	rent	<st>	must
<lt>	halt	<pt>	apt	<xt>	text

Rarer initial clusters include <pt> (*ptomaine*), <tm> (*tmesis*), <ts> (*tsetse*), and <tz> (*tzar*, a variant of *czar*). The spellings <ts> and <tz> also occur initially in transliterations of Yiddish and Hebrew words that begin with *sadhe* (e.g., *tzimmes*, *tzitzis*), but in these cases <ts> and <tz> could be treated as alternates of a separate functional unit. Rarer final clusters include <lct> (*mulct*), <ltz> (*waltz*), <ntz> (*chintz*), and <tz> (*blitz*). In *first*, *excerpt*, and related spellings, <r> composes part of the vowel spellings and therefore does not form part of a final cluster with <t>.

The sound mappings for <t> exhibit both a regular set of patterns deriving from sound changes and scribal restorations, and a marginal mess of partially patterned exceptions. Let us work our way from least to most regular. The silent <t>'s are the first plateau; these include the following:

1. French borrowings such as *depot, debut, hautboy, rapport, savant, mortgage*, and the group with final <et> (*buffet, valet*, etc.).
2. The <stl> clusters: *apostle, bristle, castle, nestle, whistle*, and so on. There are perhaps 20 of these among the 20,000 most frequently occurring words in English, and no exceptions except across syllable boundaries (*beastly, costly, listless*, etc.).
3. The <sten> endings: *fasten, glisten, hasten*, and *listen*. That this is not phonological conditioning is demonstrated by words like *piston, Boston*, and *Austin*, where <t> is pronounced in the identical phonological environment.
4. Oddities such as *often*, where spelling pronunciations occasionally restore a /t/ pronunciation.

Once the flotsam and jetsam of silent <t>'s are cleared, the next hurdle is to separate the classical substitutions of <t> for earlier <s> or <c> from the true cases of <t>. The former (e.g., *nation, caution*) are invariably realized as /š/; the latter are pronounced as either /t/ or /č/ (e.g., *bastion, mature*), except for *equation*, where /š/ is voiced as /ž/.

The correspondence <t> → /č/ is found when <t> is followed by unstressed <u> (e.g., *armature, capitulate, fatuous, fortune, mutual*) or when <st> is followed by unstressed <io> or <ia> (*bastion, celestial*). In both cases, the sequence

/tj/ + vowel (unstressed) has palatalized to /č/ + vowel.[24] In the <tu> forms, the <j> results from the <u> → /ju/; in the <ion> cases, /j/ results from the <i>. After palatalization, the remaining (unstressed) vowel usually became /ə/. Thus, in words such as *fortune*, the sequence of sound changes is presumed to be /fór tjun/ → /fór čun/ → /fór čən/. In *posthumous*, an unetymological <h> disguises the <t> + <u> pattern.

In words such as *nation*, an earlier <s> or <c> spelling (e.g., *naciune, nasion*) was replaced by <t> during the Renaissance to show the classical origins of the words affected. Before this spelling change, which became established in the 16th century, /sj/ + vowel (unstressed) had shifted to /š/ + vowel.

Where not covered by any of the patterns just described, <t> corresponds to /t/.

<tch>

The trigraph <tch> is a 15th-century replacement for doubled <ch>, just as <dg> is a replacement for doubled <g> corresponding to /ǰ/, and <ck> a replacement for <kk>. As with <dg> and <ck>, <tch> occurs almost invariably after single-letter checked vowel spellings (e.g., *kitchen, match*), the one exception being the letter name *aitch*. However, recent borrowings have resulted in a handful of word-initial <tch>'s: *Tchaikovsky, Tchebycheff* (Russian); *Tchambuli* (Papua); *tchotchke* (Yiddish); and *Tchoupitoulas* (Native American).[25] The unit <tch> forms no clusters and is mapped without exception to /č/.

<th>

The digraph <th> occurred in the earliest English texts for [θ] and [ð], which were allophones of a single phoneme. Before 700, however, a new letter for these sounds, eth, was formed by adding a horizontal bar to a lower-case <d>. Then in the eighth century, the runic letter thorn was adopted for these same functions and used in parallel with eth. The digraph <th> was not used again until the late 15th century, when the first English printer, Caxton, adopted it to replace forms that were not found in the Continental type case. In Scotland <y> was occasionally used for thorn, particularly in initial position in function words, leading to the miscreation *ye* for *the*.

This digraph occurs in all word positions and in a small number of common clusters: initial <thr> (e.g., *thrash, through, throw*), final <nth> (e.g., *labyrinth, month, tenth*), and final <rth> (e.g., *fourth*). It also occurs in three rare initial clusters: <sth> (*sthenic*), <thw> (*thwack, thwart*), and <phth> (*phthisis, phthisic*). In addition, it occurs in a group of rarely occurring final clusters mostly formed by suffixation of <th> to form ordinal numbers or abstract nouns. From the former process come <fth> (*fifth*), <lfth> (*twelfth*), and <xth> (*sixth*),[26] from the latter <dth> (*breadth, width*), <ngth> (*length, strength*), and <pth> (*depth*).[27] Two Greek borrowings, *logarithm* and *rhythm*, have brought final <thm> into English. In *Matthew*, <tth> may be treated as parallel to <cch>, <pph>, and <rrh>, but it does not occur in any other words commonly used in English.

Most words with initial <th> in Modern English derive from Old and early Middle English (e.g., *thaw, the, theft, thick*) or from Greek (e.g., *theater, thematic, theology, theory*). The latter, however, may have been borrowed directly (e.g., *therapeutic*) or indirectly (e.g., *theorem*) via Latin. A few <th> words were borrowed from other languages (e.g., Hindi *thug*), and at least one was formed by imitation (*thwack*).

In all function words except *through*, <th> corresponds to /ð/. In content words, <th> is silent in two borrowings (*asthma* and *isthmus*), corresponds to /t/ in a few Greek and Latin forms (*thyme, phthisis, Anthony, Esther*), and corresponds to /tθ/ in *eighth*. Otherwise <th> corresponds either to /θ/ or /ð/, with only a limited number of cases where the choice is predictable. These include the following:

1. Before final <e>, <th> corresponds to /ð/ (*bathe, breathe, scythe, teethe*, etc.).
2. Derivatives of final-<th> words formed by adding <ern, erly>, and <y> tend to have /ð/ (*northern, northerly, smithy, worthy*, etc.).
3. Some words that end in voiceless <th> tend to voice <th> with the addition of the plural ending (*baths, laths, mouths*, etc.). However, most of these plurals also have voiceless pronunciations, and many plurals of <th>-ending words have not voiced to /ð/ (e.g., *faiths, growths, months*).
4. Words that end in <ther> tend to have /ð/ (e.g., *either, father, mother*), the exceptions being *anther, ether, panther*, and a few proper names (e.g., *Esther, Luther*).

<u>

The 21st letter of the modern Roman alphabet and the 20th letter of the classical Roman alphabet, <u> derives from the Hebrew vav via the Greek upsilon. It was used in Latin as well as Old English for both a vowel (/u/) and a consonant or semivowel (/w/). In late Latin /w/ became /v/, and thus <u> came to represent in English /u/, /v/, and /w/. In Modern English <u> occurs regularly as a consonant spelling after <q> (e.g., *acquire, quick*), less often after <g> (e.g., *anguish, guano*) and <s> (e.g., *persuade, suite*), and after a few other letters in a small number of borrowings (*ennui, pueblo, puissance, tuille*). In the endings <que> (e.g., *torque*), <quet> (e.g., *bouquet*),[28] <quette> (e.g., *maquette*), and <quee> (e.g., *marquee*), and in *quay, queue, liquor, marquis, piquant,* and *turquoise,* consonantal <u> is silent. Otherwise it corresponds to /w/.

<v>

The 22nd letter of the modern Roman alphabet, <v> derived ultimately, like <u>, from the Hebrew vav. The letter <v>, like <j>, was a late addition to the English alphabet, first appearing as a separate letter in the 16th century but not established until the early 19th century. Before this time <u> and <v> were used interchangeably for vowel and consonant sounds, even though, according to Scragg, "As early as the fifteenth century the best scriveners tended to use only <v> for /v/ in medial position at least."[29] Over 75 percent of all occurrences of <v> in Modern English are found in medial position; almost all of the remainder occur in initial position. In word-final position, <v> is restricted to a small group of shortened forms (e.g., *rev–revolution, gov–government*), slang terms (e.g., *shiv*), and Slavic borrowings (*Slav, Kiev, Pavlov, leitmotiv*).[30] It also rarely doubles, the exceptions being a handful of orthographic outcasts: *chivvy, civvies, divvy, navvy, revving, savvy, skivvies.* Similarly, it rarely occurs in consonant clusters, the most common being <lv> (as in *shelve*) and the least common <sv> (as in *svelte*).

For mappings to sound, <v> regularly corresponds to /v/, the only exceptions being borrowings such as *leitmotiv* in which a final voiced consonant has been devoiced.[31]

<w>

The 23rd letter of the modern Roman alphabet, <w> is an invention of the Old English period. In the earliest English texts, the sound /w/ was represented by a doubled <u> (or <v>); hence the name "double <u>." Beginning in the eighth century, this spelling was replaced by a runic letter called wynn (<Ρ>), which eventually became the standard spelling for <w> until after the Norman Conquest, when <w>, which had been brought to the Continent by Germanic and French scribes, was reintroduced by the Normans. By the end of the 13th century it had completely replaced wynn.

In syllable-initial positions as in *window, beware,* and *reward,* and in the initial clusters <dw> (*dwarf*), <sw> (*swim*), <schw> (*schwa*), <tw> (*twin*), and <thw> (*thwack*), <w> is a consonant.

In the initial cluster <wr> and in *answer, sword, two,* and *toward,* <w> corresponds to /ø/. Otherwise it corresponds to /w/.[32]

<wh>

Most modern <wh> spellings are reversals of Old English <hw>. This change started at the beginning of the 12th century and was completed by the late 13th century. Some philologists argue that the change was promulgated by Anglo-Norman scribes to limit sequences of letters written with short downstrokes (e.g., <wun>, <win>), but others find the evidence for this argument less than compelling.[33] The digraph <wh> occurs today in morpheme-initial position only; in most American dialects it is pronounced /hw/, except in *who, whom, whoop, whore,* and *whole,* where it is pronounced /h/.[34]

<x>

The 24th letter of the modern Roman alphabet and the 21st of the classical Roman alphabet, <x> derives from the Greek chi. It was used in Old English in medial and final positions for what today is pronounced /ks/ as in *mix.* Greek borrowings such as *xylophone* constitute the main source of initial <x> in Modern English. Today <x> occurs in only a few monomorphemic clusters, with no more than a handful of words occurring with any of them: <lx> (*calx*), <nx> (*Bronx, jinx, larynx, sphinx,* etc.), <xl> (*axle*), and <xt> (*betwixt, context, next, pretext, text*). Across morpheme boundaries, <x> clusters with a number of other letters: <xc, xch, xcl, xcr, xh, xp, xpl, xpr, xqu> (*exceeds, exchange, exclaim, excretion, exhaust, expand, explain, express,* and *exquisite*).

In initial position <x> corresponds to /z/, in final position to /ks/, and otherwise (i.e., in medial position) to either /ks/ or /gz/. In general, medial <x> will correspond to /gz/ if the main word stress is on the vowel after <x> and to /ks/ otherwise, but there are exceptions to this pattern (e.g., *doxology, proximity*), and a few words such as *exit* have both /ks/ and /gz/ pronunciations.

<y>

The 25th letter of the modern Roman alphabet and the 23rd of the classical Roman alphabet, <y> derives ultimately from the Hebrew vav via the Greek upsilon. In its earliest Roman appearance, it had the shape of <v> and represented both /u/ and /w/. Before the earliest English records, Roman <v> was reformed into <y> to represent upsilon in Greek borrowings. Although it was used in Old English to represent various vowels, <y> was not used to represent a consonant until the middle of the 13th century, when it began to replace yogh to represent a voiced palatal fricative. Today consonantal <y> occurs in about 100 words among the 20,000 most common in English, and over 90 percent of these occurrences are in initial position (e.g., *yet*, *yoke*, *Yukon*). The only medial occurrences are *banyan*, *beyond*, *buoyant*, *canyon*, *halyard*, *lanyard*, and a few <yer> forms (e.g., *bowyer*, *lawyer*, *sawyer*). No <y> consonantal clusters exist. All occurrences of consonantal <y> correspond to /j/.

 <z>

The 26th and last letter of the modern Roman alphabet, <z> corresponds to the 7th letter of the earliest Roman alphabet and the 23rd letter of the classical Roman sequence. It derives from the Hebrew zayin via the Greek zeta, and occurred in Old English as a spelling in loan words for /ts/. With sound and spelling changes in French in the 12th century, <z> became available for /z/—a role that became established in English spelling by the end of the 13th century. In Modern English <z> is the least frequently used of the 26 letters, occurring primarily in medial position. It is generally avoided in final position, occurring mainly after a consonant (e.g., *adz*, *blitz*, *chintz*, *quartz*, *waltz*), in foreign names and loan words (*Agassiz*, *fez*, *Suez*, *topaz*), and in a few English creations (e.g., *quiz*, *whiz*).

In the medial and final cluster <tz>, <z> corresponds to /s/ (*howitzer*, *pretzel*, *waltz*); in Agassiz it is /ø/; otherwise it corresponds to /z/. The cluster <zz>, which occurs in about 30 different words among the 20,000 most frequent in English, corresponds to /ts/ in a few Italian borrowings (e.g., *mezzo*, *pizza*, *piazza* [also pronounced with /z/]); otherwise it corresponds to /z/ (*blizzard*, *grizzly*, *jazz*, *pizzazz*).

LOOKING AHEAD

This completes a rather lengthy trek through the world of consonants—an extended chapter by anyone's measurement. The next chapter, covering the vowel patterns, completes the presentation of the grapheme–phoneme patterns in American English. With the patterns in hand, the reader will be able to consider English morphophonemics, the subject of Chapter 10.

NOTES

1. This is the word corpus that has been described in the Preface. The exact word count is 19,697.

2. When a wider vocabulary is considered, exceptions to these patterns are found—for example, <tch> in word-initial position, as in Tchaikovsky and tchotchkes.
3. On the complexities of specifying rules for English onset (syllable-initial) and coda (syllable-final) clusters, see Giegerich (1992), 153ff.
4. Before <e, i>, or <y>, <cc> is either /ks/ as in *accede* or <č> as in *cappuccino*.
5. As a reminder, the *Collegiate* is *Merriam–Webster's Collegiate Dictionary*, 10th edition (see Chapter 2, note 1), and the *OED* is *The Oxford English Dictionary* (see the Preface, note 9). For a colorful survey of 18th- and 19th-century grammatical literature on this topic, see Brown (1859), 188–195.
6. The basic rule is that <c> before mid- or high-front vowels corresponds to /s/ and otherwise to /k/. In Old English <œ> was used for a mid-front rounded vowel, the *i*-umlauts of /o/ or /o:/. These vowels later lost their rounding. Modern <oe> spellings (sometimes written as a ligature, particularly in British English) represent the Latin spelling of Greek <oi>. In French, <oe> sometimes substitutes for <e> (*oeil, oeuf, coeur*). The "<c> before <oe>" rule applies almost exclusively to (rare) Greek borrowings (*coelacanth, coeliac, coelom*). In *coeducation, coefficient, coequal*, and so on, <o> and <e> are separate vowel units.
7. The presence of the final sequence /skəl/ in *rascal* and *fiscal* demonstrates that no general leveling rule can be applied to delete /k/ in *muscle* and *corpuscle*.
8. A small number of words end with <c> rather than <ck> after a single-letter checked vowel spelling. These include a number of homophones of final-<ck> spellings (*bloc, floc, lac, roc, sac, sic, tic, tac*), as well as the back-formation *doc*.
9. The Greeks developed two letters from the Hebrew vav: the digamma, which was used for the semivowel /w/, and eventually became Roman <f>, and upsilon (bare "u"), which was used in Greek for a vowel, and in classical Latin for both /w/ and /u/.
10. Kurath (1964), 67.
11. *OED*, under the letter <h> (Murray et al., 1933, vol. 5, p. 1).
12. *Hospital, heritage*, and *humble* also had silent <h> up to the 18th century.
13. *Exhale* and its compounds are the primary exceptions.
14. *Marijuana* also has <j> → /ø/.
15. In words with final <ng> (e.g., *long, strong*), the /g/ that shifted /n/ to /ŋ/ has been lost (cf., however, *stronger* and *longer*, where the /g/ is retained).
16. For more on this assimilation process, see Katamba (1989), 91, and Kurath (1964), 71.
17. Not included here are interjections such as *pshaw, pst/psst, psa, psht*, and *ptui*, where <p> is usually pronounced /p/.
18. The letter <q> represents the Chinese /č/ in Pinyin, a Romanization scheme for Chinese characters, and therefore appears without <u> in Chinese borrowings: *Qin, Qing*. Similarly, <q> transliterates Arabic *qaf* and the corresponding *qoph*: *Qatar, Qadhafi, qibla*.
19. Two nonmedical occurrences are *myrrh*, an aromatic gum resin, and *catarrhine*, a division of primates.
20. Note that in *myrrh* <yrrh> spells an /r/-colored vowel, /ʌr/.
21. A more detailed explanation of this process is given in Chapter 4.

22. Although *Illinois* is of Algonquian origin, its spelling was established by French traders and clerics.

23. *Isle*, which in Middle English was *ile* or *yle*, was borrowed from Old French *ile*, which itself derives from Latin *insula*. In France in the 15th century *ile* began to be spelled *isle* as a result of the classical enthusiasm of the Renaissance, and by 1700 this spelling was established in English. *Aisle*, which was spelled without an <s> in Middle English, was confused with *ily/yle* ("island"), and was refashioned with an <s> as early as the 15th century. By about 1700 the spelling *isle* was established, only to be modified later to *aisle*.

    Island, in contrast, derives from Old English *iland*, but in the 15th century its first part was erroneously associated with the French-derived *ile*. Consequently, when *ile* was respelled with an <s>, *ile-land* followed, becoming *isle-land*, and before 1700 was established as *island*. The full story, with copious examples of these etymologies and orthographic histories, can be found in the *OED* under *aisle*, *isle*, and *island*. A more abbreviated version is given by Scragg (1974), 57.

24. *Righteous* also has <t> + vowel (unstressed) to /č/, but no pattern can be discerned from this single example.

25. A street name in New Orleans.

26. This group can be extended by the addition of <dth> (*hundredth*), <ndth> (*thousandth*), and further <nth> exemplars (*millionth*, *billionth*, *trillionth*, *quadrillionth*, etc.).

27. The use of the suffix <th> to form abstract nouns from verbs and adjectives began in the Old English period and continued into Modern English. In the process of adding /θ/, free vowels became checked, and occasionally a vowel or consonant was lost: *born* → *birth*, *gird* → *girth*, *heal* → *health*, *spill* → *spilth*, *steal* → *stealth*; *dear* → *dearth*, *deep* → *depth*, *foul* → *filth*, *long* → *length*, *merry* → *mirth*, *strong* → *strength*, *wide* → *width*.

28. But <u> in *banquet* corresponds to /w/.

29. Scragg (1974), 81.

30. By the late Middle English period, <u> and <v> were generally avoided in word-final position; where they would occur, an <e> was added.

31. *Leitmotiv* is also spelled *leitmotif*.

32. Comparable to the cases of silent <w>, such as *write* and *toward*, are the spelling problems for /w/ in *one* and *once*, where no <w>'s occur. French borrowings such as *reservoir* present a similar spelling problem.

33. See Venezky (1993), 9f.

34. Dialectal variants of /hw/ are not treated here.

CHAPTER 9

Vowel Patterns

Mechanical mincing cramps the vowels, and
deprives consonants of vocal power.
—JAMES E. MURDOCH (1884), iii

Our regularity principle (Principle 5) continues to be explored in this chapter, but now we switch to vowel patterns. English orthography has two sets of vowel patterns that, like different forms of music, derive from different time periods, have different structures, and appear in different environments. The first set, called the *primary vowel spellings*, dates from the earliest English records. These are the single-letter spellings <a, e, i/y, o, u>, and they appear with great frequency in English words and have the most complex set of correspondence patterns (and exceptions) among all the functional units. The second set, called the *secondary vowel spellings*, occurs less frequently, dates from more recent times, and tends to have rather simple correspondence patterns. These are the digraph and trigraph spellings, such as <ea, ou, eau>. In this chapter the machinations and meanderings of both sets of patterns are discussed.[1]

PRIMARY VOWEL SPELLINGS

The primary vowel spellings carry the major burden of vowel representation in the current orthography. They occur in all word positions and have a vast complexity of correspondences and alternations, which reflect an even more complex history. When viewed from the direct spelling-to-sound standpoint, the patterns for these units reveal no regularity. The letter <o> corresponds to at least 17 different sounds, <a> to 10, <e> to 9, and the combined group to 48. When the morphemic structure and consonant environments of the words in which these units appear are considered, however, a single major pattern emerges, with a bevy of subpatterns. Exceptions still remain (large numbers of them in some cases), but the underlying pattern still dominates, giving a sense of order and tranquility to what originally appeared chaotic and without reason. In the discussion that follows, the major pattern for the stressed primary vowels is introduced in a general form and then refined through the introduction of its regular subpatterns, alternations, and exceptions.[2]

MAJOR PRIMARY PATTERNS

Each of the primary vowel units corresponds regularly to two different phonemes, a checked one and a free one, according to the morphemic structure of the word in which it occurs and the consonant and vowel units that follow it. These correspondences are shown in Table 9.1.

In monomorphemic words, a stressed primary spelling unit corresponds to its free alternate when it is followed by (1) a functionally simple consonant unit that in turn is followed by another vowel unit (including final <e>); or (2) a functionally simple consonant unit, followed by <l> or <r>, and then by another vowel unit (including final <e>).[3] It also corresponds to its free alternate in final position (stressed). It corresponds to its checked alternate in the remaining cases, i.e., when followed by (1) a functionally compound consonant unit (e.g., <x>, <dg>), (2) a cluster of consonant units (e.g., <nm>, <lth>), or (3) a word-final consonant unit or units. Examples of these correspondences are shown in Table 9.2. The column numbers correspond to the numbered qualifications in the sentences above.

A simple vowel spelling, followed by a simple consonant spelling and then <le>, corresponds to its free alternate—for example, *table*. But a geminate consonant cluster before the <le> marks the checked alternate—for example *apple*. Table 9.3 illustrates this pattern, which has a limited distribution. Only <b, p, t, d, f, g, ng> occur more than once before final <le>, and of these, only <b, p, d, t, f> double in this position (<s> and <x> occur before <le> in *measles* and *axle*; <ss> occurs in *tussle*). *Treble*, an exception for the pronunciation of <e>, is the only example in Modern English of the spelling <e> + consonant + <le> in final position. The other common exception to this pattern is *triple*, which has a checked vowel where a free one is indicated.

TABLE 9.1.   Major Pattern for Primary Vowels

Spelling	Free alternate	Checked alternate
<a>	/e/	/æ/
	sane	sanity
	mate	mat
	nation	national
	table	babble
<e>	/i/	/ɛ/
	athlete	athletic
	mete	met
	penal	pennant
	discrete	discretion
<i>	/ai/	/ɪ/
	site	sit
	malign	malignant
	silage	silly
	title	tittle
<o>	/o/	/a/
	cone	conic
	robe	rob
	probity	possible
	verbose	verbosity
<u>	/ju/*	/ʌ/
	induce	induction
	rude	rudder
	lucre	luxury
	runic	run

*The pronunciation of /ju/ alternates with /u/ and /ɪu/.

TABLE 9.2.   Examples of Primary Vowel Correspondences for Selected Environments

Spelling	Free alternate		Checked alternate		
	1	2	1	2	3
<a>	canine	ladle	badge	saddle	sat
<e>	median	zebra	exit	antenna	ebb
<i>	pilot	microbe	chicken	epistle	hitch
<o>	vogue	noble	pocket	cognate	sod
<u>	dubious	lucre	luxury	supper	rug

TABLE 9.3.   The <le> Pattern

Spelling	Free alternate	Checked alternate
<a>	*ladle*	*addle*
<e>	—	*pebble*
<i>	*rifle*	*riffle*
<o>	*noble*	*cobble*
<u>	*ruble*	*rubble*

The vowel spellings in stressed final position, which are not shown above, are few in number and admit a few exceptions. The article *a* can be either /e/ or, more commonly when unstressed, /ə/. The first-person singular pronoun, *I*, is only /aɪ/. Among the two- and three-letter spellings with final vowels, the tones of the diatonic scale—*do*, *re*, *me*, *fa*, *so* (also spelled *sol*), *la*, and *ti*—represent a special group. All are borrowings from Italian, but only two, *re* and *ti*, are irregular. Among the other two- and three-letter spellings, the spellings with final <a> are all pronounced /a/, as in *ma* and *pa*. The <e> spellings are totally regular except for the unstressed variant of *the*, which has /ə/ when spoken in phrases or sentences. The letter <i> in final, stressed position is rare; *bi*, *di-*, *hi*, and *pi* are regular, and *ski* is not. Spellings with final <o>, particularly among the monosyllabic words, have four familiar exceptions: *do*, *to*, *two*, and *who*. To be regular, these should be spelled with <u> rather than <o>, but <u> is generally not allowed at the end of English words, so <o> was substituted several centuries ago. The common occurrences of final, stressed <u> are the spelling reform creation *thru*, which is labeled "informal" in some dictionaries; *flu*, a back-formation from *influenza*; and two late 18th-century borrowings, *gnu* (African) and *tabu* (Polynesian, but more commonly spelled *taboo*).

PRIMARY SUBPATTERNS

The two most important subpatterns that can be derived from the major pattern are those for final <e> and for geminate consonants. Examples of these are shown in Table 9.4.

Final-<e> Pattern

Although the pattern for final <e> applies primarily to monosyllabic words, it also holds for many polysyllabic words, even when the vowel before the final <e> is unstressed, as in *microbe*, *decade*, and *schedule*. Besides the patterns

TABLE 9.4. Examples of the Patterns for Final <e> and Geminate Consonants

Spelling	Final-<e> pattern	Geminate consonant pattern
<a>	*rate–rat*	*anal–annals*
<e>	*mete–met*	*Peter–petter*
<i>	*site–sit*	*diner–dinner*
<o>	*pope–pop*	*coma–comma*
<u>	*cute–cut*	*super–supper*

mentioned above (vowel + consonant + <e>, vowel + consonant + <le>, vowel + consonant + <re>), <a> + <ste> is also part of the final-<e> pattern, as in *baste*, *chaste*, and *haste*. Examples of regular correspondences are shown in Table 9.5.

Geminate Consonant Pattern

The primary vowel spellings <a, e, i/y, o, u> occur frequently before geminate consonants; the digraph (secondary) spellings rarely do.[4] (The French borrowings *Braille*, *chauffeur*, and *trousseau* are the only common exceptions.) Before geminate consonant clusters, primary vowel spellings correspond to their checked alternates (see Table 9.6), with the following exceptions:

1. <a> in *mamma* corresponds to /a/, and <a> in *marshmallow* corresponds to /ɛ/.
2. <o> in *across*, *albatross*, and *boss* and before <ff> corresponds to /ɔ/ (e.g., *coffee*, *offer*).
3. <o> in *gross*, and before final <ll> (except for *doll*), corresponds to /o/.
4. <u> in *butte* corresponds to /ju/, and <u> in *pudding* and *pussy* corresponds to /ʊ/.

TABLE 9.5. Examples of the Final-<e> Pattern

<a> → /e/	<e> → /i/	<i/y> → /ai/	<o> → /o/	<u> → /ju/
bake	*accede*	*cycle*	*cove*	*cube*
decade	*impede*	*domicile*	*erode*	*duke*
fable	*obsolete*	*five*	*globe*	*mule*
gage	*scheme*	*prize*	*joke*	*produce*
haste	*serene*	*profile*	*mediocre*	*resume*
shake	*theme*	*sublime*	*smoke*	*secure*

TABLE 9.6. Examples of Regular Correspondences before Geminate Consonants

\<a\> → /æ/	\<e\> → /ɛ/	\<i/y\> → /ɪ/	\<o\> → /a/	\<u\> → /ʌ/
abbess	*appellate*	*artillery*	*accommodate*	*button*
accent	*beggar*	*bacillus*	*collar*	*funnel*
apple	*bellow*	*blizzard*	*college*	*funny*
Babbittry	*cellar*	*cribbage*	*comma*	*hullabaloo*
cabbage	*cheddar*	*issue*	*commerce*	*hummock*
callow	*dilemma*	*million*	*dollar*	*mummy*
fallacy	*pebble*	*dinner*	*hobby*	*puddle*
flabby	*fellow*	*symmetry*	*hollow*	*pummel*
grammar	*kennel*	*vanilla*	*lobby*	*rubber*
happen	*lesson*	*village*	*sonnet*	*shutter*
mammal	*message*	*willow*	*toboggan*	*supper*
rattle	*tennis*	*wriggle*	*toggle*	*tunnel*

CONSONANT INFLUENCES

\<r\>

Postvocalic \<r\> is the source of not only a wide variation in vowel pronunciations across dialects, but also a complex and sometimes irregular development of spelling-to-sound correspondences. The selection of transcriptions of postvocalic \<r\> words is arbitrary in some cases. One speaker may alternate freely between such forms as /ziro /and /zɪro/, /mɛri/and /meri/, /born/ and /bɔrn/. Some speakers use contrasting pronunciations for *horse–hoarse*, *for–four*, *marry– merry–Mary*, and some do not. In the transcriptions used here, /e/ and /i/ have coalesced with /ɛ/ and /ɪ/ before /r/. Dialect and idiolect variation between /a/ and /o/ and between /ɔ/ and /o/ is indicated by /a/ ~ /o/ and /ɔ/ ~ /o/, as in *orange*, *forest*, *glory*, and *orient*; the syllabic peak in words such as *bird*, *word*, and *urge* is symbolized phonemically as /ʌr/.

Correspondences

The correspondences of a primary vowel spelling before \<r\> (in the same syllable) depend on the environment following \<r\>. Three cases must be considered:

1. Following a vowel unit, which in turn is followed by a vowel unit or juncture.
2. Following a vowel unit, which in turn is followed by a consonant, or \<r\> followed by \<r\>.
3. Following a consonant or juncture.

The correspondences for the primary vowel spellings are shown in Table 9.7. Environments 1, 2, and 3 refer to the descriptions just given. The "<r>" columns contain the correspondences for the vowels before <r>; the "Normal" column contains the correspondences normally anticipated for that environment, but with any consonant except <r>. Where /ʌ/ is shown, the actual vowel is /ɜ/.

Examples:

Environment 1

<a>	beware, malaria, nefarious, secretary
<e>	adhere, cereal, exterior, sphere
<i>	dire, inquiry, hire, wire
<o>	adore, glory, more, shore
<u>	bureau, cure, mature, spurious

Environment 2

<a>	arid, arrogate, marriage, tariff
<e>	austerity, errand, peril, terrace
<i>	empiric, irrigate, miracle, mirror
<o>	borrow, foreign, horrid, orange
<u>	burr, current, furrier, hurry

Environment 3

<a>	alarm, carve, gargle, star
<e>	herb, erstwhile, her, infer
<i>	bird, girl, virtue, whirl
<o>	adorn, formula, or, storm
<u>	cur, spur, urge, urn

TABLE 9.7.   Vowel Correspondences before <r>

Spelling	Environment 1		Environment 2		Environment 3	
	<r>	Normal	<r>	Normal	<r>	Normal
<a>	/ɛ/	/e/	/æ/	/æ/	/a/	/æ/
<e>	/ɪ/	/i/	/ɛ/	/ɛ/	/ʌ/	/ɛ/
<i>	/aɪ/	/aɪ/	/ɪ/	/ɪ/	/ʌ/	/ɪ/
<o>	/ɔ/ ~ /o/	/o/	/a/ ~ /o/	/a/	/o/ ~ /ɔ/	/a/
<u>	/ju/	/ju/	/ʌ/	/ʌ/	/ʌ/	/ʌ/

Exceptions:

Environment 1

\<a\>	*are, aria, safari*
\<e\>	*very*
\<i\>	*delirium*
\<u\>	*bury*

Environment 2

\<a\>	*alarum, catarrh, harem*
\<e\>	*err*
\<i\>	*iris, irony, siren, spiral, squirrel, stirrup, tirade, virus*
\<o\>	*borough, thorough, worry*
\<u\>	*mural, urine*

Environment 3

\<a\>	*scarce*
\<e\>	*concerto, sergeant*
\<o\>	*attorney*

\<l\>

Before final \<ll\> and medial or final clusters composed of a pronounced \<l\> plus another consonant, \<a\> corresponds not to /æ/ but to /ɔ/, as in *almanac, alternation, call, chalk, mall, psalm,* and *walk.*[5] This shift does not occur before medial \<ll\>, however. Compare, for example, *call–calliper, fall–fallacy,* and *mall–mallard.* Before a silent \<l\> plus another consonant, \<a\> usually corresponds to /a/ (*almond, balm, calm,* etc.). The letter \<o\> before final \<ll\> or \<l\> plus consonant corresponds to /o/ rather than to /a/ (*bold, folk,* etc.).[6] Once again, however, medial \<ll\> does not have the same influence as final \<ll\>: Compare *boll–bollard, poll–pollen.* That the other three vowels are not influenced by final \<ll\> can be seen from examples such as *bell–bellow, fill–filly,* and *gull–gullet.* The letter \<i\>, however, does correspond to its free alternate before \<ld\>, as explained below under "Miscellaneous Consonant Influences."

\<w\>

With the exception of the \<a\> + \<l\> patterns discussed above, \<a\> preceded by initial \<w\> in a checked environment corresponds to /æ/ before spellings for velars (/k, g, ŋ/) and to /a/ otherwise. Compare *swath, wad, waffle, wander*; *wax, wag, waggle, wangle* (but not *swam*). This pattern also holds when <a> occurs between <qu> and <l>: *equality, squall, squalid*. With many of the <w> + <a> words, there is considerable dialectal variation (e.g., *want, wash, water*).

The sequence <o> + <r> preceded by <w> corresponds to /ʌr/ (e.g., *worm, worth*), except for *worn*, which has <o> → /o/.

Miscellaneous Consonant Influences

The letter <i> before final <nd, ld, gn>, or <gm> corresponds to its free alternate (/aɪ/) rather than its checked alternate (/ɪ/).

<nd>	*behind*	*grind*	*remind*
	bind	*hind*	*rind*
	blind	*kind*	*wind* (verb)
	find	*mind*	
<ld>	*child*	*mild*	*wild* (but *gild*)
<gn>	*align*	*design*	
	assign	*malign*	
	benign	*resign*	
	consign	*sign*	
<gm>	*paradigm*		

Before <ff, ft, ss, st, th>, <o> corresponds to /ɔ/ rather than /a/: *off, coffee, loft, loss, lost, moth*. Exceptions occur primarily for <st>: *ghost, host, most, post*.

<gh>

Of the simple vowel spellings, only <i> occurs before <gh>, and in this environment <i> corresponds invariably to /aɪ/ and <gh> to /ø/: *blight, light, thigh*.

SUFFIX PATTERNS

A number of suffixes signal a shift from a free to a checked alternate—for example, *cone–conic, align–malignant, verbose–verbosity*. These patterns are discussed in Chapter 10.

STRESS PATTERNS AND SCHWA

In unstressed positions, simple vowel spellings sometimes retain their stressed correspondences (e.g., *nomadic*); more often, however, they reduce to schwa, the neutral, unstressed vowel heard in the first syllable of *away* and the last syllable of *soda*. This is the most difficult sound to predict in the entire orthographic system. In many words, furthermore, schwa alternates with /ɪ/ or /ɛ/. For example, in *civil* the last syllable tends to reduce to schwa in fast speech, but to remain /ɪ/ when pronounced more deliberately. In *business* the last syllable is generally /ɛ/ or /ə/, but is also occasionally /ɪ/ in less careful speech.

In some unstressed prefixes and suffixes, schwa occurs regularly. Examples include initial <a> (*ahead*, *across*), <un> (*unable*, *unkind*), and final <tion> (*function*, *nation*). In some stress patterns schwa is also generally predictable—for instance, in the first syllable in trisyllabic words with stress on the middle syllable (*appellate*, *configure*, *successive*). But exceptions occur (e.g., *location*, *prudential*). Similarly, in trisyllabic words with primary stress on the first syllable and secondary stress on the last syllable, the middle syllable usually reduces to schwa (e.g., *analyze*, *homophone*, *paradigm*, *strategy*). In English the main word stress can often be predicted by eliminating, as candidates for the main word stress, prefixes and suffixes that are rarely stressed. Final <y> in multisyllabic words, for example, falls into this category, with the exception of *ally*, *apply*, *awry*, *comply*, *decry*, *deny*, *descry*, *imply*, *reply*, and *supply*. In multisyllabic words, final <ity> is never stressed, nor are final <ing, ness, hood, ment, ance, ence, ist, ism, ist>, among others.

Certain spellings tend to require the primary word stress, such as the endings <oon, aire, ade, ette, and ique>.[7] However, exceptions occur (e.g., *palette*, *etiquette*, *solitaire*). Other endings tend to require that the primary stress be fixed on a different syllable. For example, final <nal> generally requires the main word stress on the third syllable from the end (e.g., *diagonal*, *phenomenal*, *vocational*), with the penultimate syllable generally reduced to schwa. But several exceptions occur: *autumnal*, *communal*, *tribunal*, and words that have /ʌr/ in the penultimate syllable (*diurnal*, *eternal*, *maternal*, etc.). For final <ique>, the main word stress is always on the <i> (*oblique*, *physique*, *technique*, etc.), while final <ize> and <ist> behave like final <nal>: *apologize*, *equalize*; *oxidize*: *empiricist*, *idealist*, *psychiatrist* (but *extremist* and *propagandist*). Other suffixes that determine stress patterns include <ity> and <ic>. More complex patterns can be described for predicting stress, but these move us far beyond orthography and are not pursued further here. The interested reader should consult the works cited in notes 1 and 3.

EXCEPTIONS

For reasons that remain unresolved—but that are probably tied both to the different articulation movements for consonants and vowels, and to the cortical organization for speech perception—vowels tend to vary, both across dialects and across time, far more than consonants. This distinction holds even across languages. Therefore, the exceptions that exist to the various vowel patterns just described represent a formidable list in comparison to the consonant exceptions. Most can be explained through appeal to historical changes or to borrowings, but each word and each exception has its own history, and a volume or two could be filled with these explanations. What follows is a general treatment of exceptions, with highlighting of many that occur in common words. For more exhaustive treatments, see the works cited in note 1.

For the primary spellings in checked environments, correspondences are relatively consistent. The major difficulty occurs with primary spellings in free environments; primarily because of borrowings and phonological shortenings (many of which occurred almost 1,000 years ago), quite a number of such spellings correspond to their checked rather than their free alternates. Thus we have *study*, *body*, and *copy*, which are irregular, alongside *baby*, *bony*, *tiny*, and *zany*, which are regular. Similarly, we have *comet*, *edit*, *model*, and *solid* alongside *coma*, *edict*, *modal*, and *solar*. Most irregularities occur with a stressed vowel before a simple consonant unit, followed by another vowel. In all other environments, given the subpatterns just described, correspondences are more regular.

One small group of words merits special attention, because what appear to be exceptions can be explained through the marking system of English orthography. In words like *acre*, *lucre*, *mediocre*, and *ogre*, a stressed vowel before a consonant cluster has its free pronunciation where the checked pronunciation is expected. However, these are special cases where the normal final spellings <cer> and <ger> cannot be used, because the <e> after <c> or <g> would mark a soft rather than a hard pronunciation. Phonologically, these are still environments in which the free pronunciations of the vowels are expected.

Exceptions to the Final-<e> Pattern

For the final-<e> pattern, a number of irregularities exist, although in general this is a rather regular pattern. The letter <a> corresponds to /æ/ in *bade*, *forbade*, *have*, and *morale*. It corresponds to /a/ in *are*, *barrage*, *camouflage*, *corsage*, *facade*, *garage*, *massage*, *mirage*, and *sabotage*. In the ending <ate>, <a> corresponds to /e/ in verbs, but alternates to /ɪ/ in nouns and adjectives. Compare *duplicate* (verb) with *duplicate* (adjective, noun). (The stress patterns are also different in these forms.)

The letter <e> corresponds to /ɛ/ in *allege, clientele, ere, there, treble,* and *where*;[8] to /ɪ/ in *renege;* to /ʌr/ in *were;* and to /e/ in *fete.* The letter <i> corresponds to /i/ in *bastile,*[9] *caprice, elite, machine, marine, police, prestige, ravine, regime, routine, sardine, tangerine,* and *valise,* and to /ɪ/ in *give* and *live.* (The spelling <i> is highly irregular in the ending <ine> when it does not receive the primary word stress; compare *canine–examine, marine–margarine.*)

The letter <o> corresponds to /ʌ/ in *above, come, done, dove, glove, love, none, shove,* and *some;* to /u/ in *lose, move, prove,* and *whose; and* to /ɔ/ in *gone.* The letter <u>, surprisingly, has no exceptions in the final-<e> pattern among common words.

Other Exceptions

<a>

One of the largest groups of exceptions to the vowel patterns occurs for <a> → /a/, as in *father* and *spa.* Most of these correspondences are in relatively recent borrowings. Besides the examples already noted in the final-<e> exceptions and in the <l> and <w> subpatterns, <a> → /a/ also occurs at the end of a number of two- and three-letter words, where it is the only common correspondence for <a> (*bra, ma, spa*); in several imitative words (*mamma, papa*); in many Italian borrowings (*adagio, bravado, cantata,* etc.); and in a handful of borrowings from other languages: *drama* (late Latin), *padre* (Spanish), *pajamas* (Hindi), *wigwam* (Algonquian), *yacht* (Dutch). In eastern New England speech, many more /a/ pronunciations for <a> occur, but the details of such dialect variation are beyond the scope of this book.

A smaller group of exceptions for <a> occurs before <mb>, where an /e/ pronunciation generally occurs: *cambric, chamber, Cambridge* (but not in *gambit* and *gambol*). Similarly, stressed <a> before final <nge> is usually pronounced /e/: *change, grange, range* (the one exception being *flange*). The pronunciation /e/ is also found before final <ste>: *baste, chaste* (compare *chastity*), *paste.* This is not a general pattern for <a> before <st> (note *aster* and *disaster*), but it does hold for final <ste> and for *pastry.* Among the miscellaneous exceptions for <a> are /e/ in the musical term *bass,* and /ɛ/ in *any* and *many.*

<e>

The letter <e> tends to be better behaved than <a>, at least for stressed positions within a word. Most common among exceptions, besides the few mentioned already, are French borrowings where <e> is pronounced /e/. Many of these are marked in French (and occasionally in English) with an acute (é) or grave (è) accent or circumflex (ê) over the <e>: *ballét, crêpe, née, suède*. This letter is also pronounced /e/ in *Beowulf,* which derives from Old English. In another group of French borrowings, <e> is pronounced /a/, as in *encore* and *entrée* (first <e>); in *England, English,* and *pretty,* it is pronounced /ɪ/.

<i>

The letter <i> is also relatively well behaved, the most common exceptions being the free pronunciation, /aɪ/, where a checked pronunciation is expected: *Christ, climb* (but *limb*), *indict, island, isle, ninth,* and *viscount.* In a miscellaneous group of borrowings, it is /i/: *chic, fatigue, kilo* (French); *lido, primadonna* (Italian); and *Sikh* (Hindi). And in a small group of French borrowings, it is /a/: *lingerie, Rodin.* (But note the exceptions listed in the introduction to this section and under the final-<e> exceptions.)

<o>

The letter <o> has the notorious exception /ɪ/ in *women,* along with four other pronunciations besides its free and checked alternates, /a/ and /o/. A number of <o> spellings for /ʌ/ (*son, money, wonder,* etc.) result from a Middle English respelling of <u> in certain letter environments (see Chapter 6). Next in number are the /o/ → /ɔ/ patterns, which occur before <st> (*acrostic, cost, lost*—but not *ghost, most, post*), final <th> (*moth, Roth*—but not *both*), <ff> (*coffee, off, office*), final <ft> (*loft, soft*), and final <ss> (*boss, loss, moss*—but not *gross*). The pronunciation /ɔ/ also occurs in a number of American English dialects for words like *dog, log,* and *logarithm,* but the pattern is often highly irregular. Finally for the alternate pronunciations, <o> is pronounced either /u/ or /ʊ/ in a small number of words: *lose, move, movie, tomb* (/u/); *bosom, wolf, woman* (/ʊ/).

Among the exceptions to the checked–free patterns for <o> that have not already been discussed is an exceptional group where the free pronunciation, /ʊ/, occurs before final <l>: *control, extol* (also spelled *extoll*), *patrol.* These may be influenced by the vowel pronunciations in words with final <ll, ld, lt>, such as *roll, cold,* and *bolt.* The free pronunciation for <o> also occurs exceptionally in such French borrowings as *apropos, chaperon,* and *depot.* Before consonants that typically do not double (e.g., <v>), and before a number of suffixes (e.g., <logy, nomy, ic>), <o> has its checked pronunciation where its free pronunciation is expected: *novel, poverty, cosmology, economy, tropic, velocity.*

<u>

The letter <u> is silent in the ending <que>, as in *plaque* and *unique*, and occasionally elsewhere after <q>, as in *liquor* and *mosquito*. It is also silent in *build*, *guard*, and *guarantee*, but in *circuit*, *guide*, and similar <c> and <g> environments, it is a marker for the "hard" pronunciations of these two consonants. In *lettuce* and *minute* (of time), it has the pronunciation /ɪ/; after the labial consonants /b/, /p/, and /f/ and generally before /l/, <u> is pronounced /ʊ/ (*bull, bulb, pulpit*). But /ʊ/ also occurs before other consonants, as in *butcher, pudding, bush,* and *cushion*. Finally, the free pronunciation, /u/, occurs in a few words where the checked pronunciation is expected: *impugn, lubricant, lugubrious* (second <u>), and *nuclear*.

SECONDARY VOWEL SPELLINGS

The secondary vowel spellings differ from the primary vowel spellings in several important ways. First, the secondary spellings occur less frequently and have a more limited distribution. None appears commonly before geminate consonant clusters; some, such as <ai, au, ei, eu>, rarely occur in word-final position; others, such as <ie>, rarely occur in word-initial position. Second, although each primary vowel spelling has two basic correspondences, according to the graphemic environment and the morphemic composition of the word in which it occurs, each secondary vowel spelling generally has a single major correspondent. Third, the correspondences based upon the secondary vowel spellings tend not to alternate in quality with reduction in stress. Compare, for example, the first vowels in *neutral–neutrality* and *cause–causation* with those in *melody–melodious* and *telegraph–telegraphy*.

Historically, the secondary spellings also differ from the primary ones. Primary vowel spellings are found in the earliest English records, and their correspondences can be traced through a complicated chain of sound changes from Old English to the present. Most secondary vowel spellings, on the other hand, were introduced during the late Middle English period and consequently have been involved in considerably fewer sound changes.

Correspondences for the secondary vowel spellings follow, divided into major and minor categories on the basis of frequency of occurrence in different English words. These correspondences are arranged alphabetically within categories, with the exception of spellings that end in <w> or <y>. As explained in Chapter 3, <u> and <w>, and <i> and <y>, alternate as second elements of secondary vowel spellings, <u> and <i> typically occur before consonants, and <w> and

<y> occur before vowels and in word-final position. Thus we have *day* but *daily*, *caw* but *cause*. Exceptions do occur, especially for <w> spellings before consonants (e.g., *dawn, pewter, town*) and for <u> in final position (e.g., *you, thou, bureau*), but the pattern is so pervasive that the various spellings can be treated as positional alternates (with the exceptions of <ui> and <eau>, which have no related <y> or <w> forms.)[10]

MAJOR SECONDARY PATTERNS

<ai> and <ay>

The digraphs <ai> and <ay> commonly correspond to /e/, as in *aim, trait, day*, and *player*. Before /r/, however, /e/ shifts to the lax form /ɛ/, as in *air, chair*, and *prairie*. The correspondence <ai> → /ɛ/ also occurs in *again, against*, and *said*. With rare exceptions, <ai> appears before consonants, whereas <ay> appears before vowels and in final position.

In 16 relatively common multisyllabic words, an unstressed <ai> is reduced to /ə/ or /ɪ/. These include four nautical compounds (*boatswain, coxswain, mainsail, topsail*), plus *captain, certain, Chamberlain, chaplain, curtain, fountain, mountain, plantain, porcelain, portrait, villain*, and *wassail* (and their inflected and compounded forms). That this reduction occurs primarily before /n/ and /l/ is curious; too few examples are available, however, to suggest a rule.

Other uncommon pronunciations include:

/æ/   *plaid*
/i/   *plait*,[11] *quay*,[12] and days of the week (*Monday, Tuesday*, etc.)[13]
/ai/ *aisle, aye, bayou, cayenne, Kaiser, Taiwan, Shanghai, Sinai*

<au> and <aw>

The digraphs <au> and <aw> commonly correspond to /ɔ/, as in *audience, cause*, and *thaw*. The spelling <au> almost always occurs before consonants, while <aw> occurs before vowels and at the ends of words. Exceptions are few: French borrowings with /o/ (*chauffeur, chauvinist, hautboy, mauve*); German borrowings with /au/ (Faust, sauerkraut, umlaut); *gauge* (/e/); and *aunt, draught*, and *laugh* (/æ/).

<ea>

About 63 percent of all common <ea> spellings not occurring before /r/ are pronounced /i/, as in *each, beam*, and *meat*. Another 27 percent are pronounced /ɛ/, as in *bread*, *leather*, and *weapon*. The remaining 10 percent are spread across three pronunciations:

/e/   *break, great, steak, yea*
/ə/   *hydrangea,*[14] *ocean,*[15] *pageant, sergeant, vengeance*
/ɪ/   *Chelsea, Guinea*

Before /r/, /i/ shifts to the lax form /ɪ/, as in *ear*, *dreary*, and *shears*. In about a dozen <ear> words, /ɪr/ has shifted to an /r/-colored vowel, /ʌr/ (*earl*, *early*, *earn*, *earth*, etc.). Other <ear> pronunciations include the following:

/a/   *heart, hearken, hearth*
/ɛ/   *bear, pear, swear, tear* (verb), *wear*[16]

The /i/ ~ /ɛ/ variation for <ea> (e.g., *bead* ~ *bread*) generally cannot be predicted from other features of a word's spelling. The sequence <eal>, however, is usually pronounced /ɛl/ (*health, realm, wealth*), and <ea> before <sure> is usually pronounced /ɛ/ also (*measure, pleasure, treasure*). For a few spellings (e.g., *lead, read*), both pronunciations occur as distinct words. The <ea> → /ɛ/ words that occur among the 20,000 most common words in English (aside from the <eal> and <ea> + <sure> words) are shown here. These words do not include inflectional and derivational forms, such as *abreast, ahead,* and *zealot.*

bread	dread	leaven	sweater
breadth	dreamt	meadow	thread
breakfast	endeavor	meant	threat
breast	feather	peasant	treachery
breath	head	pheasant	tread
cleanliness	heaven	read	treadle
cleanly	heavy	ready	wealth
cleanse	instead	realm	weapon
dead	jealous	spread	weather
deaf	lead	stead	zealous
death	leather	sweat	

<ee>

The digraph <ee> occurs primarily in medial and final position, the only common initial occurrences being *eel* and *eerie*. Before /r/, <ee> corresponds to /ɪ/, as in *beer* and *deer*; otherwise it corresponds to /i/, as in *absentee* and *seed*. Rarer correspondences include French borrowings with final <ee> → /e/ (*matinee*, *melee*), and a handful of words with <ee> → /ɪ/ (*been, breeches, creek* [dialect], *Poughkeepsie*) *levee, toffee, Yankee; Milwaukee* (in fast speech).

<ei> and <ey>

The digraph <ei> almost always occurs before consonants; <ey> occurs before vowels (e.g., *abeyance*) and in final position. Before /r/, <ei> is either /ɛ/ (*heir, their*) or /ɪ/ (*weird, weir*). The sequence <eir> is rare, however. Otherwise stressed <ei> or <ey> is generally pronounced /e/, as in *obey, reign,* and *veil*; final, unstressed <ey> is almost always pronounced /ɪ/, as in *abbey, alley, donkey,* and *money.*

One group of exceptions include French borrowings with <ei> → /ɪ/ (*foreign, forfeit, surfeit*) and German borrowings with <ei> → /aɪ/ (*Frankenstein, gneiss, Holstein*[17]). Another group includes /aɪ/ forms, such as *eye, geyser* (Icelandic), *height,* and *Oneida* (Iroquoian); /i/ forms, such as *caffeine, conceit,* and *key*; and /ɪ/ and /ɛ/ forms such as *Raleigh* and *heifer.*

<eu> and <ew>

The digraphs <eu> and <ew>, which correspond generally to /u/ or /ju/, alternate as do the other <u> ~ <w> pairs: <eu> before consonants, <ew> before vowels and at the end of words. Only a few exceptions exist to the /ju/ ~ /u/ pronunciation: /o/ in *sew* (*sewn, sewing,* etc.) and *shew,* and /ər/ in unstressed position in *chauffeur, grandeur,* and *pasteurize.*

The pronunciation of *sew* dates from at least the 14th century, although occasional rhymes with *clue* and *new* are found as late as the 17th century.[18] *Shew,* an obsolete spelling for the verb *show,* was prevalent in the 18th century, but occurs today in the United States only in legal documents. The <ew> in *sew* may have been retained to avoid confusion with *sow* and *so.* Regardless of its origin, it ranks, along with <ew> in *shew,* as one of the great oddities of English orthography.

<ie>

The digraph <ie> occurs only in medial and final position, but has a complicated set of correspondences. To sort these out, two types of pseudodigraphs needed to be identified. The first occurs in such words as *allied, applied,* and *dried,* where <ie> results from a <y> → <i> shift with suffixation: *ally* + <ed> → *allied.* These are treated as <i> → /aɪ/ with silent <e>. Then <ie> in *ancient, brazier, crosier, glacier, patience*, and *transient* is treated similarly, with the vowel (/j/ or /ɪ/) mapped from <i> absorbed in the palatalization of /s/ or /z/.

This leaves one major correspondence for <ie>, /i/, which shifts to the lax form /ɪ/ in unstressed positions at the end of polysyllabics (*achieve, diesel, niece, yield; calorie, collie, eerie, movie*) and before /r/ (*fierce, pier*, etc.). Exceptions include monosyllables that end in <ie> → /aɪ/ (e.g., *die, lie, pie, tie*) and the following flotsam and jetsam:

/e/	*lingerie*
/ɪ/	*sieve*
/ɛ/	*friend*

The monosyllables that end in <ie> could be treated as <i> → /aɪ/, with <e> as a silent letter, added to avoid expansion of the list of two-letter words (cf. *doe, hoe*, etc.). For practical reasons, the <ie> solution is preferred here.

<oa>

As a digraph spelling, <oa> occurs only in initial and medial position and has almost invariantly a single pronunciation, /o/ (*oak, oath, boat, soap*, etc.). The exceptions are *broad* and its compounds, which have /ɔ/, and *board* as an unstressed second element in noun compounds (*clapboard, cupboard, larboard, starboard*), which has /ər/.

<oi> and <oy>

The digraphs <oi> and <oy> alternate, as do the other <i> ~ <y> digraphs, with <oi> occurring before consonants and <oy> occurring before vowels and at the ends of words. The only exceptions are *oyster* and *gargoyle*, where <oi> is expected. Generally <oi> or <oy> corresponds to /ɔɪ/ as in *oil, oyster*, and *toy*. The exceptions are *coyote* (/aɪ/) and a group of French borrowings that have various pronunciations:

/i/	*chamois*
/waɪ/	*choir*
/ə/	*mademoiselle,*[19] *porpoise, tortoise*
/wa/	*boudoir, coif, memoir, niçoise, patois, reservoir, repertoire, soirée*
/ər/	*avoirdupois*

<oo>

The digraph <oo> occurs mostly in medial position, with smaller numbers of exemplars in initial and final positions: *oodles, oompah, ooze; igloo, taboo, too, zoo*. Its most common pronunciation is /u/, as in *boot, proof,* and *tycoon*. (Unlike other /u/ spellings, <oo> is never <ju>.) The most common exception is /ʊ/, which occurs in about 20 common words (e.g., *book, boor, brook, good, shook*). The other exceptions are /ʌ/ (*blood, flood*), /o/ (*brooch, Roosevelt*), and /ər/ (*whippoorwill*).

<ou> and <ow>

The digraphs <ou> and <ow> alternate as do the other <u> ~ <w> digraphs, but with exceptions: Both <ou> and <ow> occur before consonants (*could, ounce, our; owl, own, town*) and in final position (*caribou, manitou, you; cow, show, tow*).[20] The correspondences for <ou> and <ow> are equally challenging, given that besides the major correspondence, /au/, there are a variety of minor correspondences as shown here:

1. /o/: a. In final position, /o/ correspondences far outnumber /au/ correspondences (*arrow, glow, pillow*, etc. vs. *how, trow,* etc.).

   b. In a number of words, <ou> or <ow> before <l> or <gh> maps to /o/: *boulder, mould, soul, although, borough, furlough.*

   c. The correspondence <ou>/<ow> → /o/ also occurs in a miscellaneous group: *bouquet,[21] cantaloupe, owe, own.*

2. /ɔ/: Before <gh> and <ght>, /ɔ/ also occurs: *bought, fought, wrought.*

3. /ʌ/: About a dozen <ou> spellings are pronounced /ʌ/, including *enough, tough, country, touch.*

4. /ʊ/: The correspondence <ou> → /ʊ/ occurs in about a dozen words, including *should, boulevard, detour, velour.*

5. /u/: a. In final position, <ou> → /u/ is common: *bayou, bijou, caribou, you.*

   b. The correspondence <ou> → /u/ is also common in about two dozen French borrowings other than the words with final <ou>: *accouter, coupon, group, troubadour, vermouth.*

   c. This correspondence also occurs in a miscellaneous group of words, including several from Old and Middle English, where /u/ failed to change to /aʊ/ during the Great Vowel Shift: *croup, ghoul, route, stoup, through, uncouth, wound* (noun).

6. /ə/: The pronunciation /ə/ occurs in the ending <ous> and in *camouflage, Marlborough, limousine, Monmouth, Newfoundland, Portsmouth,* and *tambourine.*

7. /ər/: The British spellings *colour, honour, neighbour*; also *glamour.*

8. /ʌr/: *Bourbon, bourgeois, courage, courier, Missouri, tournament.*

9. /a/: *Knowledge* (compare *know*).

10. /w/: *Bivouac.*

<ui> and <uy>

Although <ui> and <uy> are presented together here, their occurrences do not parallel the other <i> ~ <y> digraphs. For example, <uy> occurs only in *buy* and *guy*, and its pronunciation (/aɪ/) does not occur for <ui>. In addition, many <ui> occurrences are pseudodigraphs, in that the <u> has been inserted to mark a hard pronunciation of <c> or <g>: *biscuit, beguile, guidance, guillotine, roguish.* Of the remaining correspondences, <ui> → /u/ (*bruise, fruit, juice, recruit*) represents the regular correspondence. The correspondence <ui> → /ɪ/ occurs only in *build* and its various inflected forms.

MINOR SECONDARY PATTERNS

<aa>

The spelling <aa> occurs in a few Afrikaans borrowings (*aardvark, aardwolf, kraal, laager*), in a few German borrowings (e.g., *Saar*), and in transliterations of a few Hebrew names and Yiddish words (e.g., *Aaron, meshugaas*). Except for *Aaron*, where it is pronounced /æ/ or /ɛ/, <aa> is pronounced /a/.

<ae>

The digraph <ae> occurs in a small number of borrowings and with several different pronunciations. It is /e/ in *Gaelic*, in *maelstrom* (Dutch), and in Greek names such as *Phaedra*. It is also /e/ in the name *Mae* (e.g., Mae West). In the Latin *maenad*, <ae> is pronounced /i/; in the Italian *maestro*, it is pronounced /aɪ/.

<eau>

In most French borrowings with <eau>, the spelling occurs in word-final position and is pronounced /o/: *beau, bureau, chateau, plateau, portmanteau, tableau, trousseau*. It is also /o/ in other positions in some French borrowings (e.g., *beaux arts*), but in *beauty* it is /ju/ and in *bureaucracy* it is /a/, changing to /ə/ in unstressed derivatives (e.g., *bureaucrat*).

<eo>

A common Old English spelling that was borrowed after the Norman Conquest into French, <eo> then returned to English in a few loan words: *jeopardy* (/ɛ/), *leopard* (/ɛ/), and *people* (/i/). *Yeoman* (/o/), a Middle English invention, was spelled with <eo> from the 15th century.

The digraph <eo> also occurs in *escutcheon, luncheon, puncheon,* and *truncheon*, corresponding to /ə/. In *bludgeon, dungeon, gudgeon, pigeon, sturgeon,* and *surgeon,* <e> is a marker for <g> → / ǰ/, and therefore <eo> is not treated as a secondary vowel spelling in these words. (This is not strictly true historically for all <dg> words, but common spelling practices, as reflected in the retention of <e> in words such as *knowledgeable,* treat <e> as a required marker after <dg>.)

<ieu> and <iew>

The spellings <ieu> and <iew> occur in a few French loan words, all with /u/ or /ju/ pronunciations: *adieu, lieutenant, lieu, purlieu; view (interview, preview, review)*.

<oe>

The digraph <oe> is a marginal unit, because most of its examples are three-letter words where the final <e> was added to avoid expansion of the two-letter stock (*doe, foe, hoe, roe, toe, woe*). It does occur with the pronunciation /u/ in *canoe* and *shoe*, however, and with /i/ in Greek borrowings such as *amoeba, Oedipus, pharmacopoeia, and Phoenix*. In Greek borrowings, British English tends to retain <oe> spellings more often than American English. Thus *esophagus* is found in the United States but *oesophagus* in England, although the U.S. spelling does occasionally occur there also.

\<ue\>

Like \<oe\>, \<ue\> has marginal status as a single functional unit, because the final \<e\> was added to avoid having \<u\> in final position. Included are *cue*, *blue*, *clue*, *due*, *glue*, *hue*, *Sue*, *subdue*, and *true*, all with /u/ or /ju/.

\<ye\>

If \<ue\> is elevated to the status of a functional unit, then so should \<ye\> (*bye*, *dye*, *lye*, *rye*), which has the identical origin. In all such occurrences, \<ye\> corresponds to /aɪ/.

Marginalia

If one tramps far afield in the lexicographic landscape, a few rare digraphs and trigraphs will be encountered, all in borrowings. The spelling \<ao\> occurs in the British spelling *gaol* and in *pharaoh*; \<aou\> occurs in the Quechua term *caoutchouc* ("rubber"), borrowed through Spanish; and \<oeu\> occurs in the British spelling of the French *manoeuver*. Only a small distance separates these spellings from some of the minor secondary spellings. Perhaps in time more words will be borrowed with one or another of them, and a status upgrading will result.

\<gh\> Influence

Although secondary vowel spellings before \<gh\> and \<ght\> have been mentioned here and there, a full summary of these is merited by the attention \<gh\> words receive in reading and spelling instruction. Of the secondary vowel spellings, \<ai, au, ei, ou\> occur before \<gh\>, but the correspondences for these vowels or for \<gh\> in these environments are not entirely predictable. Shown below are the correspondences for each compound vowel, along with exhaustive word listings from the research corpus for each correspondence.

$\quad$ \<ai\> → /e/ $\quad\quad$ *straight*
$\quad$ \<au\> → /æ/ $\quad\quad$ *draught, laugh*
$\quad$ \<au\> → /ɔ/ $\quad\quad$ *caught, naughty, taught, daughter,*
$\quad\quad\quad\quad\quad\quad\quad\quad$ *naught, fraught, slaughter*

(Note that \<au\> → /æ/ implies \<gh\> → /f/, while \<au\> → /ɔ/ implies \<gh\> → /ø/.)

<ei> → /aɪ/	*height, sleight*	
<ei> → /e/	*freight, inveigh, inveigle, neighbor, sleigh, weigh, weight*	
<ou> → /ʌ/	*clough, enough, rough, slough, tough*	
<ou> → /o/	*although, borough, dough, furlough, thorough, though*	
<ou> → /a/	*hough*	
<ou> → /u/	*through*	
<ou> → /au/	*bough, slough, sough*[22]	
<ou> → /ɔ/	*bought, brought, cough, fought, ought, nought, sought, thought, trough, wrought*	

ORIGINS OF THE VOWEL LETTERS

The vowel letters <a, e, i, o, u, y>, like the consonant letters, derive mostly from Hebrew by the familiar route of Greek, Etruscan, and Latin. The letter <a> traces its family heritage back to the Hebrew letter aleph, which in Biblical Hebrew represented a glottal stop. In Greek this form became the letter alpha, and without a glottal stop to represent it, was available to become a vowel sign—which it continued to be in Etruscan, Latin, and then English.

The letter <e> began as the Hebrew letter he, which represented a voiceless fricative similar to Modern English /h/. In Greek it represented a short /e/ and in later Greek times was renamed epsilon to distinguish it from long /e:/, which was named eta. From Greek it then was borrowed into Latin and eventually into English, where it was used, as in Latin, for both long and short <e>.

The letter <i> began as the Hebrew letter yod, a sign for the semivowel /j/. In Greek it was renamed iota and associated with <i>—a function it retained into Latin and then English, representing both a long and a short <i> in Old English.

The letter <o> developed from the Hebrew letter ayin, which represented in Biblical Hebrew a laryngeal consonant. Since Greek did not have this same consonant, ayin became available for representing a vowel and was applied to both long and short <o>. In later Greek, omega was developed to represent /o:/, and the descendent of the Hebrew ayin became known as omicron, or small <o>. In Latin and then in English, it represented both a long and a short vowel.

The letter <u> derives from the Hebrew letter vav, a symbol for Hebrew /w/. However, in Greek it came to represent /u/ and was named upsilon. In Latin it was used to represent both /u/ and /w/, as it was in Old English.

The letter <y> was a readoption in Latin of the Greek upsilon, and was used for Greek borrowings. The added vertical line at the bottom was also a Latin innovation. In Old English it originally represented a high-front rounded vowel.

LOOKING AHEAD

Here we finish with the vowel patterns, both primary and secondary, and both major and minor, along with a brief historical note. This completes the long and arduous journey through the complete set of letter–sound patterns for English. Now you are ready to explore a model for mapping spelling into sound, and to learn about morphophonemic alternations.

NOTES

1. For catalogs of specific correspondences and exceptions, the reader is encouraged to browse Cummings (1988) and Wijk (1966).
2. Word stress patterns play a significant role in the relationship of spelling to sound, especially in the correspondences of the primary vowel spellings. Most of this chapter focuses on stressed vowels; however, an all-too-brief section later in this chapter discusses unstressed vowels and schwa. Throughout this chapter (and this book), three levels of stress are assumed: primary, secondary, and tertiary (unstressed). Although some forms of English word stress are predictable, no extensive analysis of this topic has ever been published. Two older publications of interest in this area are Waldo (1964) and Kingdon (1958). See also the newer works cited in note 3 of this chapter.
3. The difference between monomorphemic and polymorphemic words—a difference unfortunately neglected in the teaching of reading—is too complex to be discussed adequately here. For the prediction of sound from spelling in a large number of words, however, the distinction is crucial. What are involved, primarily, are the alternations that occur with suffixation, as in /ˈʌrbən/–/ərbˈænɪtɪ/, /kon/–/kánɪk/. On this topic, see Giegerich (1992) and Kreidler (1989). For a pedagogical approach to suffixation, see Thorndike (1941a).
4. See Chapter 8 for a summary of the geminate consonants in English.
5. Some exceptions are *alkali, altitude, contralto, palmetto,* and *shall.*
6. Exceptions are *doll, dolphin, olfactory, revolve, solve,* and *volcano.*
7. These patterns may not apply in compound words.
8. In some words, final <e> is not a marker, but a relational unit corresponding to /ɪ/ (*adobe, coyote, epitome, extempore, facsimile, finale, hyperbole, nike, posse, recipe, sesame, simile, ukulele*), or corresponding to /e/ (*café, protége*).
9. *Bastile* is an alternate spelling of *Bastille* or *bastille.*
10. The digraph <uy> occurs as a secondary vowel spelling only in *buy* and is unrelated to <ui> (as in *build, circuit,* etc.). In *colloquy* and *soliloquy,* <u> corresponds as a separate functional unit to /w/, and <y> corresponds to /ɪ/. *Buy* is an

early 16th-century spelling for earlier *by*, *bye*, *bie*, and so on. It may have been adopted to distinguish this word from *by* and *bye*. *Guy*, as used in the United States for a man or person, derives from the proper name Guy Fawkes; the <u>, which is silent, marks the /g/ pronunciation of <g>, as in *guild*, *guise*, and *guillotine*.

11. A variant spelling of *pleat*.
12. Also pronounced /ke/ or /kwe/.
13. Days of the week are also pronounced with a final /ɪ/, and in overstressed speech as /e/.
14. In <gea> words where <ea> corresponds to /ə/, the <e> could be treated as a marker for <g> → /ǰ/ (e.g., *hydrangea*).
15. Historically, <e> and <a> in *ocean* represented separate vowels. With the palatalization of /s/ to /š/, the vowel corresponding to <e> was absorbed. Notice, however, that in *oceanic* this vowel is retained, and therefore <ea> is not a single-vowel spelling.
16. These words vary across dialects as either /ær/ or /ɛr/.
17. *Holstein* is also pronounced with /i/, particularly by farmers in the United States.
18. See the *OED*, under *sew*.
19. Also /wə/.
20. Some occurrences, however, such as *fowl*, are required for homophone discrimination.
21. Also /u/.
22. Also pronounced /sʌf/.

CHAPTER 10

Morphophonemics

I have been at a loss what to say of the sound
signified by *oi* and *oy*, as in *voice* and *boy*. It
may be looked upon as a dipthongal tonic,
consisting of the radical *a*-we, and of the
vanishing monothong *i*-n, when the quantity of
the element is short, and of *ee*-l when long. But
from the habit of the voice, it is difficult to give
a-we without adding its usual vanish of *e*-rr; and
this makes the compound a tripthong.

—JAMES RUSH (1855), 88

Principle 6 in Chapter 1 is that "Visual identity of meaningful word parts takes precedence over letter–sound simplicity." What is implied by this principle is that the same meaningful word part—that is, the same morpheme—will often be spelled the same even though its pronunciation changes. The results are alternation patterns such as *sign–signal*, *sane–sanity*, and *electric–electricity*. These provide an advanced lesson in relating spelling to sound, and a base for studying English morphology and morphophonemics. The present discussion begins with a model that introduces a morphophonemic level in the translation from spelling to sound. This extra layer is then justified and used to discuss various alternation patterns. Throughout this chapter, curly brackets are used to enclose morphophonemic entities—for example, {s}.

A DESCRIPTIVE MODEL

Whatever system of rules is chosen to relate spelling to sound must be not only as accurate and as simple as possible, but also revealing, allowing a differentiation of the various patterns in the system. To present the <x> patterns, which depend on a graphemic distinction and stress placement, as parallel to the <w> pattern discussed in Chapter 8, for example, is an unsatisfactory account of the current orthography. In the spelling-to-sound model employed here, graphemic words are divided into morphemic constituents, and then these are related to intermediate (morphophonemic) units by an ordered set of rules. Other rules then relate the morphophonemic units to phonemic forms. All rules that are based upon nongraphemic features are applied in an ordered sequence on the morphophonemic level, yielding various sublevels of intermediate forms for each word. The final morphophonemic form is then mapped automatically onto the phonemic level. Although the intermediate level is not strictly a morphophonemic level, it is labeled as such hereafter. Its primary function is to separate graphemically dependent rules from grammatically and phonologically dependent ones. The steps in applying this model are as follows:

1. Parsing of compound words. For example, the boundary between *hot* and *house* in *hothouse* needs to be marked so that <t> and <h> are treated as two separate relational units, rather than as the single relational unit <th>.

2. Identification of inflectional and derivational affixes. For example, <s> at the end of *boys* must be identified as an inflection, while <ing> at the end of *trafficking* must be recognized as a derivational ending. Similarly, *running* must be recognized as *run + ing*. Notice that steps 1 and 2 require extensive knowledge of the English lexicon.

3. Parsing of relational units and markers. For example, *treatment* can be divided into an initial consonant cluster, <tr>; a compound vowel unit, <ea>; a consonant, <t>; and a suffix, *ment* (which at some stage may be subdivided). To achieve this step, long exception lists need to be developed so that, for example, <ea> in *idea* can be treated as a sequence of <e> + <a> rather than as the single compound vowel <ea>.

4. Initial mapping from spelling to morphophonemes. Once again, long exception lists are needed, especially for vowel correspondences.

5. Repeated cycles of morphophonemic changes, including stress placement.

6. Final mapping from the morphophonemic level to the phonemic level. This can be viewed as the last morphophonemic change.

For a computer-based translation system, the exception lists need to be complete for whatever lexicon is selected. For humans, somewhat less accuracy and completeness are required, because alternate mappings can be tried until either a match is made to an entry in a listening lexicon or the viable options are exhausted without a match. In the latter case, no definitive statement can be made about the pronunciation of the letter string.

The existence of many exceptions to patterns does not make English spelling–sound correspondences impossible or unnecessary to teach. Given the high degree of regularity of consonant patterns and the general predictability of selected vowel patterns, coupled with the limited range of mappings for most units in common words, close approximations or exact matches can often be made.

WHY A MORPHOPHONEMIC LEVEL?

How do we justify yet another level of analysis in the transition from spelling to sound, given William of Occam's admonition, "Entities are not to be multiplied without necessity."[1] The answer is that it helps to distinguish what is due to orthographic conventions and what is due to English phonology. Consider the pronunciations of <n> in words like *uncle, synchronize,* and *anger.* In each case <n> is ultimately mapped into /ŋ/. If rules that mapped spellings directly into sound were the only ones allowed, a complicated rule would be required, based not only on the graphemes following <n> but also on their pronunciations. Note that in *angel, ranch,* and *rancid,* <n> is mapped into /n/ and not into /ŋ/. A more parsimonious statement is that at a subphonemic level, {n} shifts to {ŋ} before velar stops ({g} and {k}). (There is a further complexity to this rule, involving syllable boundaries, but this is ignored here.)

Consider further the mapping of noun plural <s> and <es> into sound, and recall that three different pronunciations are possible, as represented by *cats, dogs,* and *horses.* We could write rules on the graphemic level for these mappings, but these rules would need to reference sound either directly or indirectly. If directly, than a morphophonemic representation is probably required; if indirectly, than clumsy and complex mechanisms will be needed to work strictly on the graphemic level. Notice, for example, the pronunciations of the plurals in *aches* and *arches.* In *aches,* because <ch> is pronounced /k/, the plural is /s/. In contrast, *arch* has <ch> → /č/, so the plural is /ɪz/ as it is in all words that end in sibilants (/s, z, š, ž, ǰ, č/). If we want to avoid mention of sound, then we must enumerate all of the possible spellings for relevant sounds; this requires that we identify all spellings for sibilants, and for the remaining sounds identify which spellings are for voiced and which are for voiceless ones. Rules exist for part of this task, but a list of exceptions is also required: words that end in <ch>

→ /k/, or in silent <t> (*valet*), or silent <p> after a voiced sound (*corps*), and so on.

For resolving this pattern on the morphophonemic level, the plural spellings <s> and <es> are mapped into the plural morphophoneme {S}. A set of regular rules then converts {S} to the appropriate phonemic representation:

1. If the preceding sound is a sibilant, map {S} to /ɪz/.
2. Otherwise, if the preceding sound is voiced, map {S} to /z/.
3. In all other cases, map {S} to /s/.

Geminate consonants are another justification for a level between spelling and sound, although in Chapter 8 this topic has been treated, without justification, on the phonemic level. Within a single syllable, most geminate consonants are mapped into a single sound. However, for <cc> and <gg>, the immediately following letter determines whether these clusters are mapped into one or two sounds (cf. *acceded–accord, aggravate–exaggerate–suggest*). Thus a general rule that maps all geminates into a single sound would not be accurate. On a morphophonemic level, however, such leveling can be done because the basic phonemic mapping is available, thus requiring only a single rule: For example, $\{C_1C_2\}$/single morpheme → $\{C_1\}$, where $C_1 = C_2$; that is, where two identical morphophoneme consonants occur in sequence within the same morpheme, reduce them to the first consonant. The "same morpheme" qualification is required because of words such as *misspell*, where the consonants occur before and after a morpheme boundary, and therefore both are retained. For direct spelling–sound correspondences, either each cluster must be specified separately (e.g., <bb> → /b/), or a general rule with a complex sequence of exceptions must be developed.

The solution described in Chapter 8, which does the leveling of geminate consonants on the phonemic level, is not adequate for a formal system because different levels of phonemic transcription are assumed, but no mechanism for distinguishing them is provided. For example, in the mapping of <bubble> to sound, /bʌbbəl/ would appear at some stage, to be leveled to /bʌbəl/. How do we know that /bʌbbəl/ is not the final phonemic representation, but a penultimate one, to which consonant leveling rules still need to be applied? How do we know that /bʌbəl/ is the final stage?

We could label the first phonemic representation as nonfinal, but this is equivalent to creating a new level between graphemes and final, output phonemes. In other words, we would have the equivalent of the morphophonemic stage, but with a different label. Other examples could be adduced, but it should be clear already that a level between spelling and sound is needed to simplify grapheme–phoneme mappings. Labeling this a morphophonemic level is consistent with modern linguistic practice. But, having created a need for a morphophonemic level, we must now place some limits on its application. Why, for example, shouldn't the silent <p>'s in *cupboard* and *receipt* both be treated on the morphophonemic level, perhaps with a {P} morphophoneme? In *cupboard* the dropping of /p/ occurs as a phonological process. Sequences of stops that are articulated in the same position in the mouth are simplified to the second stop under certain stress conditions (e.g., *Campbell*, *cupboard*).[2] Even though the deletion took place hundreds of years ago for *cupboard* and similar words, the same process appears to be active today in English phonology. For *receipt*, however, silent <p> is a scribal restoration that has never been pronounced in formal speech. (In Middle English it was spelled without a <p>: *receite*.) If both were mapped directly into silence, this distinction would be lost.

One of the goals of the spelling–sound organization presented here is to treat all patterning as generally as possible—that is, to discover separate patterns that can be explained by a single, general principle. A second goal is to separate clearly the layers of patterning in the various systems that are involved in spelling–sound translation. To create new systems is inefficient in this enterprise when existing ones will do. Therefore the silent <p>'s and <b>'s in *receipt*, *doubt*, and *subtle* remain on the graphemic level, while the mapping of <n> to /ŋ/, the mappings of plural <s> and <es>, past-tense <d>/<ed>, and various other patterns are treated on the morphophonemic level. To facilitate discussion, however, I use the convention of <*x*> → /*y*/ to designate "spelling <*x*> mapped ultimately into pronunciation /*y*/" when the intervening morphophonemic levels are not of interest.

MORPHOPHONEMIC ALTERNATIONS

Fricatives

The alternations {s} ~ {z}, {f} ~ {v}, {θ} ~ {ð}, and {š} ~ {ž} reveal a number of problems in translating from spelling to sound. These problems, though encountered here in moving from orthography toward sound, also occur in the construction of models for English phonology, so that the considerations presented below have a much wider significance than in spelling-to-sound studies alone. In the discussion that follows, I assume that spellings have been mapped onto an initial morphophonemic level, so that our next objective is to describe alternations in terms of regular and irregular rules. In this section I will assume that an alternation that is both productive and high-frequency is *regular*. The specific problems discussed in relation to the voiceless–voiced fricative alternations are these: (1) What generalizations can be made about these alternations? And (2) What relevant differences exist among the nonproductive (irregular) patterns? Whether or not an alternation is marked in the orthography is relevant for both reading and spelling. This fact is mentioned for each pattern, but not discussed thoroughly.

A Rehashing of the Alternations

1. Noun plural {s} ~ {z} ~ {ɪz} *cats–dogs–horses* (unmarked)
2. Noun–adjective
   a. {š} ~ {ž} *luxury–luxurious* (unmarked)
   b. {s} ~ {z} *louse–lousy* (unmarked)
   c. {θ} ~ {ð} *north–northern* (unmarked)
3. Verb–verb
   {s} ~ {z} *sound–resound* (unmarked)
4. Noun–verb (infinitive)
   a. {f} ~ {v} *belief–believe* (marked)
   b. {θ} ~ {ð} *breath–breathe* (marked)
   c. {s} ~ {z}
      1. *house* (noun)–*house* (verb) (unmarked)
      2. *glass–glaze* (marked)
5. Noun singular–noun plural
   a. {f} ~ {v} *wife–wives* (marked)
   b. {θ} ~ {ð} *bath–baths* (unmarked)
   c. {s} ~ {z} *house–houses* (unmarked)
6. Verb (past)–verb (present)
   {f} ~ {v} *left–leave* (marked)
7. Noun–noun
   {θ} ~ {ð} *smith–smithy* (dialectal) (unmarked)
8. Ordinal–cardinal
   {f} ~ {v} *fifth–five* (marked)

Of these alternations, only a few are invariant. The noun plural <s> or <es> certainly is. It is a phonetically conditioned alternation that is describable by a single rule. It is generally not marked in the spelling, as shown by houses {háuz-ɪz}, boys {bɔɪz}, and cats {kæts}, all of which add only <s> to the singular. Where <es> is added for the plural, the alternate {ɪz} is marked.

Class 8, the ordinal–cardinal alternations, is also invariant, since the only two members that end in voiced {v} in the cardinal have unvoiced {f} in the ordinal: *five–fifth, twelve–twelfth*. One rule for the generation of the ordinal forms from the cardinal forms, therefore, can be stated as "final {v} → {f}." It is also possible to state this rule as "voiced fricative → unvoiced fricative" because no other cardinals end in a voiced fricative. Such a generalization, however, is probably not acceptable unless there are other major patterns in the orthography that show a similar voiced–voiceless alternation.

Class 4b, the {θ} ~ {ð} alternations in noun–verb, is nearly invariant, but since it has so few examples, there is a temptation to base its classification upon those of the other class 4 alternations. Almost all the nouns that end in {θ} and can also be used as verbs alternate {θ} to {ð} in the verb form (e.g., *cloth–clothe, teeth–teethe*). One exception is *earth*, whose related verb form, *unearth*, retains {θ}. In addition, *froth* has either {θ} or {ð} in its verb form.

The {f} ~ {v} alternations for noun–verb are not nearly so regular; for instance, *belief–believe* and *proof–prove* exist alongside *dwarf–dwarf* and *leaf–leaf*. It would be stretching a point considerably to say that in general nouns ending in {f} change {f} to {v} in forming the corresponding verb. At best, it can be said that there is a class of nouns (which must be enumerated in the lexicon attached to the model) in which the voiceless–voiced alternation occurs for this production.

The case for a {s} ~ {z} alternation in this class is even more tenuous. *Abuse, grease* (dialectal), *house*, and *use* have this alternation, as do, in an extended sense, *brass* (*braze*), *glass* (*glaze*), and *grass* (*graze*). But there is an even longer list of forms like *class, curse, mass*, and *witness*, in which no such alternation occurs. In general, nouns ending in {s} do not change {s} to {z} in forming the corresponding verb.

On the basis of this evidence, there is no justification for establishing a regular voiceless–voiced alternation for this class. This indicates, furthermore, that no special status should be assigned to the {θ} ~ {ð} alternation, even though it occurs in the majority of the <th> words. The only conclusion that can be drawn is that nouns ending in voiceless fricatives generally retain these voiceless fricatives in forming the verb. There is, however, a productive subpattern in which the voiceless fricative is voiced.

Class 2a, which has only one example in the corpus used for this book (and probably not very many more in the entire English language), might also be classed as regular. But this depends upon whether the alternation {ks} ~ {gz} is classed as regular. If spelling is used as the starting point, then this is possible, but not necessarily desirable. Intervocalic <x> could be mapped into {ks}, and then a stress rule could be applied to convert {ks} to {gz} when the primary stress is not on the preceding vowel: *execute–exist*. This {ks} must be distinguished from {ks} derived from <cc>, because the latter does not shift to {gz} under any circumstances: *access–accessible, accept–acceptable.*

Under the classifications of <x>-derived {ks} and <cc>-derived {ks}, the {š} ~ {ž} alternation in *luxury–luxurious* is regular; the actual alternation, however, is not {š} ~ {ž}, but {s} ~ {z}. The morphophonemes {š} and {ž} result from the palatalizations {sj} → {š} and {zj} → {ž}. This means, first, that the alternation {š} ~ {ž} is actually the alternation {s} ~ {z} from the standpoint of a generative model; and, second, that it is regular only if the identity of <x>-derived {ks} is maintained until after stress is applied. If this identity is not maintained, then there is no reason to call {ks} → {gz} regular. In lieu of the lack of other criteria to apply, frequency favors the invariantly voiceless cluster: *accent–accentuate, accident–accidental.* Therefore the alternation in *luxury–luxurious* is not classed as regular here.

Class 3 could, and probably should, be designated as regular. At present only three pairs reflect this alternation: *sign–design, solve–dissolve (absolve),* and *sound–resound.* The rule for the voicing of {s} is based on the stress pattern; that is, where {s} occurs between an unstressed and a stressed vowel (in that order), {s} → {z}.

Class 5 is the largest of the remaining classes, containing about 20 examples for {f} ~ {v} (e.g., *calf–calves, loaf–loaves, shelf–shelves*), about 7 for {θ} ~ {ð}[3] (e.g., *bath–baths, moth–moths, wreath–wreaths*), and one for {s} ~ {z} (*house–houses*).

The lack of a {š} ~ {ž} alternation in this class and the rarity of the {s} ~ {z} alternation eliminate the possibility of a general voicing rule for final fricatives in forming the noun plural. This leaves the possibility of labeling the {f} ~ {v} and {θ} ~ {ð} alternations as regular. But the regular label implies either that there is a phonetic or a grammatical factor that will allow the prediction of the alternation or that this alternation occurs frequently. That the {f} ~ {v} and {θ} ~ {ð} alternations are not phonetically or grammatically predictable can be seen from pairs such as *gulf–gulfs, reef–reefs, breath–breaths,* and *month–months.*

The frequency question is also answered in the negative, although the {f} ~ {v} alternation does occur in almost one-third of the nouns that end in {f}. The remainder retain {f} in forming the plural. This would imply that the *leaf–leaves* alternation should be classed as irregular, just as is the petrified alternation represented by *smith–smithy.* A native speaker's intuition, however, is uncomfortable with this solution. Not only is the *smith–smithy* alternation uncommon, but it would be rarely invoked as a model for forming new English words. *Leaf–leaves,* on the other hand, appears more productive. We would suspect, for example, that voiced fricative plurals of such words as *dwarf, fife*, and *roof* occur in American speech. Furthermore, the formation of the noun plural from the noun singular is one of the most common forms of word formation in English. Formation of one noun from another by the addition of <y> is much less productive.

The issue here is that a model that concerns itself strictly with regular and irregular categories fails to account for some features of the language. Although some work remains to be done, the irregular class is divided here into *productive* and *petrified* subclasses. At best, we can say that alternations like *leaf–leaves* fit into the *productive irregular* class, while those like *smith–smithy* fit into the *petrified irregular* group.

Finally, all {f} ~ {v} alternations are marked in the orthography by a change in spelling, while in the {s} ~ {z} alternations only the one represented by *glass–glaze* is marked by a spelling change. In the {θ} ~ {ð} alternations, only the noun–verb one is marked, and this by the addition of final <e> as a marker, which is the only possible device for marking the voiced pronunciation of <th>.

A reclassification of these alternations, based on the newly adopted classes, is shown below.

I. Regular
    A. Noun plural {s} ~ {z} ~ {ɪz})   *cats–dogs–horses*
    B. Verb–verb {s} ~ {z}   *sound–resound*
    C. Ordinal–cardinal {f} ~ {v}   *fifth–five*
II. Irregular
    A. Productive
        1. Noun–adjective {θ} ~ {ð}   *north–northern*
        2. Noun–verb {θ} ~ {ð}   *breath–breathe*
           {f} ~ {v}   *belief–believe*
           {s} ~ {z}   *house* (noun)–*house* (verb)
        3. Noun singular–noun plural
           {f} ~ {v}   *wife–wives*
           {θ} ~ {ð}   *bath–baths*
           {s} ~ {z}   *house–houses*
    B. Petrified
        1. Noun–adjective {s} ~ {z}   *louse–lousy, luxury–luxurious*
        2. Noun–verb {s} ~ {z}   *glass–glaze*
        3. Verb (past)–verb (present)
           {f} ~ {v}   *left–leave*
        4. Noun–noun {θ} ~ {ð}   *smith–smithy*

Silent Consonants

In a small group of words, certain consonant spellings alternate between silence and their normal phonemic values. The largest subgroup of these consists of words that end in the clusters <mn> and <mb>. When certain suffixes are added, the silent last letter remains silent (e.g., *autumns, bombing*); before other suffixes, the silent last letter shifts to its more common form (*autumn–autumnal, damn–damnation, bomb–bombard*, etc.). Two pairs of words have a similar alternation based on an initial cluster, *gnostic–agnostic* and *know–acknowledge*, although the second is stretching a point somewhat. Internal (medial) silent letters can also shift to a full value: *sign–signal, malign–malignant, debt–debit*. The morphophonemic alternations involved can be expressed as {ø} ~ {g}, and {ø} ~ {b}.

Syllabic Consonants

Syllabic consonants at the ends of words also shift to their normal consonant values with the addition of certain suffixes: *juggle–juggler, muffle–muffler, peddle–peddler, prism–prismatic, schism–schismatic*. This is a small group, however.

Primary Vowel Spellings

The major pattern for the primary vowel spellings in stressed positions depends upon two basic features: environment, which has been discussed in Chapter 9, and morphemic structure, which is discussed briefly in this section. Morphemic structure forms the basis for describing the alternations based upon the primary vowel spellings. For example, the word *sanity*, if considered solely on the basis of the rules given in Chapter 9, would be an exception to the major pattern, since <a> before a simple consonant unit followed by a vowel corresponds to its checked rather than to its free alternate. If the word is viewed, however, in relation to the pairs *sane–sanity, humane–humanity*, and *urbane–urbanity*, another regular feature can be seen. Starting with the forms *sane, humane*, and *urbane* enables us to write regular rules for changing the free alternate (/e/) to the checked alternate (/æ/) when the suffix <ity> (/ɪtɪ/) is added.

This rule also holds for the spellings <e, i, o>, as can be seen from the following examples:

<e>   *extreme–extremity*
       obscene–obscenity
       serene–serenity

<i>   *asinine–asininity*
       divine–divinity
       malign–malignity
       senile–senility
<o>   *mediocre–mediocrity*
       precocious–precocity
       verbose–verbosity

Alternations based upon stressed <u>, which are absent for final <ity>, are rare in Modern English, the most common being those that occur when verbs are converted to nouns with final <tion>: *assume–assumption, presume–presumption, reduce–reduction.* Even with loss of stress, <u> → /ju/ tends not to change to /ə/. Thus we have *compute–computation* and *utilize–utility.*

Although a complete survey of vowel alternations is beyond the scope of this book, a few of the more common alternations are presented below:

1. Final <ic>		Free	Checked
	<a>	*angel*	*angelic*
		state	*static*
	<e>	*athlete*	*athletic*
		hygiene	*hygienic*
		meter	*metric*
	<i/y>	*cycle*	*cyclic*
		mime	*mimic*
		paralyze	*paralytic*
	<o>	*cone*	*conic*
		neurosis	*neurotic*
		phone	*phonic*

2. Final <ion>		Free	Checked
	<e>	*concede*	*concession*
		convene	*convention*
	<i>	*collide*	*collision*
		decide	*decision*
		provide	*provision*

3. Final <ian>		Checked[4]	Free
	<a>	*mammal*	*mammalian*
	<e>	*comedy*	*comedian*
	<o>	*custody*	*custodian*

Secondary Vowel Alternations

Only a small number of alternations involve secondary vowel spellings, and most of these result from the {i} and {ɛ} pronunciations of <ea>: *heal–health*, *steal–stealth*, and so on. *Dear–dearth* also involves <ea>, but the pronunciation of <ea> in *dearth* has been modified by {r}.

Miscellaneous Alternations

A great many alternation patterns exist for different forms of Latin and Greek roots in English words. For example, from the Latin word for year, *annus*, a number of words now in common use have variations on this root, spelled *anni, annu,* or *enni* (*annual, biannual, anniversary, annuity, biennial, centennial, millennium, perennial*). Similarly, the Greek word for star, *astron*, yields roots with *aster* and *astro* spellings (*aster, astrology, astronaut, astronomical, disaster*). And the Latin *fallere* ("to deceive") has English derivatives with *fal, fail,* and *faul* spellings (*fail, failure, fallacy, fallible, false, falsetto, fault*). In some cases the same spelling maps into different pronunciations—for example, the <a> in *false* and *fallible*. In other cases both spelling and sound change—for example, *biannual–biennial*. Although an extensive treatment of such forms is not attempted here, language arts teachers in particular should examine this area for ideas on teaching vocabulary.

A second group of alternations derive from the {k} and {s} pronunciations of <c>. These consist of several subgroups, based on the addition of different suffixes. When final <ity> is added to words ending in <ic>, the pronunciation of <c> shifts from {k} to {s} (*elastic–elasticity, electric–electricity, periodic–periodicity*). With the addition of final <ian>, an identical shift occurs (*clinic–clinician, optic–optician, phonetic–phonetician*). Similarly, the replacement of final <ic> (or <tic>) with final <acy> causes the same shift (*diplomatic–diplomacy, numeric–numeracy*). Remaining are a few miscellaneous endings such as *medic–medical–medicine*.

A Note of Caution

So that the reader does not assume more regularity with alternations than exists, a few failures of alternation are offered. For reasons mired in the history of English spelling, as explained in Chapter 6, the sound /e/ is often represented by <ea> and <ee> as well as by <e>. Notice the pairs *bereave–bereft, cleave–cleft,* and *leave–left,* as well as *deep–depth, feed–fed,* and *sleep–slept.* For the *bereave* group, <ea> could also be used for /ɛ/, so that an alternation in which the spelling remained constant was possible. For the <ee> spellings, an <e> with a final, silent <e> added would have been required to keep the spelling constant (e.g., *depe–depth*, *fede–fed*). (Notice, nevertheless, that even with the vowel changes, morpheme identity is largely preserved.) More examples could be offered, such as pairs like *declaim–declamation* and *curious–curiosity*, but the point should already be established. No hand of consistency ever stroked the spelling system for English. Patterning? Yes. Full, consistent patterning? No!

LOOKING AHEAD

This is a preliminary basis for understanding English morphophonemics and a small part of English morphemics. The interested reader can pursue this topic with other texts; the plan here, however, is to close this book with chapters on two applied areas—spelling reform and the teaching of phonics.

NOTES

1. According to Bertrand Russell (1945, 472), what William of Occam actually said was, "It is vain to do with more what can be done with fewer."
2. See Chapter 4.
3. Most of these plurals vary between the voiced and unvoiced forms according to dialect and idiolect.
4. All of these also have /ə/ pronunciations.

CHAPTER 11

Spelling Reform

Uncle Cadmus sat down, and the Opposition [to
simplified spelling] rose and combated his
reasonings in the usual way. Those people said
that they had always been used to the
hieroglyphics, that the hieroglyphics had dear
and sacred associations for them; that they loved
to sit on a barrel under an umbrella in the
brilliant sun of Egypt and spell out the owls and
alligators and saw-teeth . . . and weep with
romantic emotion at the thought that they had at
most but eight or ten years between themselves
and the grave for the enjoyment of this ecstasy.
        —SAMUEL L. CLEMENS [Mark Twain]
        (1909/1975), 11

According to Principle 7 in Chapter 1, English orthography is oriented more toward word recognition and the initiated speaker than it is toward exact pronunciation and the nonspeaker. Yet spelling reformers for several centuries have assumed just the opposite. With this misconception as a base, these reformers then
assumed that the present system is full of imperfections and greatly in need of repair. This chapter discusses a number of the spelling reformers and spelling reform movements, mainly to explore the reforms proposed.

PHILOLOGISTS, LINGUISTS, AND SPELLING

The earliest writings on English orthography are based on an alphabetic principle derived from the fourth- and sixth-century Roman grammarians Donatus and Priscian. Each letter of the alphabet has, besides its name (*nomen*) and appearance (*figura*), a power (*potestas*) or sound, and a description of the orthography involves a classification of the letters according to their powers.[1] Thus English orthography from the time of King Alfred (849–899) to the present day has been delimited by the letters and their powers. So ingrained has this principle become that some contemporary linguists have attempted, by substituting *grapheme* for *letter*, to sanctify it with the countenance of linguistic science without examining how unsound it is.

The relationship between spelling and sound ranked high among the problems the first Indo-European comparative philologists faced at the end of the 18th century and through most of the 19th. The works of the early 19th-century philologists, such as Franz Bopp and Rasmus Rask, show classifications of sounds based on orthographic rather than phonetic data. On Bopp, the Swiss linguist Ferdinand de Saussure wrote, "Even Bopp failed to distinguish clearly between letters and sounds. His works give the impression that a language and its alphabet are inseparable."[2] The first 20th-century linguists were so adamant in pointing out the 19th-century confusion of sound and spelling that they reduced the orthography to a secondary, subservient role, from which it has not always emerged in the writings of contemporary linguists.

Part of the early failure to distinguish clearly between phonology and orthography stemmed from the lack of an adequate vocabulary for discussing phonological phenomena. Jacob Grimm, for example, titled his discussion on sound changes "Changes of the Letters."[3] By the beginning of the fourth quarter of the 19th century, philologists had resolved most of the confusion between spelling and sound. Nevertheless, Saussure still inveighed against the orthography as an obfuscation of the true language: "Language and writing are two distinct systems of signs; the second exists for the sole purpose of representing the first. . . . The preceding discussion boils down to this: writing obscures language; it is not a guise for language but a disguise."[4]

To Saussure can also be attributed the first exposition on the so-called grapheme–phoneme parallel—a superficial relationship that is frequently invoked without critical comment by some contemporary linguists. In a brief note on phoneme and grapheme, Stetson claimed that to understand written forms one must understand writing movements, just as, apparently, one must understand articulatory movements to understand spoken forms.[5] Bazell, disagreeing with

Pulgram in particular, objected to the phoneme–grapheme parallel on the grounds that phonemes contain simultaneous distinctive features, while graphemes contain nonsimultaneous ones.[6] Bazell's solution was to create a parallel between letter and morpheme, an idea not pursued further.

Considerations of the orthography by linguists, from the time of Saussure through World War II, were directed mostly toward spelling reform. Many scholars who demonstrated adeptness and unbiased critical ability in all other phases of linguistic investigation could, in their passion for reforming English spelling, see nothing in the prevailing orthography except a defective alphabetic system, badly in need of repair. Leonard Bloomfield is probably more responsible than any other 20th-century linguist for the view that writing is secondary and subservient to speech. This notion was espoused not only in his seminal 1933 work *Language*, but also in several later articles.[7] Bloomfield held that writing is not a part of language, but simply an imperfect image of speech, and even though he wrote at length on the teaching of reading, he maintained that English orthography is simply a grossly irregular alphabetic system.

Some critical exceptions to this view are found in the writings of a few modern linguists. Hockett, for example, wrote in 1958: "The complexities of English spelling cannot be accounted for completely on the assumption that the system is phonemic with irregularities of the sort listed [above]. It is necessary to assume that the system is partly phonemic and partly morphemic."[8] In a series of articles, the Czech linguist Joseph Vachek, who has been mentioned in Chapter 1, has advanced one of the most critical analyses of the English spelling-to-sound relationships ever done. Vachek first distinguished the aims of the traditional writing system of a language from its phonetic transcription: "While any system of phonetic transcription provides means for an optical recording of the purely acoustic make-up of spoken utterances, the traditional writing system increasingly tends to refer to the meaning directly without necessarily taking a *detour* via the corresponding spoken utterance."[9] He then went on to give definitions of the spoken and written norms of language and to develop, in a general fashion, the hierarchical relation of the two norms of English.

In enumerating the nonphonemic features of English writing, W. Nelson Francis pointed out not only the graphemic differentiation of homophones, but also the use of graphemic markers to show the phonemic correspondences of other graphemes, and the tendency in English spelling to preserve morphemic identity regardless of phonemic differences.[10] Francis's most important observation was his pointing out the strong tendency in English orthography to preserve the identity of morphemes. "We may state this in terms of a general principle which, while admitting many exceptions, is what governs and systematizes many of the apparent inconsistencies of our writing system: The English writing system tends to employ a single combination of graphemes to represent a given morpheme, disregarding for the most part all except the grossest phonemic differences between allomorphs."[11]

Similarly, Henry Bradley, one of the editors of the original *OED*, claimed that writing does not attempt to relate directly and solely to speech. In commenting on graphic distinctions of homophones, Bradley noted: "It is because the expression of meaning is felt to be the real purpose of written language that these distinctions still survive, in spite of the disastrous effects that they have had on the phonetic intelligibility of written words."[12] In summarizing his views on writing and speech, Bradley stated further that "speech and writing are two organs for the expression of meaning, originally co-ordinate and mutually independent."[13]

Spelling reformers in the 20th century, who have contributed an enormous quantity of literature on English orthography, have ignored the opinions of linguists like Vachek and Hockett, seldom analyzing the object of their scorn beyond the more common examples of scribal pedantry. Their arguments were, and are still, based on the a priori assumption that alphabets should, and by some right ought, to be perfectly phonetic. It is no surprise, therefore, that most spelling reformers have concerned themselves with direct letter-to-sound relationships and have ignored all other facets of the writing system.

EARLY EFFORTS AT SPELLING REFORM IN BRITAIN

A Medieval Spelling Scheme

The orthography of Orm, preserved in a holograph manuscript written about 1200 (*The Ormulum*), is the earliest extant example of English spelling reform.[14] Orm's goal, considering that he was an Augustinian canon writing at a time when many non-English-speaking priests held parish positions in England, was probably to facilitate the reading aloud of religious texts. The orthographic regularity in *The Ormulum* was unmatched until well after the introduction of printing; among other things, Orm attempted to indicate vowel quantity through consonant doubling and accent marks. As a spelling reformer, he was a little clumsy, but as an analyzer of spelling-to-sound correspondences in the 13th century, he was unique. If, however, Orm advocated a general spelling reform (which is doubtful), then he failed, because the text of *The Ormulum* is the only evidence we have of this spelling system.

Reformers in the 16th Century

From *The Ormulum* until the middle of the 16th century, we have no evidence of spelling reform attempts. Then, suddenly, spelling reformers flourished in England. Sir Thomas Cheke and Sir Thomas Smith, codefendants in the great Greek controversy of the 16th century, were the first; they were followed closely by John Hart, the most competent by far, and then by a long succession of others. Although most of the spelling reformers viewed writing as a mirror for speech, William Bullokar, Alexander Gill, and a few others proposed alphabets based at least in part on etymology and on the desire for a graphic distinction of homophones, and recognized nonphonemic elements in the orthography.[15]

The earliest 16th-century spelling reformers, Cheke and Smith, did not wage reform campaigns. That Cheke was interested in spelling reform is known only from his translation into a reformed English alphabet of the Gospel according to St. Mark (c. 1550), and from a letter he wrote to Sir Thomas Hoby, which was published in 1561.[16] Except for a special symbol that he substituted for the spelling <oo>, Cheke employed only Latin letters, using, among other devices, geminate vowels to show vowel length, geminate consonants to show a preceding short vowel, and <sch> for /š/. Although he was inconsistent in the employment of his orthography, Cheke attempted to devise a phonetic transcription system, as did Smith, who saw writing only as the imitation of speech. Smith published his views on spelling reform in *De Recta et Emendata Linguae Anglicae* (1568), but did not advocate a particular spelling system. Rather, he offered variant spellings for the writer to choose from.[17] Smith worked from sound to spelling, employing at least 34 unique letter forms, along with the dieresis, circumflex, and hyphen.

John Hart was the most competent phonetician of the early reformers, and also the most evangelistic. He saw in the orthography the vices of "diminution" (lack of enough letters), "superfluite" (use of superfluous letters), "usurpation of one letter for an other," and "mysplacing and disordering [of letters]" (failure of the order of the spelling to correspond to the order in which the letters are pronounced).[18] In three major works published between 1551 and 1570, Hart enumerated and then attacked the arguments against spelling reforms, set forth a reformed alphabet based entirely on the existing Latin alphabet, and transcribed some popular texts in his system.[19] Although his system was more consistent than those of the reformers who followed him in the next two centuries, his chief value today is in the record he left of the speech of his time. Although claiming that the purpose of writing "is to signifie their mindes unto the absent,"[20] Hart could see no other way to achieve this goal than to write phonetically.

The major spelling reformers who followed Hart in Britain contributed little to the understanding of writing and the relation between writing and speech.

Some of the later reformers based their systems on etymology and analogy, but the majority advocated phonetic systems and cited, to establish a need for reform, such worn-out examples of scribal pedantry as *debt*, *doubt*, and *victuals*. The works of two, however—Alexander Hume (c. 1617) and James Douglas (c. 1740)—are especially important for understanding British attitudes toward spelling in the 17th and 18th centuries. Hume was one of the first grammarians to discuss orthographic practices and to explain such early Modern English innovations as the substitution of <t> for <c> and <s> in words of Latin origin like *nation* and *congregation*. Douglas was one of the few grammarians ever to attempt a complete description of English spelling-to-sound correspondences, and although his rules generally neglected nonphonetic features like morpheme identity, his results were as successful as many of the modern letter-to-sound descriptions.

Alexander Hume

Alexander Hume's *Of the Orthographie and Congruitie of the Britan Tongue*, written around 1617, is one of the earliest English works in which spelling patterns are discussed.[21] Although born a Scotsman, Hume spent 16 years in England, studying, teaching, and serving as a schoolmaster in Bath. On returning to Scotland, he became rector of a secondary school and later Master of the grammar school of Dunbar, where he wrote *Of the Orthographie and Congruitie*, dedicating it to King James I. This book was apparently designed as a spelling book and grammar for use in the Dunbar schools. Hume also wrote a Latin grammar that was, by declaration of Parliament and the Privy Council, to be used in all the schools of the kingdom. There is no evidence, however, that the injunction was carried out.

In the dedication to *Of the Orthographie and Congruitie*, Hume noted the "uncertentie in our men's wryting," and claimed to have devised a "remedie for that maladie," which he said he put aside when he learned of Sir Thomas Smith's spelling reform proposal.[22] He divided the book itself into two sections: "Of the Orthographie of the Britan Tongue" and "Of the Congruitie of Our Britan Tongue." Spelling matters occupied approximately one-third of the first section, the remainder of this section being devoted to the sounds of the "Latine" and "Britan vouales" and "consonantes," and the syllable. The basis of orthography, according to Hume, consists of "the symbol," "the thing symbolized," and "the congruence between them" (he defined *congruence* as follows: "the instrument of the mouth, quhilk [which], when the eie sees the symbol, utteres the sound").[23] As for the symbols, Hume recommended that <i> and <u> be used only for vowel sounds and <j> and <v> only for consonants, and he assigned the names "jod" and "jau" to the latter two. This separation was not widely adopted until almost 100 years later. It was not, for example, advocated in Ben Jonson's grammar, which was published at least 15 years after *Of the Orthographie and Congruitie* appeared.[24]

Two short chapters in the first section of Hume's book were devoted to spelling rules. The first is interesting because it stated a rationale for the Latin spellings that were adopted into English orthography during the 16th century. According to one rule, Latin derivatives written in Latin with <c, s>, or <sc> for /s/ should retain their original spellings as a means for distinguishing homophones. Hume cited such pairs as *council–counsil* and *cel* (*cell*)*–sel* (*sell*). He stated that Latin verbals (gerund, participle, etc.) in <tio>, (e.g., *oration, visitation,* and *vocation*) should be written with the <t>, but that Latin verbals in <tia> and <tium> should be written with <ce> (as in *justice,* from Latin *justitia*).

In the second spelling chapter, Hume discussed the symbolization of the syllabics /l/ and /n/, as well as final <e>. He rejected the idea that final <e> marks the quantity of a preceding vowel, because he did not believe that one vowel can change the sound of another if they are separated by a consonant. Hume did, however, approve of the final <e> to "break the sound" of <c> and <g> as in *peace* and *savage,* and after <s> as in *false* and *case,* for which he gave no reason.[25] The <e> here is probably to show that <s> is pronounced /s/ rather than /z/, as it would be in *false* and *case* if the <e> were not present. As Wheatley pointed out in his notes to the Early English Text Society edition of Hume's *Of the Orthographie and Congruitie,* Hume's spelling itself is occasionally inconsistent.[26] *Judge,* for example, is rendered alternately as *judge, juge,* and *judg.* Nevertheless, Hume's work is valuable for what it reveals about the development of orthographic practices.

James Douglas

One of the more thorough treatises now in existence on English spelling-to-sound correspondences was written by James Douglas about 1740.[27] Douglas, physician, anatomist, and fellow of the Royal Society, wrote drafts of (but never published) Latin, Greek, French, and English grammars. In writing his treatise on spelling-to-sound correspondences, Douglas attempted to record the upper-class speech of London. He was a competent phonetician, but, more important for the interests of this chapter, he gave hundreds of rules for predicting sound from spelling and illustrated his rules with over 6,500 different words. His rules were based mostly on the syllable position in the word and the letter position in the syllable. More sophisticated ideas (such as those based on accent position and morpheme identity) were also used, but not frequently. Typical of his rules was the following: "When the vowel A makes a compleat syllable in the beginning of a word, & is not a preposition, it is sounded long & slender, as . . . A-BLE."[28]

In spite of his insights into spelling, Douglas's rules were somewhat primitive. His selection of graphemic units was not based on any discernible criteria; <ya, ye, wa, wi>, for example, were classed as diphthongs, and <awe, ewe, eye, way>, and numerous others were classed as triphthongs. He also claimed that certain consonants were sounded double, such as the <b> in *cabin* (then spelled *cabbin*). The effects of certain consonant groups such as <ld> and <ft> on preceding vowels were recognized, although the effect of accent on the pronunciation of intervocalic <x> was not. The merit of Douglas's work lies more in the intent than in the results, although the 358 rules he presented, along with the lists of examples and exceptions, represent an extremely thorough attempt to analyze English spelling-to-sound correspondences.

SPELLING REFORM IN THE UNITED STATES

Spelling reform engaged the attention of independent writers such as Noah Webster, Benjamin Franklin, James Elphinston, and William Thorton in the formative years of the United States, but an active and organized movement for reform began only toward the last quarter of the 19th century.[29] National committees were founded in America (and in England), with the most prominent names from science, education, industry, and public life listed on their governing boards. But the fragility of the reform movement was exposed by its greatest triumph—an executive order in 1906 by President Theodore Roosevelt, directing the U.S. Government Printing Office to employ 300 simplified spellings in White House publications. Both the U.S. Congress and a vocal segment of the public expressed immediate and firm opposition, and a well-organized and highly financed drive sputtered off course, never regaining its momentum. A little more than a decade later, its principal financial support was severed, and its highly visible offices on Madison Avenue in downtown Manhattan moved to the exclusive obscurity of the Lake Placid Club in upstate New York.

In the period from Webster's first speller in 1783 to Roosevelt's executive order in 1906, the unique character of American spelling was firmly implanted, and the U.S. public's attitude toward spelling reform was clarified. Yet much more can be learned from a careful analysis of this period. In the arguments and practices of Webster and his main antagonist, Lyman Cobb, are portrayals of linguistic science of the late 18th and early 19th centuries, containing as they do phonologies of English and justifications for different renderings of sound into spelling. In the spelling reform proposals of both Webster and the early 20th-century reformers are attitudes about orthography and its role in national life. There are also excellent case studies for historiography, and particularly for the influence of great men on historical events.

Noah Webster

Noah Webster, Jr., was born in Connecticut in 1758, the son of a farmer who later rose to be deacon of his West Hartford parish and a local justice of the peace.[30] Young Noah attended Yale University, graduating in 1778 after several brief stints in the Connecticut militia. Although he was admitted to the Connecticut bar three years later, he found employment primarily as a school teacher. Sometime in the early 1780s he began work on a three-part series of texts for improving American education, the first of which, a speller, was published in 1783 under the title *A Grammatical Institute of the English Language*, Part I.[31]

The "Blue-Back Speller," as this text was soon called, was motivated by equal measures of patriotism and educational reform. In the introduction Webster wrote, "We find Englishmen practicing upon very erroneous maxims in politics and religion; and possibly we shall find, upon careful examination, that their methods of education are equally erroneous and defective." He attacked the "clamour of pedantry in favour of Greek and Latin," as well as the lack of attention to standards for American pronunciation.[32]

Webster, though quick to point out even the most minor inconsistencies in other authors, produced a continually changing set of spellings in his major works. In the introduction to his first speller, he proudly announced his compliance with respectable British spelling norms: "In spelling and accenting, I have generally made Dr. Johnson's dictionary my guide; as in point of orthography this seems to be the most approved authority in the language."[33] On the failings of the English grammarians to articulate a correct set of rules for syllabication and pronunciation, Webster was unreserved in his criticism. But the remoteness of spelling reform from his educational plan was unmistakably revealed in his criticism of those who would delete the <u> from <our> endings—a practice that Webster himself was not only to adopt within a few years, but to defend as if it had been culled from divine revelation:

> There seems to be an inclination in some writers to alter the spelling of words, by expunging the superfluous letters. This appears to arise from the same pedantic fondness for singularity that prompts to new fashions of pronunciation. Thus they write the words *favour*, *honour*, &c. without *u*. But it happens

unluckily that, in these words, they have dropped the wrong letter—they have omitted the letter that is sounded and retained one that is silent; for the words are pronounced *onur, favur*.[34]

But while the first part of *A Grammatical Institute*, with its conservative spellings, was rapidly becoming an American standard, Webster was changing into a radical spelling reformer. Moreover, in the style that characterized most of his commercial ventures, he was attempting through personal appeal to America's elder statesmen to have his views imposed on the country. In 1786 Webster sent a plan for a phonetic alphabet to Benjamin Franklin, soliciting his aid in convincing Congress to adopt the scheme as a national printing standard. Franklin—in part because he favored his own phonetic alphabet, and in part because of common sense—gave little encouragement to Webster's plan. Webster apparently dropped the phonetic alphabet completely, but he proceeded to advocate a less radical reform, based on three principles that were first presented in *An Essay on a Reformed Mode of Spelling*:[35]

1. Omission of all superfluous or silent letters;
2. Substitution of a character that has a definite sound for one that is more vague and indeterminate.
3. Small alterations in a character or the addition of a point to distinguish different sounds.

The first principle gave, for example, *bred*, *hed*, *giv*, and *bilt* for Modern English *bread*, *head*, *give*, and *built*. The second produced *greef* (*grief*), *kee* (*key*), *laf* (*laugh*), *dawter* (*daughter*), *korus* (*chorus*), and *masheen* (*machine*). The third added a stroke across <th> to indicate a voiced sound, points and macrons over vowels, and the joining of some digraphs. These principles were used, although not consistently, in *A Collection of Essays and Fugitive Writings*—for instance, *ritten* (but *writings*), *az*, *hiz*, and *haz* (but *peeces*, *times*, and *excused*); and *guvernment* (but *of*).[36] With this well-confined experiment, Webster withdrew from his extremist position and, according to one of his biographers, concentrated on reform derived from "uniformity on analogical principles."[37]

In 1804 Webster brought out the first major revision of the Blue-Back Speller (since 1788, formally titled the *American Spelling Book*), which now included the beginnings of Webster's publicly advocated spelling reforms, here limited to deletion of <u> from terminal <our> and <k> from terminal <ick> in polysyllabic words. Two years later, however, he published his first dictionary, *A Compendious Dictionary of the English Language*, with the fullest range of spelling reforms that he would advocate for the remainder of his lifetime. The "pedantic fondness for singularity," which he had accused other writers of suffering from 23 years earlier, now was in full corporal control of the father of American lexicography. The endings <or, ic, er> were now preferred over the British endings <our, ick, re>, as were stress placement as a determiner of whether or not a final consonant is doubled before a suffix that begins with a vowel (*rebelling*, but *traveling*). These and several other Webster reforms have become standard spellings, in contrast to such forms as *ake, crum, fether, ile,* and *spunge,* which were also advocated in the 1806 dictionary.

The man who had found earlier that Johnson was "the most approved authority in the language" now could find little to praise in Johnson's orthography. And where spelling reform was once undesirable, now it was indispensable, at least under the proper constraints:

> No great change should ever be made at once, nor should any change be made which violates established principles, creates great inconvenience, or obliterates the radicals of the language. But gradual changes to accommodate the written to the spoken language, when they occasion none of these evils, and especially when they purify words from corruptions, improve the regular analogies of a language and illustrate etymology, are not only proper, but indispensable.[38]

In time Webster rested his reforms on two principles: etymology and the practices of great writers. It is a tribute to Webster's marketing capabilities that his major reforms were finally adopted, because the etymologies he invoked were often inconsistent or faulty, and his citations of great writers were obviously selective. For example, terminal <k> after <ic> was rejected because it was a Norman innovation, but <ch> for <c> when pronounced /č/, <sh> for earlier <ss> (or <ssc>), and <th> for eth and thorn, which were also Norman innovations, were silently retained.[39] On the one hand Webster justified continual change to bring spelling in line with current pronunciation, but on the other hand he justified specific respellings, such as *fether* and *lether,* by reference to Old English spellings for sounds that these words no longer contained.[40]

Webster's use of analogy was equally inconsistent, as pointed out by his most vocal critic of the time, Lyman Cobb. For example, Webster justified final <or> for <our> on the basis of the <u> deletion in such derived forms as *laborious, rigorous, invigorate,* and *inferiority.* But the same argument could be applied also to the <u> in final <ous> (*curious–curiosity, generous–generosity,* etc.), the <i> in final <aim> and <ain> (*declaim–declamation, explain–explanation,* etc.), and the <a> in final <eal> (*congeal–congelation, reveal–revelation,* etc.).[41] Similarly, <re> should be justified over Webster's <er> (*centre–central, fibre–fibrous, lustre–lustrous,* etc.).

Webster's analysis of letter–sound correspondences, which he included in the introduction to his speller, showed little improvement over the analyses already published at the time, with minor exceptions. He noted, for example, that although <h> is written after <w> in words like *whale*, the <h> is pronounced first. He tabulated, as did others, the various pronunciations for letters like <c, g, x>, and showed an awareness of the problems of determining syllable divisions in words like *magic* and *acid*. Some of his patterns, however, such as the syllable-dependent subpatterns for <c> and <g>, were faulty. His exceptions to letter–sound rules often included the bizarre, the arcane, or the obsolete. To Webster, nevertheless, must go credit for the first pedagogically oriented tabulation of letter–sound correspondences.

Reform Efforts in the Late 19th and Early 20th Centuries

Webster died in 1843 at the age of 85, having lived long enough to see many of his spelling reforms become American standards and to see his speller become an all-time best seller. The lingering controversy in the United States over Webster's reforms and over the relationship of American to British spelling created a receptive climate for a spelling reform movement in the last quarter of the 19th century. An American Philological Association committee, working in cooperation with a similar committee appointed by the Philological Society of England, reported an urgent need for spelling simplification and made specific proposals for achieving this goal. In 1876 an International Convention for the Amendment of English Orthography was held in Philadelphia, resulting in the formation of the Spelling Reform Association in the United States, and shortly thereafter in a companion organization in England (which counted numerous distinguished authors and philologists among its vice-presidents).

After several of its annual meetings, the U.S. Spelling Reform Association printed the records of its meetings in one or another of the simplified spellings that it was advocating. An excerpt from the meeting at Chautauqua, New York, in 1880 read: "The Missouri Pres Asociation, meeting at Sedalia in May, unanimously past the following resolutions: Hweraz the iregyularitiz ov Inglish orthografi ar a great obstacl tu the progres ov the pepl. . . ."[42] The previous year's record was printed with modified letters, complete with diacritics and shadowing. One writer described the appearance of these pages as that of "a very ancient or an obscure foreign language."[43]

Through the 1880s, both the Philological Society of England and the American Philological Association issued broad recommendations for simplifying thousands of spellings, but little progress in actual reform was made until 1898, when the board of directors of the National Education Association (NEA) adopted 12 simplified spellings for use in its proceedings: *tho, altho, thoro, thoroly, thorofare, thru, thruout, catalog, prolog, decalog, demagog,* and *pedagog.*[44] Both the moderation displayed by the NEA proposal and the presence on the proposing committee of W. T. Harris, U.S. Commissioner of Education, gave the reform movement an acceptability and rationality that the philologists had failed to achieve with their endless lists of reforms. The next major boost for spelling reform came in 1906 when, with a subsidy of $10,000 per year from Andrew Carnegie, the Simplified Spelling Board was created.[45] Like the previous associations, boards, and committees, this one also sported a star-studded list of officers and collaborators, including Andrew Carnegie, Samuel Clemens, Melvil Dewey, William James, and the editors of most English-language dictionaries. At once the board issued a series of circulars in which it advocated the use of the simpler spellings of 300 particular words that were already spelled in two or more ways.[46]

Most of the reforms were based on principles that rational people would have found acceptable—for example, dropping the <e> after <dg> in words like *abridgment, lodgment,* and *acknowledgment,* and preferring <ense> over <ence> in *defense, offense,* and so on.[47] Many of the reforms, such as final <er> in *center* and *theater,* and final <or> in *honor* and *labor,* were already preferred American spellings. Others were acceptable alternatives (e.g., *catalog, acknowledgment*) if not the preferred spellings. Only a few, such as *pur* and *bur* and the <t> preterite after <s, sh, p> (e.g., *dipt, husht*), could be considered radical. The degree of departure that these reforms represented from current practice was summarized by the head of the U.S. Government Printing Office, Charles Stillings, in the introduction to the basic word list: "The seeming difficulties of adopting copy to the new method will become greatly minimized when it is realized that of the three hundred words recommended for immediate adoption one hundred fifty-three are at present in preferred use in the Government Printing Office; forty-nine of the others in this list are not preferred in Webster's Dictionary, but are used in the Government Printing Office wherever the author requests copy to be followed."[48]

As careful as the society was in selecting noncontroversial spellings for reform, and in eschewing the radical and wide-sweeping proposals that had doomed previous simplification movements, it could not totally resist the hyperbole that has characterized most orthographic evangelists. "Intricate and disordered spelling" was the only barrier to English's becoming the "dominant and international language of the world," announced Circular 1 of the Simplified Spelling Board. The consequences of this chaos were frightening to behold: "It wastes a large part of the time and effort given to the instruction of our children, keeping them, for example, from one to two years behind the school children of Germany. . . . Moreover, the printing, typewriting, and handwriting of the useless letters which our spelling prescribes, and upon which its difficulty chiefly rests, waste every year millions of dollars, and time and effort worth millions more."[49] The financial theme was to be picked up in a later circular, with estimates of the savings that would accrue to education and industry through simplified spelling.

The Simplified Spelling Board deliberately chose a policy of gradual simplification, beginning with changes that had a high probability of popular acceptance. Success seemed to have been ensured when, as soon as the 300 simplified spellings were published, President Roosevelt ordered the U.S. Government Printing Office to follow the board's recommendations in all documents from the executive branch, and urged Congress to make them the standard for all government publications. In Teddy Roosevelt, the simplified spelling movement could not have hoped for a more sympathetic ally. A graduate of Harvard and the author of several American histories (including *The Naval War of 1812* and *The Winning of the West*), Roosevelt became a progressive reformer in the late 1890s while governor of New York. As president, he frequently entertained artists, writers, and professors; he also "wrote introductions to dissident books like Ross's *Sin and Society* [and] named that persistent nonconformist, Oliver Wendell Holmes, to the Supreme Court."[50] Spelling reform was a natural addition in 1906 to the reforms that Roosevelt had already initiated in antitrust procedures, conservation, workmen's compensation, food and drug sales, and meat inspection.

According to one of his biographers, Roosevelt's interest in spelling reform may have come from early difficulties in spelling.[51] Whatever the validity of this claim, the link from the spelling reform movement to Roosevelt was certainly Brander Matthews—professor of literature at Columbia University; prolific writer of novels, reviews, essays, and other belles lettres; and chairman of the trustees of the Simplified Spelling Board. Matthews was a close friend of Roosevelt for many years before Roosevelt became president. It was at Matthews's invitation that Roosevelt had written an article on the history of New York City for the American Historic Towns Series in 1891, and it was Matthews who urged him to assist in promoting the Simplified Spelling Board's first list of offerings.[52]

The changes accepted by Roosevelt were described in the Simplified Spelling Board's 1906 pamphlet, which it entitled *The Roosevelt Fonetic Spelling Book*. As Roosevelt claimed in his contribution to the word list's introduction, "If the slight changes in the spelling of the three hundred words proposed wholly or partially meet popular approval, then the changes will become permanent . . . if they do not ultimately meet with popular approval they will be dropt and that is all there is about it."[53]

But the glory of the world has made no quicker transit than it did in 1906 for spelling reform. Roosevelt's order of August 27, 1906, to the U.S. Government Printing Office evoked an immediate and vociferous opposition from the public.

In November of that year, Congress received the President's special message on his visit to the isthmus of Panama and on plans for the Panama Canal in the reformed spelling, and quickly expressed its outrage. The Louisville *Courier-Journal* captured the flavor of the opposition in an editorial entitled "Nuthing Escapes Mr. Rucevelt," noting that "No subject is tu hi fr him to takl, nor tu lo for him to notis. . . . He now assales the English langgwidg."[54]

Roosevelt's political acumen had improved immensely from the time 11 years before when, as New York City police commissioner, he had stubbornly attempted to enforce Sunday liquor laws. On this occasion he decided that combat with Congress should be reserved for more important issues, and committed himself to rescind his order if the House of Representatives went on record against it. The House did just that on December 13, 1906, and Roosevelt, with Matthews protesting, fulfilled his promise immediately. "I could not by fighting have kept the new spelling in," he replied to Brander Matthews on December 16: "It was evidently worse than useless to go into an undignified contest when I was beaten. . . . But I am mighty glad I did the thing anyhow."[55]

Roosevelt's backing, rather than accelerating the acceptance of spelling reform, produced the opposite effect by stirring to action the traditionalists who until then had considered spelling reform to be distant and abstract. Congress's refusal to go along with Roosevelt, and the public outcry that resulted from his executive order, were as much reactions to the arrogation of linguistic authority on his part as they were to the 300 innocent spellings that the Simplified Spelling Board had offered. In the coming years Carnegie raised the board's subsidy to $25,000 a year, and various organizations, including the NEA and the Modern Language Association, officially adopted the board's reforms; however, the damage done by Congress and the public airing of the reform issue blocked the full acceptance that had seemed so close at hand.

A few years prior to Carnegie's death in 1919 the board's subsidy ended, and the staff was forced to move out of its Madison Avenue offices to a distant upstate New York resort.[56] In 1921 the NEA withdrew its support for reformed spelling, and in time most other organizations and publications did the same. The last holdout in the United States was the *Chicago Tribune*, which finally conceded in a front-page announcement and editorial on September 29, 1975, that *thru*, *tho*, and *thoro* were through: "From now on Webster's Third will be our guide, first variants preferred. Sanity some day may come to spelling, but we do not want to make any more trouble between Johnny and his teacher."[57] Reform movements continued, and several exist today; still, the potential for success that existed in 1906 has not existed since, and neither the academic community nor the public seems at all interested in the issue of spelling reform.[58]

EPILOGUE

In retrospect, the spelling reform movement deserves some credit for the current acceptance of spellings like *program*, *acknowledgment*, and *catalog*. Even *thru* can be found on road signs and in other places where space for letters is limited. Yet it is undeniable that in terms of its own goals, the reform movement has failed. Why? Part of the answer lies in most people's naturally conservative attitude toward language. Just as we resist rapid changes in our phonology, syntax, and vocabulary, so do we resist changes in spelling. Furthermore, schools, libraries, publishers, and the general public have large investments in printed materials that embody the current orthography; spelling reform is a potential threat to the utility of these holdings. Yet phonology, syntax, and vocabulary do change, and spelling reform need not be so abrupt and extensive as to render existing materials obsolete.

Some of the fault for the failure of spelling reform must be placed on the tactics of the reformers themselves, and particularly on the excesses of rhetoric that have usually pervaded the spelling reform tracts. The spelling reform movement has also suffered from an obsession with phonemic writing—a bias that has occasionally led it to inconsistent and misleading defenses of its proposals. English spelling now, as in 1906, is a phonemically based system that preserves morphemic identity wherever possible. It is not—nor was it ever, even in the beginning, a one-letter, one-sound system, as most reformers claim or imply. Nor is there evidence for claiming that a phonemic writing system may significantly alter the rate at which children acquire literacy.[59] After nearly a century of active reform agitation, no evidence has been produced to demonstrate that words with silent letters, as an example, are significantly more difficult to learn to read than words without silent letters.

Even more important, however, is the concern that if English spelling is pushed more toward a phonemic system, the skilled reader will lose the advantage offered by the morphemic components of the present system. If *cone* and *conic*, for example, were spelled *kon* and *kanic*, their shared semantic base would not be so immediately obvious. Whether this feature has a significant influence on reading rate (or accuracy) has never been determined. If it does, then the gains from a more phonemic system will need to be weighted against the losses from removal of morphemic features. But since this argument does not apply to spellings like *gnat* and *psychology*, where no morphologically related forms are involved, we might ask why these spellings should be suffered. Given our tolerance of the current forms and the lack of convincing evidence for benefits from change, support for change is minimal at best. It might be generated if research could demonstrate that learning to read in a modified English alphabet progresses at a more satisfactory rate than is presently observed in the United States, and especially that children considered at risk for learning to read succeed at a significantly higher rate than they do now.

Some cross-language studies have shown interesting differences between regular and not-so-regular orthographies in the initial stages of learning to read, but much remains to be explored in this area. If anything, we have learned that the perceptual and memory systems can tolerate considerably more complexity and exception than English spelling presents to them, and that the variation in reading abilities across any sizable population of learners is attributable to a host of factors, orthography being at most just one of many.

So we continue with an orthography that was last tampered with 200 years ago by Noah Webster, and that by the beginning of the 20th century was so solidly woven into the national fabric that even Teddy Roosevelt—who led the charge up San Juan Hill, broke up the Northern Securities Company, and resolved the Russo-Japanese War—could not alter a thread of it. Spelling reform does not occupy a central role today in education or in public life. No major funding agency in the last 25 years has included among its highest priorities the development of a simplified spelling system, and few cognitive psychologists have confessed an interest in spelling processes based on reformed orthographies. With the abandonment by the *Chicago Tribune* of the remaining reformed spellings it had adopted 41 years earlier went the last token allegiance to a once grand and glorious movement.

LOOKING AHEAD

Thus ends the spelling reform story. The last chapter of this book follows obliquely from this issue, because one of the arguments of the spelling reformers has been that children in the English-speaking world are confronted with an unnecessary burden in learning to read because of the irregularities in English spelling. Chapter 12 addresses the issue of teaching letter–sound correspondences—that is, the initial stages of learning to read in any sensible literacy curriculum. The issue discussed there is not so much the pedagogical methods to employ as the content (which patterns to teach and in what order). This will not be the last word on this topic, but I do hope it is viewed as a rational statement on a topic that for too long has been left to polemic, misinformation, and at times plain ignorance.

NOTES

1. See Haugen (1950).
2. Saussure (1916/1959), 10.

3. Grimm (1822–1827).
4. Saussure (1916/1959), 23, 30.
5. Stetson (1937).
6. Bazell (1956).
7. See especially Bloomfield (1942).
8. Hockett (1958), 542.
9. Vachek (1959), 8.
10. Francis (1958), 450–469.
11. Francis (1958), 468.
12. Bradley (1928), 176.
13. Bradley (1928), 186.
14. See Burchfield (1956).
15. Bullokar (1580); Gill (1619/1972).
16. See Dobson (1957), I, 38–46.
17. Smith (1568/1913). See also Dobson (1957), I, 46–62.
18. Hart (1569/1955), 121.
19. Hart (1569/1955).
20. Hart (1569/1955), 118.
21. The text was edited by Henry B. Wheatley and issued as Publication No. 5 of the Early English Text Society (Hume, c. 1617/1865).
22. Hume (c. 1617/1865), 1.
23. Hume (c. 1617/1865), 7.
24. Jonson (1634/1972).
25. Hume (c. 1617/1865), 21.
26. Wheatley (Ed.), in Hume (c. 1617/1865), 35.
27. Douglas (c. 1740/1956).
28. Douglas (c. 1740/1956), 128.
29. For a description of the early spelling reform efforts in the United States, see Tauber (1958).
30. Of the various biographies of Noah Webster, Warfel (1936), although sycophantic, is generally the most accessible. Less available generally are Scudder (1881) and Shoemaker (1936). Skeel and Carpenter (1958) is a complete catalog of Webster's works.
31. The history of Webster's Blue-Back Speller is traced by Monaghan (1983) in her comprehensive study.
32. Webster (1783/1968), 4.
33. Webster (1783/1968), 11.
34. Webster (1783/1968), 11, fn.
35. Webster (1789/1908), 387f.
36. Webster (1790), cited in Warfel (1936), 138.
37. Warfel (1936), 158.
38. Webster (1806), vii.
39. Several examples of faulty etymologies can be found in Webster's preface to the 1806 dictionary. See, as an example, the historical sketch for <c> (p. vii). Malone (1925) has pointed out the faulty derivation of *provable*, *movable*, and the like. (Webster incorrectly derived these from French verbs rather than French adjectives.)

40. Although Webster claimed to have studied ancient languages intensely in preparation for writing his major dictionary, he remained unaffected by the philological revolution that was occurring in Europe at the time. He either ignored or was unaware of the work of Sir William Jones, Jacob Grimm, and Franz Bopp in comparative phonology (Morgan, 1975, 168). So far as his writings reveal, Webster never modified his Biblically-based view that all of the world's languages derived from the Semitic, with the three sons of Noah being the progenitors of the major language branches evidenced in Webster's time. The introduction to the 1828 dictionary was devoted almost entirely to establishing this view, complete with etymologies based on Hebrew roots for English words.

41. Cobb (1831).

42. Wesley (1957), 218.

43. Quoted in Wesley (1957), 218.

44. Wesley (1957).

45. Andrew Carnegie, who was born in a weaver's cottage in 1835 in Scotland and died near Lennox, Massachusetts in 1919, was one of America's most generous and diverse philanthropists. The $311,594,230 that he is known to have given away, either personally or through the Carnegie Corporation of New York, went to every imaginable human pursuit—from art, to research on radium, to the strengthening of educational institutions like the Tuskegee and the Hampton Institutes (see Lester, 1941, and Carnegie Endowment for International Peace, 1919, for a listing of benefactors). Carnegie established a $280,000 endowment for the Simplified Spelling Board and became himself an advocate of reformed spelling. He used simplified spellings, although not consistently, in personal correspondence and in the parts of his will that appear in his own hand (Hendrick, 1932, II, 263).

46. References to Circulars 1–6 of the Simplified Spelling Board are to their reissue by the U.S. Government, Office of the Public Printer in 1906, with continuous pagination. They are referenced here as Stillings (1906).

47. Stillings (1906), 14.

48. Stillings (1906), 3.

49. Stillings (1906), 7.

50. Goldman (1956), 127.

51. Pringle (1931).

52. Roosevelt (1951), II, 147, fn. 1.

53. Simplified Spelling Board (1906), 3. This pamphlet, which includes Roosevelt's portrait on the cover, consists of most of Roosevelt's letter of August 27, 1906 to the Public Printer (Charles A. Stillings), directing that the Simplified Spelling Board's 300 simplified spellings be used in "all Government publications of the Executive Departments" (p. 5), plus most of Circular 2 of the Simplified Spelling Board.

54. Quoted in Gardner (1973), 71.

55. Roosevelt (1951), V, 527.

56. By 1915 Carnegie had soured on the Simplified Spelling Board. To Henry Holt he wrote, "A more useless body of men never came into association, judging from the effects they produced. Instead of taking twelve words and urging their adoption, they undertook radical changes from the start and these they can never

make. . . . I have much better use for Twenty-five thousand dollars a year" (quoted in Wall, 1970, 893). When the initial endowment ran out in 1917, Carnegie did not renew it. Wall (1970, 893) claims that "Of all of Carnegie's various ventures into reform, this proved to be his most complete failure."

57. Quoted in Vivian (1979).
58. For an example of a current and rational simplified spelling proposal, see Rondthaler & Lias (1986).
59. Psychological studies of reading rates and reading fatigue with modified spelling systems are rare. Among the few that merit attention are Yule (1986) and Yule & Greentree(1986).

CHAPTER 12

Teaching Phonics

The human fledgling—
barely out of the egg—
grasps at a book,
at quires of exercise paper.
But I learned my alphabet from signboards,
leafing through pages of iron and tin.
—VLADIMIR MAYAKOVSKY
(1922/1960), 157

Now begins the final chapter, the terminus of this long journey over the orthographic trail. This is where I venture into instruction and pedagogy, presenting a plan for teaching decoding patterns, or what others often call *phonics*. What is presented here is a rationale for teaching phonics and a sketch of the content of such instruction. What are not included are teaching strategies—the paradigms, games, activities, and other devices that experienced teachers have developed to make learning take place. Nevertheless, the reader is not spared a few opinions about how these should be deployed, derived from many years of designing prereading, reading, spelling, and language arts programs, and from both doing and reading research on the same.[1] All seven principles presented in Chapter 1 serve as the foundation for teaching phonics, but the emphasis here is primarily on the early stages, where mainly the simpler patterns presented in Chapters 8 and 9 are introduced.

FUNCTIONS OF PHONICS

Phonics is a means to an end, not an end itself. Its functions are somewhat speculative, but most scholars agree that at least three are crucial to the acquisition of competent reading habits. One is to provide a process for approximating the sound of a word known from listening but not recognized quickly by sight. For this to work, decoding patterns need not generate perfect representations of speech. Instead, they need to get the reader close enough that, with context, the correct identification can be made. Readers of all levels of experience attempt to use decoding patterns when they are confronted with unfamiliar words or with words that are visually obscured, such as a street sign in a dark location.

Another function is to focus the reader on the letters and letter strings of a word, so that visual word recognition can develop properly for that word. If readers did not need to recognize the functional units of a word—<ee, tch, b>, and all the others—there would be no compelling reason to focus on these in learning to recognize words visually. Consequently words might be approached as if they were Chinese characters, instead of sequences of letters and letter units. From what we know about visual word recognition, familiar sequences of letters facilitate recognition much more than overall word shape does. That is, through learning to decode, readers develop a familiarity with letters, functional units, and other familiar sequences of letters, and these help speed word recognition. One proof of this is the *word superiority effect*, which is the advantage in speed of recognition that a letter within a letter string has when it is embedded within a regular sequence as opposed to an irregular one (e.g., the letter <c> in *acroming* vs. *mcnunxh*).

One could also speculate that because of the extra effort required to determine pronunciations, learning a complex orthography like English leads to faster word recognition than does learning a simple orthography such as Finnish, which can be pronounced in a left-to-right scan without considering units larger than a single letter. On this, however, little evidence is currently available.

A third function of phonics is to generate a pronunciation for a word unknown either by sight or by sound. This function is problematic, in that the imperfections in English orthography make such generation uncertain. If a word is totally unknown, the reader has little basis for deciding whether any particular pronunciation is correct or not. However, often even an incorrect pronunciation will facilitate memory for the word, and this can be easily replaced when the correct pronunciation is either encountered in listening or generated from a dictionary.

GENERAL PRINCIPLES

Since the most important function of phonics is to facilitate the development of rapid visual recognition of words, not all decoding patterns need be taught. Furthermore, all the principles of learning that have been uncovered in the teaching of other topics need not be ignored. Learners need to be motivated; learning needs to be meaningful; practice is required to fix habits; and in initial reading children learn best from exemplars, not from overtly presented rules. To learn, for example, that <c> has one pronunciation before <e, i, y> and another pronunciation elsewhere, children require lots of words with each of these patterns. Whether these words are proper nouns or any other type of word doesn't appear to matter. For children who are average or above-average learners and who have good letter and sound skills, both of these patterns may be acquired at the same time. However, for learners who are struggling to learn to read, the simultaneous introduction of the two <c> pronunciations, of the free and checked vowel patterns, or of any other variant pattern, is almost certain to depress learning. As children become more proficient decoders, however, they begin to understand how to apply rules, and can learn new patterns more quickly.

One part of learning to decode is learning the basic game—that sounds are connected with letters and letter sequences, that they are blended to make a coherent sound unit, and that the result is matched with something in listening memory. If what is first produced does not sound like something already known from listening, a child has to change one or more of the sound associations (most probably a vowel) and try again. The result, however, should make sense in the context in which it appears. This is the process for short words. For longer words, visual segmentation skills need to be acquired. Word parts need to be identified—common beginnings and endings, mostly—and sounds need to be assigned to the resulting pieces either by recall (e.g., final *ing*, initial *pre*) or by the process just described above. In addition, stress needs to be assigned to syllables.

In learning decoding patterns, children must acquire what Gibson and Levin call a *set for variability*.[2] That is, if one pronunciation does not produce a known word that makes sense for the context, a child has to try a different pronunciation, as explained above. Why some children acquire this set for diversity quickly and others only after great effort remains a mystery. Teachers should try modeling how to figure out a word through decoding, producing first a nonword and then, through successive refinement, the correct word. Students should be asked repeatedly, "What other sounds could that letter [digraph, etc.] have?" and "Do you know a word in which it has a different sound?" In addition, lots of printing and spelling activities should be used to help children focus on specific letters and sounds and to build representations for letter–sound and sound–letter patterns.

A related factor is that children need to read to become better readers. Lots and lots of books need to be available, both in school and at home. Parents, older siblings, relatives, volunteer tutors, and just about anyone else who can read should be recruited to help young children practice reading. For children having difficulties in the initial stages, rereading simple passages and stories can help build confidence and reinforce word recognitions. If sight words help keep motivation and interest high, teachers and others should prepare lots of word cards for practice.

One of the less understood parts of teaching phonics is how children deal with exceptions to patterns. For average and above-average learners, exceptions appear not to interfere with pattern acquisition. Life is full of exceptions to rules: Bedtime is 8:30 P.M., except when Grandma comes or on certain holidays; *The Simpsons* starts at 8:00 P.M., except when a special program is broadcast; and so on. Most children have no difficulty learning that words such as *the, whom,* and *woman* should be learned as whole units and not used to generalize patterns. Nevertheless, some parts of these words do follow regular patterns, and children come in time to recognize this, even though the words have been taught as sight words.

One central problem for many children in learning to read is recalling which sounds go with which letters. Some teachers try to use letter names to facilitate recall of sounds. This works for some sounds, but it has some drawbacks also. For <h, w, y> the letter names do not contain the sounds of the associated letters. For <c>, <g>, and the vowel letters, the letter names do not contain the sounds usually taught first. For the remaining consonants, seven have the pattern vowel + consonant (<f, l, m, n, r, s, x>) while the remainder are consonant + vowel. An alternative to letter names as props for recalling letter sounds is to use key exemplars (e.g., "/n/ is the *noodle* sound") or to create artificial but believable connections between the letters and the sounds: "<s> looks like a snake and makes the snake sound /s/," "<a> looks like an open mouth and has the sound /a/ that the doctor asks you to make when he looks at your throat," and so on.

SELECTING AND SEQUENCING PATTERNS

It is probably not too important which patterns are introduced first, so long as the patterns lead in short order to real words, and the features needed for deciding on their pronunciations are not complex. Checked vowels tend to be easier to introduce than free vowels, because they do not require attention to a final <e> or to a digraph spelling. Similarly, nasals, fricatives, and liquids tend to be easier to introduce than stops, because they can be sustained in isolation. (Children are able to work with sounds presented in isolation or in phonological context; furthermore, perfect pronunciation of consonants—i.e., pronunciation without a following vowel or off-glide—does not appear to be required for children to learn sounds associated with letters. Children are flexible learners when confronted with well-planned instruction.)

Some teachers have success in teaching phonics with occasional nonsense words; others shy away from this practice for fear that meaningless words will somehow confuse children. There is, so far as I know, no empirical data to support either side of this divide, although common sense would lead to judicious use of such creations. Children love nonsense words in poems such as "Jabberwocky"; decodable nonsense words can be made just as meaningful. On the other hand, a child struggling to create something meaningful from print may be confused by the lack of meaning in such words.

Mixing sight words and decoding patterns is important for ensuring that meaningful sentences can be read, but too much is made of so-called "authentic" texts. Children learning to read want and need success, and whether this success comes from real or made-up sentences is unimportant. At this stage they neither need nor appreciate great literature. "Dan has a fan" is perfectly fine for initial reading, as are any one of a number of other silly or stilted sentences. The enduring popularity of *The Cat in the Hat*, which Dr. Seuss created for teaching phonics, is ample proof of the interest children have in limited-vocabulary texts. Exercise phonics, synthetic words, repetitive sentences, and whatever else works are all highly recommended.

This is not to say that texts in the real world should be ignored. The more that communication can be stressed in teaching reading, the better the chances are that a child will remain motivated to learn. Postcards, letters, brief poems, signs, directions, labels on maps, and any other familiar form of writing should be the first choices for teaching reading. But artificial texts are fine when specific patterns and words need to be taught and no real texts can be found with them. With a little imagination, almost anything written can be presented as a "real" or "authentic" text.

GETTING STARTED

All beginnings are difficult, and initial reading is no exception. For children who do not recognize most of the letters and have difficulties making rhymes and playing sound games, considerable sound practice will be required, along with experience with the alphabet. For children ready for instruction, teachers can begin by teaching some sight words, using these to make simple phrases and sentences, and then taking apart the decodable words to teach phonics patterns. Alternatively, teachers can dive in with correspondences—perhaps short <f> → /f/, <a> → /æ/, and <n> → /n/—and then make the word *fan*. From here <m> → /m/ can be taught, making *man*, and so on through other consonants and vowels. A third strategy is to teach endings such as <an> → /æn/ and <it> → /ɪt /, and then teach consonants that allow words such as *pan*, *ran*, *sit*, and *hit* to be decoded. Eventually single-unit vowel correspondences will need to be taught, especially when the digraph vowels and the final-<e> pattern are reached.

Children who cannot attend to single sounds in words—that is, who can't isolate the first sound in *bunny* or decide whether *lamb* and *light* start with the same sound—generally need special practice before being introduced to formal reading instruction. Considerable research over the past 35 years has converged on the lack of this processing ability as a major barrier to learning to read. Most children who have extreme difficulties in learning to read cannot segment separate sounds from words or do some other tasks that require overt attention to separate word sounds. In the research literature this ability is called *phonemic sensitivity* or *phonemic awareness*—terms that are perhaps not wisely chosen.[3] Some children who become normal readers also have difficulties with these same tasks at an early age. In addition, some children who are disabled readers are still able to play with separate sounds when they are used as labels for meaningful concepts, such as saying the sound that a balloon makes when air is let out of it (/s/).

Whether the difficulty that inhibits learning to read is strictly a function of particular tasks that require meaningless sounds to be held in working memory for prolonged periods or sequenced properly, or of some other ability, is not yet determined. Nevertheless, the difficulty is frequently observed and needs overt instructional attention. For these children, extensive practice with rhymes, sorting objects by their first or last sounds, and other sound-based activities may be needed. However, many children acquire phonemic awareness through learning the alphabet.

THE CONTENT OF INSTRUCTION

There are about 100 patterns that should be taught explicitly in the first two or three years of reading instruction, not counting common prefixes and suffixes or exception words. Of these, about 58 are for consonants, about 38 are for vowels, and the remaining 4 are for spelling rules. The lists that follow are based upon an analysis of the most common 5,000 words in printed English. Although the frequency count from which these 5,000 words were drawn is quite old, nothing significant would change if a more recent list were used. In many cases, counts of the number of words that contain a particular pattern are presented. These should be taken as approximations and not as exact statistics. No effort has been made to reduce these counts to basic words or to eliminate proper nouns. For example, <ch> occurs 107 times in this corpus. Eight examples have <ch> → /k/ (*character*, *choir*, *ache*, etc.); 96 have <c> → /č/; and 3 have <c> → /š/. These 3, however, are *Chicago*, *machine*, and *machinery*; among them is only one base form that is not a proper noun. Similarly, for <ch> → /k/, both *character* and *characteristic* are counted.

For initial instruction, <ch> can be treated as regularly mapping to /č/. The /k/ and /š/ pronunciations can be treated as exceptions, since in initial reading few of them will occur. The two alternative pronunciations can be taught at later times. (In the lists that follow, both <ch> → /č/ and <ch> → /k/ are included, but not <ch> → /š/, because the latter occurs mostly in low frequency-words—*chalet*, *bouquet*, *valet*, etc.)

Checked Vowels

The checked vowel correspondences in the most common words in English have many exceptions; nevertheless, six regular patterns and two alternate ones (for <o> and <u>) are highly productive. Whether or not to teach <y> → /ɪ/ as a regular pattern is left as an option for the instructor, although it is listed here. Only three common monosyllabics contain this correspondence: *gym*, *hymn*, and *myth*. It might best be left for multisyllabics such as *cloudy*, *foggy*, and *icy*. On the other hand, since <y> → /aɪ/ is so common (*by*, *cry*, *dry*, *fry*, *my*, etc.), symmetry might lead to introducing both correspondences for <y> (but not at the same time).

Caution needs to be taken in working with words that have final <en> and <og> (*men*, *when*, etc., and *cog*, *hog*, *fog*, *log*, etc.) since these vary, often irregularly, by dialect. The safest practice is not to use these as exemplars for the vowel patterns involved.

Regular Correspondences

<a> → /æ/: *hat, man, sad, cap*
<e> → /ɛ/: *pet, bed, hem, web*
<i> → /ɪ/: *hid, dim, bit, lip*
<o> → /a/: *hot, fox, mop, rod*

<u> → /ʌ/: *fun, cut, gum, tub*
<y> → /ɪ/: *gym, hymn, myth, bunny*

Alternate Correspondences

<o> → /ʌ/: *ton, son, money, tongue*
<u> → /ʊ/: *bull, full, pull; bush, bushel, push*

Free Vowels—Final-<e> Pattern

The free vowel correspondences in the final-<e> pattern have a few rough spots for instruction. First, <e> has too few exemplars among the common words to be taught as a pattern. The digraphs <ee> and <ea> are far more common as spellings for /i/ than <e . . . e>. Then free <u> has a leading glide, /j/ or /ɪ/, according to the preceding consonant (and, in certain cases, according to dialect). Although these may not affect student ability to generalize a pattern, the instructor needs to be aware of the potential problem. But it is doubtful that any good can be done in instruction by overtly pointing out the different pronunciations. Example words are given to provide a contrast with corresponding checked vowel patterns; however, this should not be a signal to teach the two patterns simultaneously.

Regular Correspondences—Final-<e> Pattern

<a> → /e/: *cape* (*cap*), *mate* (*mat*), *made* (*mad*)
<e> → /i/: *scene* [not suggested as a pattern, however]
<i> → /aɪ/: *dime* (*dim*), *fine* (*fin*), *hide* (*hid*)
<o> → /o/: *rode* (*rod*), *note* (*not*), *robe* (*rob*)
<u> → /u/ or /ju/ or /ɪu/: *tube* (*tub*), *cute* (*cut*), *cube* (*cub*)
<y> → /aɪ/: *rhyme, hype, type*

Regular Correspondences—Other Patterns

<a> → /e/: *baby, crazy, lady, table*
<e> → /i/: *be, he, me, she*
<i> → /aɪ/: *child, mild, wild; find, kind, mind; sign, tiny; bright, fight, high, sight*
<o> → /o/: *old, hold, gold; bolt, jolt, volt; ghost, host, most; poll, roll, toll; bony, both*
<u> → /u/ or /ju/ or /ɪu/: *duty, Judy, Ruth, truth*
<y> → /aɪ/: *bye, rye; Bryan, cycle, style; by, my, sly*

Alternate Free Vowel Correspondences

<i> → /i/: *police, machine, marine*
<o> → /ɔ/: *long, song, wrong; cross, moss, toss; cost, frost, lost; broth, cloth, moth*

Digraph Vowels

Among the digraph vowel correspondences, the major ones are all free vowel patterns, while the minor ones are all checked vowel patterns. In addition, a regular alternation in spelling occurs in that <i> alternates with <y> and <u> alternates with <w> regularly (or mostly so) as the final letters in certain vowel digraphs. The letters <i> and <u> occur before consonants, while <y> and <w> occur before vowels and in final position. The only major exception to this alternation is <ow>, which occurs both in final position and before consonants: *howl, own, crown,* and so on.

Major Digraph Vowel Correspondences

<ai> or <ay> → /e/: *bait, pain, day, clay*
<ea> or <ee> → /i/: *eat, team, east; see, tree, seek*
<ew> → /u/ or /ju/ or /ɪu/: *chew, dew, flew, stew*
<ie> → /i/: *brief, chief, field, thief*
<oa> → /o/: *boat, foam, goal, toast*
<oi> or <oy> → /ɔɪ/: *boil, coin, oil; boy, Roy, toy*
<oo> → /u/: *bloom, boom, cool, food*
<ou> or <ow> → /aʊ/: *cloud, foul, out; allow, cow, howl*

Alternate Major Digraphs

<ea> → /ɛ/: *bread, breath, feather, read* (past tense)
<oo> → /ʊ/: *look, stood, took, wood*
<ou> → /ɔ/: *bought, fought, sought, thought*
<ow> → /o/: *arrow, crow, grow, slow*

/r/-Colored Vowels

English pronunciation colors certain vowel sounds when an /r/ follows in the same syllable. The checked correspondences of <e>, <i>, and <u> regularly merge with /r/ to produce a single /r/-colored vowel, which for convenience is represented as if it were still a sequence of two sounds, /ʌr/. Thus *her, sir,* and *fur* all have two phonemes and rhyme. The checked correspondence for <or> following /w/ also shifts to this same /r/-colored vowel (*work, worm, worth,* etc.). The sound /r/ also shifts the checked correspondence for <a> to /a/ as in *bar, barn,* and *farm,* and shifts the free correspondences of <e> and <u> according to dialect. Notice, however, that before <rr> the shift generally does not occur: *Barry, carry, marry; berry, cherry, merry.* Few of these patterns require overt attention in instruction, since they occur automatically for native speakers of English. (There is almost no evidence from instructional studies for deciding which of the /r/-colored vowels need overt attention and which do not. One possibility is that none does. What is presented here is the "best-guess" position.)

/r/-Colored Vowel Patterns

<er> or <ir> or <ur> → /ʌr/: *fern, her, term; birth, girl, sir; burn, fur, hurt*
<ar> → /ar/: *bar, barn, car, farm*
Initial <wor> → /wʌr/: *worm, word, worth*

Schwa

Teaching schwa is problematic because it depends on stress; that is, schwa occurs only in unstressed position, even though it is articulated otherwise identically to /ʌ/. Every single-letter vowel corresponds to schwa in some word, although in many words schwa can alternate with other unstressed vowels. For example, *civil* is pronounced either /sív ɪl/ or /sív əl/. Neither is more correct or proper than the other, although the schwa version is more common in fast speech. To introduce schwa, an instructor should use common words with unstressed initial vowels, such as *away, awake, aware, across,* and *unhappy.*

Consonants

The consonant correspondences, for instructional purposes, are classed here in four groups, representing the suggested priorities for initial introduction of the patterns. Group 1 contains the most common correspondences for <b, d, f, h, j, k, l, m, n, p, r, s, t, v, w, x, y>, plus <c> → /k/ and <g> → /g/. (The letter <x> is taught in this group only with /ks/, as in *next, fox,* and *fix.*)

Group 2 consists of the pseudogeminates, <ck>, <dg>, and <tch>; the digraphs <ch, gh, ng, ph, sh, th, wh>; the alternate correspondences for <c> and <g> (/s/ and /ǰ/, respectively); <qu> → /kw/; <z> → /z/; the common initial and final clusters; and silent <k>, as in *know, knee,* and *knot.* (For <ch>, only the /č/

correspondence is taught in this group, and for <th>, only /θ/ as in *thin* and *thick*. Whether to teach <th> → /ð/, as in *then*, *the*, *these*, etc., is left to the teacher to decide. For <gh>, only the silent correspondence as in *fight* and *night* is taught.)

Group 3 consists of the final clusters <ff, ll, ss, zz>; silent <l>, as in *half* and *walk*; <s> → /z/, as in *has*, *as*, and *was*; silent <w>, as in *write* and *wrong*; contractions (*don't*, *isn't*, *wasn't*, etc.); and the regular plural and past-tense endings.

Group 4 consists of common prefixes (*a, un, re, non*) and suffixes (*ful, ly, ment, ous, er*); stress patterns for two- and three-syllable words; <t> → /š/, as in *nation* and *caution*; <c> → /š/, as in *ocean*, *social* and *special*; <s> → /ž/, as in *measure*, *treasure*, *pleasure*, *usual*, *division* and *decision*; <ch> → /k/, as in *chord* and *mechanical*; silent <h>, as in *honest*, *hour*, *herb* and *honor*; silent <b>, as in *bomb*, *thumb* and *tomb*; and <gh> → /f/, as in *rough* and *tough*.

Spelling Rules and Contractions

For both reading and spelling, the rules for doubling final consonants, dropping or retaining final <e>, and changing <y> to <i> before suffixes should be taught as rules, along with common contractions (*aren't*, *don't*, *isn't*, etc.). Spelling rules are best taught in conjunction with suffixes such as *ing*, *er/est*, *ed*, and *y*: *run–running*, *big–bigger–biggest*, *tip–tipped*, *fun–funny*. Practice is required, however, on all of these patterns, with many exemplars for each.

Exception Words

A substantial number of words are usually taught as sight words, yet within any of these most of the letter–sound patterns are regular. For example, *is* and *has* have irregular <s> → /z/, but otherwise regular correspondences. Early in the teaching of reading, an instructor may want to teach exception words without fanfare—that is, without overt attention to what is irregular. As children begin to develop good decoding skills, however, the irregular patterns should be pointed out as a means of reinforcing both decoding in general and specific spelling units that have alternate or irregular patterns. Among the prime candidates for exception words are the following:

a/an	*has*	*their*
are	*I*	*there*
as	*is*	*to*
been	*live*	*was*
blood	*many*	*were*
come	*me*	*what*

could	*no*	*where*
creek	*of*	*who*
for	*one*	*whom*
from	*only*	*women*
give	*should*	*would*
go	*so*	
great	*the*	

This list should be treated as an initial collection, from which words should be added or subtracted according to the stories and patterns introduced in any particular program, and not as a definitive grouping of irregularities in the English lexicon. Some of these are chosen because they have patterns that are normally taught only in second or third grade, yet the words are important for building natural sentences.

Suffixes and Multisyllabic Words

Longer words—that is, words with three or more syllables—tend to have more regular letter–sound correspondences than one- and two-syllable words. Nevertheless, children need help in decoding multisyllabic words. An initial step in this teaching process is to introduce compound words such as *birdhouse, birthday,* and *shoemaker.* Children, when encountering long words, should be taught to look first for smaller words as in these compounds. Then the instructor should introduce words such as *Monday, Tuesday,* and *shepherd,* which are compounds but which have some less recognizable components.

From this point, common prefixes and suffixes should be introduced. Some have been listed already (*ing, er/est,* etc.). To this list should be added *a, ance/ence, ant/ent, able, al, be, con, ful, in, ish, ity, ly, ment, ness, ous, pre, re, un, under, ward,* and *y.* The object here is not to teach all possible affixes, but to sensitize the students to look for recurring prefixes and suffixes and to use this knowledge to decode longer words. Finally, some practice should be given in trying different stress patterns, with possible change of vowel pronunciations.

Teaching formal rules for dividing words into syllables is of doubtful value. A few rules that relate to vowel pronunciations may help, however, such as that a doubled consonant signals that a preceding vowel is checked and that the consonants close the preceding syllable rather than starting the next syllable (e.g., *manner, traffic, rabbit*). Another useful strategy is to place a single consonant that occurs between two vowels with the preceding vowel, and to give that vowel its checked correspondence. If this doesn't produce a recognizable (or believable but unfamiliar) word, a child should shift the consonant to the following syllable, give the preceding vowel its free pronunciation, and try to pronounce the entire word again. Once again, a set for diversity is critical. If one pronunciation doesn't work, the child should try another.

A CLOSING NOTE

Not all children will need extensive practice with decoding patterns. Some will come to formal reading instruction already reading simple stories. These students may be able to generalize patterns on their own from word lists arranged to reflect correspondences of interest. They do need to be encouraged, nevertheless, to read extensively at a challenge level and to demonstrate decoding knowledge with words in isolation as well as in context. Writing and spelling should be integrated with reading, so that communication can be stressed and children can use literacy functionally. This requires that language arts be taught with a balance of documents, expository texts, narrative texts, and poems. A diet of narrative fiction alone is not a healthy recipe for acquiring the skills needed for everyday reading and for academic learning.

For students who come to formal reading instruction without a beginning sight word vocabulary and without adequate prereading skills, more time must be spent in sound-processing activities (rhymes; matching spoken words by initial, medial, and final sounds; removing a sound to make a new word; etc.) and in alphabet, spoken vocabulary, and sight word teaching. These children will need more reinforcement and more rereading of familiar texts, both for learning sight words and decoding patterns and for building confidence in their own abilities to learn. Positive teacher reinforcement is critical, as is a careful, small-step sequence of instruction with repeated practice.

Among the children who learn slowly will often be some with true learning disabilities. Early diagnosis of potential difficulties is strongly advised. However, until a child fails over an extended period to respond to instruction, no diagnostic result should be taken as confirmation of inability to learn. Enlisting the help of those in the home and of volunteer tutors, if available, is also essential. Parents may need to be told that just reading stories to children is not as useful for learning to read as engaging children with print. That is, as a story is read, words and letters should be pointed out, and the children should be asked to supply names and sounds. In addition, questions about the story should be asked, but these should be questions that challenge the children to connect to prior knowledge, project into the future, and consider possible contradictions.[4]

After-school and summer reading are important for all children. Teachers should ensure that all children have interesting books to read at all times, and that parents know at the end of the school year what reading practice is required over the summer. Any type of reading that interests a child is fine, as long as it is at an appropriate challenge level. Award-winning fiction may interest some children and not others. Comic books, Westerns, romances, baseball cards, and bubble gum wrappers are all acceptable bases for reading practice and potential sources of new vocabulary. What is important is to build an interest in reading and in using print for communication and enjoyment. Few if any children arrive at this position, however, without acquiring good decoding habits.

NOTES

1. The literature on beginning reading is voluminous, but often consists of anecdotes and opinions disguised as legitimate research. A good starting point for the better part of this literature is Snow, Burns, and Griffin (1998). Especially recommended among the works cited here are various studies sponsored by the National Institute of Child Health and Human Development. Another good general source is Adams (1990). Among the separate works on this topic that any serious student should consult are Beck and Juel (1995), Biemiller (1994), Cunningham and Stanovich (1993), Ehri (1992), Ehri and Wilce (1987), Share (1995), Stanovich and West (1989), and Venezky (1995).
2. Gibson and Levin (1975), 292.
3. For more on this topic, see Snow et al. (1998).
4. For a review of this topic, see Meyer et al. (1994).

Thou hast embarked, thou has made the
voyage, thou art come to shore; get out.
—MARCUS AURELIUS

Glossary

affricate   A consonant sound initiated with closure as in producing a **stop**, but completed with air turbulence as in producing a **fricative**. English has two affricates: /č/ and /ǰ/. These can also be represented as /t š/ and /d ž/.

allophone   A phonetic realization of a **phoneme**. For example, /t/ in American English has a number of allophones, including an aspirated one, /tʰ/, which is heard at the beginning of *tin*; an unaspirated variant, which is heard in *stop*; and a glottalized variant often heard in New York City in words such as *bottle*.

alveolar   Pertaining to the ridge on the roof of the mouth just behind the upper teeth. The consonants /t, d, s, z, l, r, n/ are pronounced with the tongue tip or blade near or against the alveolar ridge.

assimilation   An articulatory process through which a sound is modified to make it more like a neighboring sound. Assimilation is either caused by or results in a smoothing of articulation. *Progressive* assimilation occurs when a sound is modified to match the sound before it better. Matching to a following sound is called *regressive* or *anticipatory* assimilation.

back-formation   A word created by reducing or shortening a related, more complex word. For example, *charge* is a back-formation, derived from *charger* ("war horse").

bilabial   Involving the lips as the main articulators. The bilabial consonants in English are /p, b, m/.

checked vowel   A vowel (in speech) that generally does not occur at the end of a morpheme when stressed; that is, a vowel that is always followed by one or more consonants when in stressed positions. The checked vowels in American English are /ɪ, ɛ, æ, ʌ, ʊ/. **Checked** vowels contrast with **free** vowels.

content word   A word whose primary function is to relate lexical meaning, as opposed to grammatical relationships (**function word**).

decoding   In reading, a process for generating the pronunciation of a word from the pronunciations of its letters or letter sequences.

diacritic   A mark such as a macron, cedilla, or circumflex, which is added to a letter to indicate that letter's pronunciation, functional status, or other property within a word.

dialectologist   A person who specializes in the study of dialects.

digraph   A two-letter **functional unit**, such as the <ch> in *chin* or the <ea> in *head*. Digraphs are distinguished from clusters, such as <cl> at the beginning of *clue* and <ea> in *idea*.

diphthong   A vowel pronounced with movement of tongue and lips from one simple (**monophthong**) position to another. American English has three vowels that are considered to be true diphthongs, /aɪ, ɔɪ, ʊ/; in addition, all of the free vowels can be pronounced as diphthongs by the addition of off-glides.

dissimilation   A pronunciation process through which a sound is changed to distinguish it more clearly from a neighboring sound. Like **assimilation**, dissimilation generally occurs gradually, requiring a relatively long period of time to become established.

etymology   The origins of a word.

free vowel   A vowel (in speech) that can occur at the end of a word or **morpheme**. All the vowels in American English that are not **checked** are free.

fricative   Consonant sounds generated by constricting the airstream so that turbulence or friction occurs.

function word   A word, such as a preposition or auxiliary verb, whose primary function is to express a grammatical relationship, as opposed to lexical meaning (**content word**)

functional unit   One or more letters that function together in such a way that the same function cannot be derived from considering the constituent letters separately. All of the single letters are functional units, as are **digraphs** and **trigraphs**.

geminate   In orthography, a doubled letter such as <bb>. In phonology, a doubled consonant or vowel sound.

General American Speech   A variety of American English accents that are marked by a lack of prominent regional characteristics, such as eastern or southern speech.

glide   A vowel-like sound that does not occur as a syllable peak and therefore is classed as a consonant. American English has two glides (also called **semivowels**), /j/ and /w/. When these occur as the second part of a vowel, they are called *off-glides*.

glottal stop   A stop consonant formed by drawing the vocal cords together to cut off the airstream. The glottal stop, represented phonetically as [ʔ], occurs most often in American English as an **allophone** of /t/.

glottis   The opening between the vocal cords.

grapheme   A class of letters, paralleling **phoneme**. In practical terms, used as a synonym of *letter*.

graphotactics   The rules or patterns that describe the allowable sequences of letters within words. For example, English prefers not to have <v> at the end of a word. When it could occur, an <e> is generally added, as in *love*.

Great Vowel Shift   A major shifting of the Middle English long vowels, which may have begun as early as the 1200s, but which was clearly evident by 1500. Through the Great Vowel Shift, the two highest long vowels became **diphthongs**, while the others shifted upward and to the front.

homograph   One of two or more words that share a single spelling but have different meanings or derivations, and sometimes different pronunciations. *Read* (the present tense of the verb "to read") and *read* (the past tense of the same verb) are homographs.

homonym   One of two or more words that share a single spelling and a single pronunciation but have different meanings. *Bar* ("straight piece of metal") and *bar* ("table-like furniture used for serving drinks") are homonyms.

homophone   One of two or more words that share a single pronunciation but have different meanings, derivations, or spellings. In this text, the homophones of most interest are those with a single pronunciation but different spellings, such as *nose* and *knows*.

idiolect   The speech patterns of a single speaker. Speakers of the same dialect or language may have different idiolects, but are by definition mutually intelligible. An idiolect includes speech patterns or accents, as well as vocabulary, morphology, and syntactic patterns.

interdentals   Consonants articulated with the tip of the tongue between the teeth (/θ/, /ð/).

IPA   International Phonetic Alphabet.

labial   Pertaining to the lips. English has both **bilabial** and labiodental consonants.

lateral   A consonant sound produced by forcing the airstream to pass laterally off the tongue. English has one lateral, /l/.

larynx   A cartilage structure at the top of the trachea (windpipe) that contains the vocal cords. It is also called the *voicebox*.

lax   A vowel that is articulated with the speech muscles relatively relaxed. The lax vowels in American English are the **checked** vowels.

liquid   A consonant sound that is voiced and, among other properties, can function as a syllable peak. American English has two liquids, /l/ and /r/.

logographic   A type of writing system in which signs represent words or other forms of meaningful units.

marker   A letter that has no direct reference to sound, but instead indicates the pronunciation of another **functional unit**, indicates its **morphemic** status, or preserves a **graphotactical** pattern.

Middle English   The period from about 1100 to about 1500. Middle English can be viewed as a transition from the form of English spoken in the first half of the Middle Ages to the form spoken at the end of the Middle Ages and the beginning of printing.

Modern English   The forms of English spoken after Middle English—that is, from about 1500 until now.

monophthong   A vowel sound that is spoken with the articulators in a steady-state position throughout its articulation.

morpheme   A minimal unit of meaning in a language. Some words are composed of a single morpheme, but some have two or more, such as *horses.*

monosyllable   A word composed of a single spoken syllable.

morphophoneme   A unit of analysis between a **phoneme** and a **morpheme**, used to represent with a single unit the different phonemic representations of a morpheme.

monomorphemic   A word composed of a single **morpheme**.

nasal   In phonology, a sound produced with air passing through the nasal cavity. English has three nasal stops, /n, m, ŋ/.

obstruents   A consonant formed by either blocking and then releasing the airstream or by constricting it. The obstruents include the **stops**, **affricates**, and **fricatives**.

Old English   The forms of English spoken from the earliest evidence of the language until about 1100.

palatal   Sounds articulated with the front of the tongue raised toward or against the hard palate (or **alveolar** ridge). English has four palatal consonants: /č, ǰ, š, ž/. A semivowel, /j/, is also a palatal.

palatalization   A form of **assimilation** whereby a tongue-tip consonant (/t, d, s, z/) shifts to a palatal (/č, ǰ, š, ž/), under the influence of a following /j/ or /ɪ/.

pharynx   An area in the neck and mouth that extends from the **larynx** to the oral and nasal cavities.

philologist   One who studies texts, writing, and language. It often refers to linguists who worked prior to the time that linguistics became a science separate from philology.

phoneme   A class of similar sounds (*phones*) that contrasts as a class with other classes of sounds to separate meaningful words.

phonemic awareness   An ability to attend to or manipulate single phonemes in spoken words; also referred to as *phonemic sensitivity*. Evidence for phonemic awareness includes the ability to determine the number of **phonemes** in a word; to determine the word created by deleting a specified sound from another word; or to match spoken words by the initial, medial, or final sounds.

phonetic   In phonology, a reference to the physical properties of a speech sound.

phonics   An approach to teaching initial reading based on pronunciation of words by translation from letters into sounds.

phonotactics   The rules or patterns that describe the allowable sequences of sounds in words.

polymorphemic   A word that has more than a single **morpheme**.

postvocalic   Occurring after a vowel. In English, postvocalic /r/ often changes the value of the preceding vowel.

pseudoword   A made-up word, often appearing like a real word. However, pseudo-words can be created with any degree of similarity to real words.

pseudogeminate   The units <ck, dg, tch>, which were created to replace the geminates <kk, gg, chch>.

primary vowel spelling   One of the single-letter vowel units: <a, e, i/y, o, u>.

r-colored vowel   A vowel sound that shifts in pronunciation under the influence of a following /r/.

relational unit   One or more letters that as a unit relate to sound. An alphabetic writing system is composed of relational units and **markers**.

runes   The symbols of the runic alphabet, a writing system that the early Germanic settlers in England brought from the Continent.

schwa   A neutral, unstressed vowel, represented as /ə/. In **General American Speech**, schwa can be treated as an allophone of /ʌ/ but generally is not.

semivowel   One of the **glides** (/j/ and /w/). Semivowels are so named because they are articulated similarly to vowels and can be the second elements of vowels. They cannot, however, be syllable peaks.

sibilant   One of the high-pitched and strident **fricatives** and **affricates**: /s, z, š, ž, č, ǰ/.

sonorant   A speech sound produced predominantly through continual vibration of the vocal cords. Sonorants include all of the vowels plus the **nasals** and the **semivowels** or **glides**.

stop   In phonology, a consonant sound articulated by closing completely the flow of the airstream for a brief period. The stop consonants in English are /p, b, t, d, k, g/, along with the nasal stops /m, n, ŋ/.

syllabary   A writing system composed of symbols that mostly relate to consonant–vowel or vowel–consonant sequences.

syllabic consonant   A consonant that functions as a syllable peak, such as the /m/ in *chasm*. In English, /l, r, m, n/ can occur as syllable peaks.

secondary vowel   A two- or three-letter vowel, such as <oi> or <eau>.

shortened form   A word created by shortening (abbreviating, clipping) a longer word. Some shortened forms, such as *extra* (*extraordinary*) and *auto* (*automobile*), have become standard English words; others, such as *gov* (*government*), are considered informal or slang.

tense   In phonology, the articulation of a vowel with the muscles of the articulators tensed. The tense vowels in English are /i, e, a, ɔ, o, u, aʊ, ɔɪ, aɪ/.

trigraph   A spelling unit composed of three letters, such as <tch> and <eau>.

velar   Pertaining to consonants articulated with the back of the tongue against or near the **velum**. English has three velar consonants: /k, g, ŋ/.

velum   A soft piece of tissue and muscle in the back of the upper part of the mouth. When raised against the back of the **pharynx**, the velum blocks air from entering the nasal cavity. When lowered, it allows air into the nasal cavity.

vocal tract   The **pharynx** and the oral and nasal cavities.

References

Adams, M. J. (1990). *Beginning to read: Thinking and learning about print.* Cambridge, MA: MIT Press.

Akmajian, A., Demers, R., & Harnish, R. M. (1990). *Linguistics: An introduction to language and communication* (3rd ed.). Cambridge, MA: MIT Press.

Albright, R. W. (1958). The International Phonetic Alphabet: Its background and development. *International Journal of American Linguistics, 24* (1, Part 3).

Anderson, I. H., & Dearborn, W. F. (1954). *The psychology of teaching reading.* New York: Ronald Press.

Barzun, J. (1991). *An essay on French verse: For readers of English poetry.* New York: New Directions.

Bateson, F. W. (1941–1957). *The Cambridge bibliography of English literature.* New York: Macmillan.

Bazell, C. E. (1956). The grapheme. *Littera, 3,* 43–46.

Beck, I. L., & Juel, C. (1995). The role of decoding in learning to read. *American Educator, 19*(2), 21–25.

Bellamann, H. (1929, September). Robots of language. *Yale Review,* pp. 212–214.

Bethel, J. P. (Ed.). (1956). *Webster's new collegiate dictionary* (2nd ed.). Springfield, MA: Merriam.

Biemiller, A. (1994). Some observations on beginning reading instruction. *Educational Psychologist, 29*(4), 203–209.

Blair, P. H. (1956). *An introduction to Anglo–Saxon England.* Cambridge, UK: Cambridge University Press.

Bloomfield, L. (1933). *Language.* New York: Holt.

Bloomfield, L. (1942). Linguistics and reading. *Elementary English Review, 19,* 125–130, 183–186.

Bloomfield, L., & Barnhart, C. L. (1961). *Let's read: A linguistic approach*. Detroit, MI: Wayne State University Press.

Bradley, H. (1928). *The collected papers of Henry Bradley, with a memoir by Robert Bridges*. Oxford, UK: Clarendon Press.

Brown, G. (1851). *The grammar of English grammars*. New York: Samuel S. & William Wood.

Buckley, C. (1996, March 11). Répondez, si vous payez. *The New Yorker*, p. 112.

Bullokar, W. (1580). *Booke at large, for the amendment of orthographie for English speech*. London: Denham.

Burchfield, R. W. (1956). The language and orthography of the Ormulum MS. *Transactions of the Philological Society*, 56–87.

Burchfield, R. W. (Ed.). (1972–1986). *A supplement to the Oxford English dictionary*. Oxford, UK: Clarendon Press.

Butler, C. (1910). *Charles Butler's English grammar*. (A. Eichler, Ed.). Halle: M. Niemeyer. (Original work published 1634)

Campbell, A. (1959). *Old English grammar*. Oxford, UK: Clarendon Press.

Carnegie Endowment for International Peace. (1919). *A manual of the public benefactions of Andrew Carnegie*. Washington, DC: Author.

Chaucer, G. (1957). The Canterbury tales: General prologue. In F. N. Robinson (Ed.), *The works of Geoffrey Chaucer* (2nd ed.). Boston: Houghton Mifflin. (Original work composed c. 1387)

The Chicago Manual of Style (14th ed.). (1993). Chicago: University of Chicago Press.

Chomsky, N. (1957). *Syntactic structures*. The Hague, The Netherlands: Mouton.

Chomsky, N., & Halle, M. (1968). *The sound pattern of English*. New York: Harper & Row.

Clemens, S. L. [M. Twain]. (1975). Simplified spelling in ancient Egypt. *Spelling Progress Bulletin*, *15*(3), 10–11. (Original work published 1909)

Cobb, L. (1831). *A critical review of the orthography of Dr. Webster's series of books for systematick instruction in the English language*. New York: Collins & Hannay.

Cook, J. (1955–1974). *The journals of Captain James Cook on his voyages of discovery* (J. C. Beaglehole, Ed.). Cambridge, UK: Published for the Hakluyt Society at the University Press. (Original works written 1768–1779)

Craigie, W. A. (1927). *English spelling: Its rules and reasons*. New York: Crofts.

Craigie, W. A. (1946). *The critique of pure English from Caxton to Smollett* (SPE Tract No. 65). London: Society for Pure English.

Cummings, D. W. (1988). *American English spelling*. Baltimore: Johns Hopkins University Press.

Cummings, E. E. (1991). *Complete poems 1904–1962* (Rev. ed.; G. J. Firmage, Ed.). New York: Liveright.

Cunningham, A. E., & Stanovich, K. E. (1993). Children's literacy environments and early word recognition subskills. *Reading and Writing*, *5*, 193–204.

Dearborn, W. F. (1906). The psychology of reading. *Archives of Philosophy, Psychology, and Scientific Methods*, No. 4.

Deighton, L. C. (1972). *A comparative study of spellings in four major collegiate dictionaries*. Pleasantville, NY: Hardscrabble Press.

Dickson, P. (1992). *Word treasury.* New York: Wiley.

Dionysius Thrax. (1874). The grammar of Dionysius Thrax (T. Davidson, Trans.). *Journal of Speculative Philosophy, 8,* 326–339.

Dobson, E. J. (1957). *English pronunciation 1500–1700* (2 vols.). Oxford, UK: Clarendon Press.

Dogdson, C. L. [L. Carroll]. (1979). Jabberwocky. In M. H. Abrams, E. T. Donaldson, H. Smith, R. M. Adams, S. H. Monk, L. Lipking, G. H. Ford, & D. Daiches (Eds.), *The Norton anthology of English literature* (4th ed., Vol. 2). New York: Norton. (Original work published 1871)

Douglas, J. (1956). *James Douglas on English pronunciation c. 1740* (B. Holmberg, Ed.). Lund: Gleerup. (Original work published c. 1740)

Ehri, L. C. (1992). Reconceptualizing the development of sight word reading and its relationship to recoding. In L. C. Ehri, P. Gough, & R. Treiman (Eds.), *Reading acquisition.* Hillsdale, NJ: Erlbaum.

Ehri, L. C., & Wilce, L. S. (1987). Does learning to spell help beginners learn to read words? *Reading Research Quarterly, 22*(1), 47–65.

Fisher, J. H. (1977). Chancery and the emergence of standard written English in the fifteenth century. *Speculum, 52,* 870–899.

Fisher, J. H. (1996). *The emergence of standard English.* Louisville: University Press of Kentucky.

Flexner, S. B. (Ed.). (1987). *The Random House dictionary of the English language* (2nd ed., unabridged). New York: Random House.

Flom, G. T. (1915). Studies in Scandinavian paleography. *Journal of Germanic and English Philology, 14,* 530–543.

Forster, G. (1777). *A voyage around the world, in His Britannic Majesty's sloop, Resolution.* London: B. White.

Francis, W. N. (1958). *The structure of American English.* New York: Ronald Press.

Friederich, W. (1958). *English pronunciation: The relationship between pronunciation and orthography* (R. A. Martin, Trans.). London: Longmans, Green.

Fries, C. C. (1963). *Linguistics and reading.* New York: Holt, Rinehart & Winston.

García Marquez, G. (1997, August 3). Words are in a hurry, get out of the way. *The New York Times,* p. E13.

Gardner, J. L. (1973). *Departing glory; Theodore Roosevelt as ex–president.* New York: Scribner.

Geisel, T. S. [Dr. Seuss]. (1974). *There's a wocket in my pocket!* New York: Random House.

Gelb, I. J. (1963). *A study of writing* (rev. ed.). Chicago: University of Chicago Press.

Gibson, E. J., & Levin, H. (1975). *The psychology of reading.* Cambridge, MA: MIT Press.

Gibson, E. J., Osser, H., Schiff, W., & Smith, J. (1963). *An analysis of critical features of letters, tested by a confusion matrix* (Final Report on A Basic Research Program on Reading. Cooperative Research Project No. 639). Ithaca, NY: Department of Psychology, Cornell University.

Giegerich, H. J. (1992). *English phonology: An introduction.* Cambridge, UK: Cambridge University Press.

Gill, A. (1972). *Logonomia Anglica.* Stockholm: Almqvist & Wiskell. (Original work published 1619)

Gneuss, H. (1972). The origin of standard Old English and Aethelwold's school at Winchester. *Anglo-Saxon England, 1,* 63–83.

Goddard, I. (1990, September 29). Time to retire an Indian place-name hoax. *The New York Times,* p. 1:22.

Goldman, E. (1956). *Rendezvous with destiny* (rev. ed.). New York: Vintage Books.

Grimm, J. (1822–1837). *Deutsche Grammatik.* Göttingen, Brunswick (Germany): Dieterich.

Hall, R. A., Jr. (1961). *Sound and spelling in English.* Philadelphia: Center for Curriculum Development.

Harris, Z. S. (1951). *Methods in structural linguistics.* Chicago: University of Chicago Press.

Hart, J. (1955). *John Hart's works on orthography and pronunciation* (B. Danielsson, Ed.). Stockholm: Almqvist & Wiskell. (Original work published 1569)

Haugen, E. (1950). *The first grammatical treatise: The earliest Germanic philology* (Language Monographs No. 25). Baltimore: Linguistic Society of America.

Haugen, E. (1951). Directions in modern linguistics. *Language, 27,* 211–222.

Henderson, L. (1985). On the use of the term 'grapheme'. *Language and Cognitive Processes, 1,* 135–148.

Hendrick, B. J. (1932). *The life of Andrew Carnegie.* Garden City, NY: Doubleday, Doran.

Hockett, C. F. (1958). *A course in modern linguistics.* New York: Macmillan.

Hockett, C. F. (1963). Analysis of graphic monosyllables. In E. J. Gibson & H. Levin (Eds.), *A basic research program on reading.* Ithaca, NY: Department of Psychology, Cornell University.

Hofstetter, W. (1988). Winchester and the standardization of Old English vocabulary. *Anglo-Saxon England, 17,* 139–161.

Hogg, R. M. (1992). Phonology and morphology. In R. M. Hogg (Ed.), *The Cambridge history of the English language: Vol. I. The beginnings to 1066.* Cambridge, UK: Cambridge University Press.

Holroyd, M. (1991). *Bernard Shaw: Vol. 3. 1918–1950: The lure of fantasy.* New York: Random House.

Hume, A. (1865). *Of the orthographie and congruitie of the Britan tongue* (H. B. Wheatley, Ed.). London: Published for the Early English Text Society by H. Milford, Oxford University Press. (Original work published c. 1617)

In Spanish, two fewer letters in the alphabet. (1994, May 1). *The New York Times,* p. 1:10.

International Phonetic Association. (1949). *The principles of the International Phonetic Association.* London: Author.

International Phonetic Association. (1989). Report on the 1989 Kiel Convention. *Journal of the International Phonetic Association, 19*(2), 67–80.

Jackson, D. (1981). *The story of writing.* New York: Taplinger.

Jaquith, J. R. (1976). Digraphia in advertising: The public as guinea pig. *Visible Language, 4,* 295–308.

Jespersen, O. H. (1946). *Essentials of English grammar.* Tuscaloosa: University of Alabama Press. (Original work published 1933)

Jespersen, O. H. (1961). *A modern English grammar on historical principles* (Part 1). London: George Allen & Unwin. (Original work published 1909)

Johnson, S. (1755). *A dictionary of the English language* (2 vols.). London: W. Strahan.

Jonson, B. (1972). *The English grammar*. Menston, UK: Scolar Press. (Original work published 1634)

Kaiser, R. (Ed.). (1961). *Medieval English* (5th ed.). Berlin: Privately published.

Katamba, F. (1989). *An introduction to phonology*. London: Longman.

Kenyon, J. S., & Knott, T. (1951). *A pronouncing dictionary of American English*. Springfield, MA: Merriam.

Kingdon, R. (1958). *The groundwork of English stress*. London: Longmans.

Kirkpatrick, E. M. (Ed.). (1983). *Chambers 20th century dictionary*. Edinburgh, UK: Chambers.

Kittredge, G. L. (1906). *Some landmarks in the history of English grammars*. Boston: Ginn.

Krapp, G. P. (1919). *The pronunciation of Standard English in America*. New York: Oxford University Press.

Kreidler, C. W. (1989). *The pronunciation of English*. Oxford: Blackwell.

Kučera, H., & Francis, W. N. (1967). *Computational analysis of present–day American English*. Providence, RI: Brown University Press.

Kurath, H. (1964). *A phonology and prosody of modern English*. Ann Arbor: University of Michigan Press.

Lester, R. M. (1941). *Forty years of Carnegie giving*. New York: Scribner.

Lounsbury, T. R. (1909). *English spelling and spelling reform*. New York: Harper.

Lyall, S. (1993, July 1). A regular guy on a laugh track. *The New York Times*, pp. C1, C5.

Malone, K. (1925). A linguistic patriot. *American Speech, 1,* 26–31.

Martin, H.-J. (1994). *The history and power of writing* (L. G. Cochran, Trans.). Chicago: University of Chicago Press.

Marcus Aurelius Antoninus. (1909). *The meditations of Marcus Aurelius* (George Long, Trans.). New York: P. F. Collier & Son. (Reprinted in *The Harvard Classics*, vol. 2; Charles W. Eliot, Ed.)

Matthews, B. (1892). *Americanisms and Britishisms*. New York: Harper and Brothers.

Matthews, B. (1919, February). The advertiser's artful aid. *Bookman*, p. 662.

Matthews, C. M. (1972). *Place names of the English-speaking world*. New York: Scribner.

Mayakovsky, V. (1960). My university. In P. Blake (Ed.) & M. Hayward & G. Reavey (Trans.), *The bedbug and selected poetry*. New York: Meridian Books. (Original work published 1922)

McLaughlin, J. C. (1963). *A graphemic-phonemic study of a Middle English manuscript*. The Hague: Mouton.

Mencken, H. L. (1936). *The American language* (4th ed.). New York: Knopf.

Meyer, D., & Romano, M. (1994). *The Union Square Cafe cookbook*. New York: HarperCollins.

Meyer, L. A., Wardrop, J. L., Stahl, S. A., & Linn, R. L. (1994). Effects of reading storybooks aloud to children. *Journal of Educational Research, 88*(2), 69–85.

Miller, G. A., Bruner, J. S., & Postman, L. (1954). Familiarity of letter sequences and tachistoscopic identification. *Journal of General Psychology, 50,* 129–139.

Mish, F. C. (Ed.). (1993). *Merriam-Webster's collegiate dictionary* (10th ed.). Springfield, MA: Merriam-Webster.

Monaghan, E. J. (1983). *A common heritage: Noah Webster's blue-back speller.* Hamden, CT: Archon Books.

Morgan, J. S. (1975). *Noah Webster.* New York: Mason/Charter.

Mossé, F. (1968). *A handbook of Middle English* (corrected ed., James A. Walker, Trans.). Baltimore: Johns Hopkins University Press.

Mulcaster, R. (1970). *The first part of the elementarie.* Menston, UK: Scolar Press. (Original work published 1582)

Murdoch, J. E. (1884). *Analytic elocution.* New York: American Book.

Murray, J. A. H., Bradley, H., Craigie, W. A., & Onions, C. T. (Eds.). (1933). *The Oxford English dictionary* (Corr. reissue). Oxford, UK: Clarendon Press.

Nabokov, V. (1989). *Pnin.* New York: Vintage International. (Original work published 1957)

Nicholson, M. (1957). *A dictionary of American-English usage, based on Fowler's Modern English usage.* New York: Oxford University Press.

Norton, D. S., & Rushton, P. (1952). *Classical myths in English literature.* New York: Rinehart.

O'Grady, W., Dobrovolosky, M., & Aronoff, M. (1989). *Contemporary linguistics: An introduction.* New York: St. Martin's Press.

Oxford University Press. (1983). *Hart's rules for compositors and readers at the University Press, Oxford* (39th ed.). Oxford, UK: Author.

Page, R. I. (1964). Anglo-Saxon runes and magic. *Journal of the British Archaeological Association* [3rd series] *27,* 14–31.

Page, R. I. (1973). *An introduction to English runes.* London: Methuen.

Page, R. I. (1990). Dating Old English inscriptions: The limits of inference. In S. Adamson, V. Law, N. Vincent, & S. Wright (Eds.), *Papers from the 5th International Conference on Historical Linguistics.* Amsterdam: John Benjamins.

Parkes, M. B. (1993). *Pause and effect: An introduction to the history of punctuation in the West.* Berkeley: University of California Press.

Penzl, H. (1947). The phonemic split of Germanic 'k' in Old English. *Language, 23,* 33–42.

Peter Pauper Press. (1951). *The world's best limericks.* Mount Vernon, NY: Author.

Peterson, G. E., & Lehiste, I. (1960). Duration of syllable nuclei. *Journal of the Acoustical Society of America, 32,* 693–703.

Pope, M. K. (1934). *From Latin to modern French with especial consideration of Anglo-Norman.* Manchester, UK: Manchester University Press.

Pound, L. (1923). Spelling–manipulation and present–day advertising. *Dialect Notes, 5*(6), 226–232.

Pound, L. (1925). The kraze for "k." *American Speech, 1,* 43–44.

Pringle, H. F. (1931). *Theodore Roosevelt: A biography.* New York: Harcourt, Brace.

Proctor, P. (Ed.). (1995). *Cambridge international dictionary of English.* Cambridge, UK: Cambridge University Press.

Publications of the English Place-Names Society. (1924–present). Cambridge, UK: Cambridge University Press.

Pulgram, E. (1951). Phoneme and grapheme: A parallel. *Word, 7,* 15–20.

Pullum, G. K. (1990). Remarks on the 1989 revision of the International Phonetic Association. *Journal of the International Phonetic Association, 20*(1), 33–40.

Pyles, T. (1964). *The origins and development of the English language.* New York: Harcourt, Brace & World.

Robinson, F. (1973). Syntactic glosses in Latin manuscripts of Anglo-Saxon provenance. *Speculum, 48*(3), 443–475.

Rondthaler, E., & Lias, E. J. (Eds.). (1986). *Dictionary of American spelling.* New York: American Language Academy.

Roosevelt, T. (1951). *The letters of Theodore Roosevelt* (8 vols., E. E. Morison, Ed.). Cambridge, MA: Harvard University Press.

Rush, J. (1855). *The philosophy of the human voice.* Philadelphia: Lippincott, Grambo.

Russell, B. (1945). *A history of Western philosophy.* New York: Simon & Schuster.

Saenger, P. (1998). *Space between words: The origins of silent reading.* Stanford, CA: Stanford University Press.

Samuels, M. L. (1963). Some applications of Middle English dialectology. *English Studies, 44,* 81–94.

Saussure, F. de. (1959). *Course in general linguistics* (C. Bally & A. Reidlinger, Eds.; W. Baskin, Trans.). New York: Philosophical Library. (Original work published 1916)

Scanlon, D. M., & Vellutino, F. R. (1996). Prerequisite skills, early instruction, and success in first-grade reading: Selected results from a longitudinal study. *Mental Retardation and Developmental Disabilities Research Reviews, 2,* 54–63.

Scragg, D. G. (1974). *A history of English spelling.* Manchester, UK: Manchester University Press.

Scudder, H. E. (1881). *Noah Webster.* Boston: Houghton Mifflin.

Shakespeare, W. (1952). Love's labor's lost. In G. B. Harrison (Ed.), *Shakespeare: The complete works.* New York: Harcourt, Brace. (Original work published 1598)

Shannon, C. E. (1951). Prediction and entropy of printed English. *Bell System Technical Journal, 30,* 50–64.

Share, D. L. (1995). Phonological recoding and self–teaching: Sine qua non of reading acquisition. *Cognition, 55,* 151–218.

Shaw, B. (1963). *On language* (Abraham Tauber, Ed.). New York: Philosophical Library.

Shepherd's Garden Seeds. (1998). *Shepherd's garden seeds.* Torrington, CT: Author.

Shaywitz, S. E., Escobar, M. D., Shaywitz, B. A., Fletcher, J. M., & Makuch, R. (1992). Evidence that dyslexia may represent the lower tail of the normal distribution of reading ability. *New England Journal of Medicine, 326,* 145–150.

Shipley, J. T. (1977). *In praise of English.* New York: Times Books.

Shoemaker, E. C. (1936). *Noah Webster, pioneer of learning.* New York: Columbia University Press.

Simplified Spelling Board. (1906). *The Roosevelt fonetic spelling book.* New York: Author.

Simpson, J. A., & Weiner, E. S. C. (Eds.). (1989). *The Oxford English dictionary* (2nd ed., 20 vols.). Oxford University Press.

Sinclair, J. (Ed.). (1987). *Collins COBUILD English language dictionary*. London: Collins.

Skeel, E. E. F., & Carpenter, E. H., Jr. (Eds.). (1958). *A bibliography of the writings of Noah Webster*. New York: Arno Press.

Smith, A. E. (1942). Stephen H. Long and the naming of Wisconsin. *Wisconsin Magazine of History, 26*, 67–71.

Smith, T. (1913). *De recta et emendata linguae anglicae* (O. Deibel, Ed.). Halle, Germany: M. Niemeyer. (Original work published 1568)

Snow, C. E., Burns, M. S., & Griffin, P. (1998). *Preventing reading difficulties in young children*. Washington, DC: National Academy Press.

Soukhanov, A. H. (Ed.). (1992). *The American Heritage dictionary of the English language* (3rd ed.). Boston: Houghton Mifflin.

Spenser, E. (1981). *The faerie queen* (T. P. Roche, Jr., Ed.). New Haven, CT: Yale University Press. (Original work published 1590)

Stanovich, K. E., & West, R. F. (1989). Exposure to print and orthographic processing. *Reading Research Quarterly, 24*(4), 402–433.

Stetson, R. H. (1973). The phoneme and the grapheme. In *Mélanges de linguistique et de phonologie offerts à Jacques van Ginneken à l'occasion du soixantiéme anniversaire de sa naissance* (pp. 353–356). Geneva: Slatkine Reprints. (Original work published 1937)

Stewart, G. A. (1945). *Names on the land: A historical account of place-naming in the United States*. New York: Random House.

Stillings, C. A. (Ed.). (1906). *Simplified spelling* (1st ed.). Washington, DC: U.S. Government, Office of the Public Printer.

Strang, B. M. H. (1970). *A history of English*. London: Methuen.

Sullivan, W. (1990, September 9). Honoring, and unearthing, Indian place names. *The New York Times*, p. 1:34.

Tauber, A. (1958) *Spelling reform in the United States*. Unpublished doctoral dissertation, Columbia University.

Thorndike, E. L. (1941a). *The teaching of English suffixes*. New York: Bureau of Publications, Teachers College, Columbia University.

Thorndike, E. L. (Ed.). (1941b). *Thorndike–Century senior dictionary*. Chicago: Scott, Foresman.

U.S. Board on Geographic Names. (1892). *First report of the United States Board on Geographic Names*. Washington: U.S. Government Printing Office.

U.S. Board on Geographic Names. (1901). *Second report of the United States Board on Geographic Names*. Washington: U.S. Government Printing Office.

U.S. Government Printing Office. (1967). *Style Manual* (rev. ed.). Washington, DC: Author.

Vachek, J. (1959). Two chapters on written English. *Brno Studies in English, 1*, 7–34.

Vachek, J. (1962). On the interplay of external and internal factors in the development of language. *Lingua, 11*, 433–448.

Vachek, J. (1973). *Written language*. The Hague, The Netherlands: Mouton.

Vachek, J. (1976). *Selected writings in English and general linguistics*. The Hague, The Netherlands: Mouton.

Vachek, J. (1989). *Written language revisited*. Amsterdam: Benjamins.

Venezky, R. L. (1970). *The structure of English orthography*. The Hague, The Netherlands: Mouton.

Venezky, R. L. (1993). History of interest in the visual component of reading. In D. M. Willows, R. S. Kruk, & E. Corcos (Eds.), *Visual processes in reading and reading disabilities*. Hillsdale, NJ: Erlbaum.

Venezky, R. L. (1995). How English is read: Grapheme–phoneme regularity and orthographic structure in word recognition. In I. Taylor & D. R. Olson (Eds.), *Scripts and literacy: Reading and learning to read alphabets, syllabaries, and characters*. Dordrecht, The Netherlands: Kluwer Academic Publishers.

Venezky, R. L., & Suraj, M. (1993). Automatic syllabication for an on-line reading tutor. *Behavior Research Methods, Instruments, and Computers, 25*(1), 67–75.

Vivian, J. (1979). Through with thru at the *Chicago Tribune*: The McCormick spelling experiment. *Journalism History, 6*(3), 84–87, 96.

Waldo, G. S. (1964). The significance of accentuation in English words. *Proceedings of the Ninth International Congress of Linguists*, 204–210.

Wall, J. F. (1970). *Andrew Carnegie*. New York: Oxford University Press.

Wallach, M. A. (1962). Perceptual recognition of approximations to English in relation to spelling achievement. *Journal of Educational Psychology, 54*, 57–62.

Webster, N. (1789). *Essay on a reformed mode of spelling, with Dr. Franklin's arguments on the subject*. Boston: Isaiah Thomas (for the author).

Webster, N. (1806). *A compendious dictionary of the English language*. New Haven, CT: Sidney Babcock.

Webster, N. (1852). *An American dictionary of the English language* (2nd ed., C. A. Goodrich, Ed.). Springfield, MA: Merriam.

Webster, N. (1968). *A grammatical institute of the English language, Part I* (Facsimile reprint No. 89). Menston, UK: Scolar Press. (Original work published 1783)

Webster, N. (1908). *The reforming of spelling*. (Old South Leaflets, Vol. 8, No. 196). Boston: Directors of the Old South Works. (Original work published 1789)

Webster, N. (1962). *Noah Webster's American spelling book*. New York: Bureau of Publications, Teachers College, Columbia University. (Original work published 1831)

Weiner, E. S. C., & Delahunty, A. (Eds.). (1994). *The Oxford guide to English usage* (2nd ed.). Oxford, UK: Clarendon Press.

Wells, J. C. (1982). *Accents of English* (3 vols.). Cambridge, UK: Cambridge University Press.

Wesley, E. B. (1957). *NEA: The first hundred years*. New York: Harper.

Whitford, H. C. (1966). *A dictionary of American homophones and homographs*. New York: Teachers College Press.

Wijk, A. (1966). *Rules of pronunciation for the English language*. London: Oxford University Press.

Williams, C. (1994). *Beans and rice*. New York: Time–Life Books.

Wloszczyna, S. (1991, October 10). Odd spelling is the hip way 2 B kool. *USA Today*, p. 4d.

Woodward, W. H. (1967). *Studies in education during the age of the Renaissance, 1400–1600* (Classics in Education No. 32). New York: Teachers College Press.

Yule, V. (1986). The design of spelling to match needs and abilities. *Harvard Educational Review, 56*(3), 278–297.

Yule, V., & Greentree, S. (1986). Readers' adaptation to spelling change. *Human Learning, 5*, 229–241.

Zachrisson, R. E. (1930). *Anglic: A new agreed simplified English spelling*. Uppsala, Sweden: Anglic Fund A. B.

Word Index

Word Index

Index